MYSTERIES OF MIND, SPACE AND TIME

Volume 6

Marshall Cavendish · New York London & Toronto

Contents

VOLUME SIX

CERGY-PONTOISE AFFAIR
MYSTERY OF THE LOST WEEK   1801
A Frenchman goes missing for a week – but was he, as a leading ufologist claimed, abducted by a UFO?
Hilary Evans

PHYSICAL MEDIUMS
APPORTS: A MOVING STORY   1806
Carnations, fruit, a plant taller than a man ... these and even stranger objects materialise in seances
Roy Stemman

ESP ON TEST
ESP UNLIMITED   1810
The Ganzfeld has successfully induced telepathy – but also spontaneous psi on a remarkable scale!
Carl Sargent

PSYCHIC SURGERY
THEATRE OF BLOOD   1814
Is the showmanship that surrounds psychic surgery indicative of fraud – or a vital part of the treatment?
David Harvey

OCCULT CHEMISTRY
A PENETRATING VISION   1818
We uncover evidence that two visionaries 'saw' the structure of atomic particles in the 1900s
Stephen M. Phillips

HOLY BLOOD, HOLY GRAIL
THE ROYAL HOUSE OF JESUS   1821
A married Christ, whose descendants are guarded by secret societies? We examine the evidence
Stan Gooch

BIORHYTHMS
A TIDE IN THE AFFAIRS OF MEN   1826
The biorhythm theory has been roundly criticised – but do our lives still obey cyclic forces?
Guy Lyon Playfair

PHYSICAL MEDIUMS
A WORD TO THE WISE   1830
We investigate the 'direct voice' phenomenon – when the dead speak in their own characteristic voices
Roy Stemman

OCCULT CHEMISTRY
THE HUNTING OF THE QUARK   1834
Two Edwardian psychics 'saw' the structure of atoms – but how right were they?
Stephen M. Phillips

PSYCHIC SURGERY
THE KINDEST CUT OF ALL   1838
What does it feel like to undergo psychic surgery? One woman recounts her experience
Anne Dooley

BORLEY RECTORY
BORLEY: A HAUNTING TALE   1841
Borley Rectory has been called 'the most haunted house in England'. What are the facts?
Frank Smyth

PHYSICAL MEDIUMS
THIS TOO, TOO SOLID FLESH   1846
We describe some famous cases of alleged materialisations of people at seances
Roy Stemman

ALTERNATIVE HEALING
THE DOCTOR'S DILEMMA   1850
Many people are becoming increasingly dissatisfied with orthodox medicine. What are the alternatives?
Ruth West

CERGY-PONTOISE AFFAIR
FACT, FRAUD OR FANTASY?   1854
Doubt is cast on this impressive abduction case by facts that have subsequently come to light
Hilary Evans

DEATH VALLEY
THE RIDDLE OF RACETRACK PLAYA   1858
On a remote plateau in the Sierra Nevada mountains in California stones move at night. How?
Bob Rickard

BIBLE MYSTERIES
FOR IT IS WRITTEN ...   1861
The Bible is full of seemingly paranormal events – we explore and anlyse them
David Christie-Murray

ALTERNATIVE HEALING
A POTENT REMEDY? 1866
Homoeopathy, the art of administering drugs that produce the symptoms of the disease they cure
Ruth West

THE SUN
A TOUCH OF THE SUN 1870
Is our physical health – and even our politics – controlled by what happens on the surface of the Sun?
Guy Lyon Playfair

HOLY BLOOD, HOLY GRAIL
THE KING AND THE COVENS 1874
We continue to examine the mystery of the crucifixion – and its relation to the deaths of certain European kings
Stan Gooch

UFO CASEBOOK
A UFO COMES TO TOWN 1878
One of the rare sightings of UFOs over London – complete with photographs
Charles Bowen

SPIRIT PHOTOGRAPHY
UNEXPECTED DEVELOPMENTS 1881
We publish a gallery of alleged 'spirit photographs' – and sift the evidence for fraud
Frederick Goodman

BIBLE MYSTERIES
HIS WONDERS TO PERFORM 1886
The miracles of the New Testament have often been explained away – but could they be the gospel truth?
David Christie-Murray

MERFOLK
A FISHY TALE 1890
Despite tall stories and blatant fakes, mermaids continue to be reported by reliable witnesses
Paul Begg

BORLEY RECTORY
BORLEY: THE TENSION MOUNTS 1894
Did the problems of one family create the phenomena of 'the most haunted house in Britain'?
Frank Smyth

THE SUN
THE HEART OF THE SUN 1898
Has the Sun gone out? Or is it merely behaving strangely? We examine the disconcerting facts
John Gribbin

DIVINATION
THE PATTERN OF THE FUTURE 1901
We examine the ancient art of geomancy: reading the future in randomly generated patterns
Brian Innes

HOLY BLOOD, HOLY GRAIL
MURDER BY MOONLIGHT 1906
Was Christ's death connected with Moon worship – part of an archaic tradition of ritual murder?
Stan Gooch

BRITISH SCARESHIPS
THE BRITISH SCARESHIP INVASION 1910
Unidentified airships were seen in large numbers over Britain in 1909. Where did they come from?
Nigel Watson

ALTERNATIVE HEALING
A TOUCHING STORY 1914
Massage, manipulation and simple touch therapy can work wonders for the sick
Ruth West

BORLEY RECTORY
BORLEY IN RUINS 1918
Price's fake phenomena were exposed and the rectory razed to the ground – but the rumours persist ...
Frank Smyth

TALKING MONGOOSE
THE MONGOOSE THAT TALKED 1921
A review of the renowned case of a small shy animal that – it was claimed – could talk
Melvin Harris

DIVINATION
I CHING: ENQUIRE WITHIN 1926
The ancient art of divination by the *I Ching* proves effective even today – we look at the method *Brian Innes*

SPIRIT PHOTOGRAPHY
AN ENTERPRISING SPIRIT 1930
Apearances of 'extras' in photographs have long been regarded as fraud. We consider alternative theories
Frederick Goodman

BIBLE MYSTERIES
THE GOSPEL TRUTH 1934
Did Christ really rise from the dead in his physical body as the Bible states? We evaluate the evidence
David Christie-Murray

BRITISH SCARESHIPS
WHO SENT THE SCARESHIPS 1938
Where did the strange airships seen over Britain in 1909 come from? And what of the next scare in 1913?
Nigel Watson

A to Z Quick Reference

A

abduction
  Cergy-Pontoise case (1979) 1801–5, **1801–5**, 1854–7, **1854–7**
acupuncture 1850
Adamski, George, 1879
Agpaoa, Antonio 1814, **1815**, 1816, 1817
airship
  British scares 1910–13, **1910–13**, 1938–40, **1938–40**
  R101 disaster 1998
  Wellman **1911**
Allen, C. W. 1911, **1913**
Ambrecht, Ernest Louis 1866
Andrea, J. Valentin 1825
apportation
  physical mediums and 1806–9, **1806–9**
Arachne 1907
Arigo José 1816, 1817
Aristotle 1851
Arles, François d' 1897, 1919
Arthur, King
  Glastonbury 1961, 1965, **1965**
  Moon worship 1908, **1909**
  sorcerer' garter 1874
Asclepius 1850, 1852, **1852**
Ashton, Hugh 1812, **1812**, 1813
astrology
  radio weather 1873
atom
  'ultimate physical atom' 1818–20, **1818–20**, 1834–7, **1834–7**

B

Bacon, Francis 1891
Bailey, Charles 1807, 1808
Balder 1908, 1909, **1909**
Barbarossa, Frederick 1071, 1073
Baring-Gould, Sabine 1893
Barlow, Fred 1883
Barnum, Phineas T.
  mermaid **1890**, 1893
Barron, Dr Donald 1914
Becker, Dr Robert O. 1827
Bender, Prof. Hans
  psychic surgery **1814**
Bennett, Sheila 1813
Benson, Dr Herbert 1916
Berossus 1890
Bes 807
Besant, Annie
  Theosophy 1818–20, 1834–7
  'ultimate physical atom' 1818–20, **1818–20**, 1834–7, **1834–7**
Bible
  Elijah **1862–3**, 1863–4
  healing miracles 1889
  Jacob's ladder **1861**, 1862
  Jonah and the whale **1865**
  Joseph's dream 1862, **1862**
  Joshua at Jericho **1864**, 1865
  'manna' 1865, **1865**
  Moses and the burning bush **1863**, 1864
  mysteries 1861–5, 1886–9, 1934–7
  New Testament 1886–9, **1886–9**
  Peter and Cornelius 1888
  pillar of cloud **1863**
  plagues of Egypt 1864, **1864**
  prediction 1887
  raising of Lazarus 1889, **1889**
  resurrection 1934–7, **1934–7**
  Saul and with of Endor **1861**, 1862
  technique of the Midrash **1886**, 1887, 1888
  tradition of Moon worship 1906–9, **1906–9**

Billon-Duplan, Luis 1855, 1856, 1857
Billot, Dr G. P. 1806
biorhythms 1826–9, **1826–9**, **1826–9**
Borley Rectory 1841–5, **1841–5**, 1894–7, **1894–7**, 1918–20, **1918–20**
  Price, Harry and 1841–5, 1895
Botta, Paul Emil 1890
Botticelli 1823
Boyd, Dr William 1867
Bozzano, Ernesto 1808
Bradley, Dennis 1831, 1832–3
Brown, Frank A. 1828
Bull, Ethel 1895
Bull, Rev. Harry **1894**, 1895
Bull, Rev. Henry 1894–5

C

cancer
  touch therapy 1915
Capra, Fritjof 1868
chemistry, occult 1818–20, **1818–20**, 1834–7, **1834–7**
chiropractic 1916–17, **1917**
Chizhevsky, A. L. 1872–3
Chou, Duke of 1927, 1928, 1929
Christ 1821–5
  possible descendants of 1821–5
  prediction 1887
Churchill, Winston
  mystery airships 1938
Cleary, Michael 1806
Cocteau, Jean 1824, 1825, **1825**
Colley, Archdeacon Thomas 1847
Combermere, Viscount 1883
Confucius 1831, 1832, 1926, 1927, **1927**
Control (UFO organisation) 1803, 1805, 1854, 1856, 1857
Cook, Roger 1815, **1816**
Corbet, Sybell 1883
Cornelius Agrippa 1903
cosmic consciousness 1240
Coulter, Harris 1866
Courcoux, Commandant 1803
Cox, Esther 1918
Crandon, Mina ('Margery')
  direct voice medium **1830**, 1832, 1833
Crane, Walter **1826**
Creighton, Gordon
  London UFO 1879
Crocker, Sir William 1920
'crosstalk' 1811, 1812
curse
  Bible mysteries 1864

D

Dagobert II **1877**
Dagon 1890
Death Valley National Park, USA 1858–60, **1858–60**
Debussy, Claude
  Prieuré de Sion 1823, 1824
Dingwall, Eric
  Borley Rectory 1842, 1844, 1918, 1919, 1920
disappearances
  Bible mysteries 1863
  divination 1901–5, **1901–5**, 1926–9, **1926–9**
  Bible mysteries 1861–5, **1861–5**
Donne, John 1891
Dooley, Anne 1838–49, **1838–40**
Douglas-Home, Hon. Henry 1842, 1895, 1919
dreams
  Bible mysteries 1862, **1862**
Druids
  ritual sacrifice **1876**

Dubos, René 1850
Dubrov, Dr Aleksandr P. 1828, 1871, 1872
Duncan, F. Martin 1925
Dunraven, Lord 1860

E

ectoplasm
  physical mediums **1809, 1830**, 1832, 1846–9, **1846–9**
  spirit photography 1932
Edmund, King 1877
Edmund Ironside 1877
Edward III, King 1874, **1874**, 1875
Edwards, Harry
  and Webber, Jack 1832
Eglinton, William
  materialisation medium 1847, **1847**, 1849
  spirit photography 1930–31, **1931**
Eisenbud, Dr Jule
  Serios, Ted 1885
electron
  micro-psi atom 1820
Elizalde, David 1814–16, **1815**
Elizalde, Helen 1814–16, **1815**
Ellison, Rev. Charles 1843
Esperance, Madam d'
  physical medium 1806–7, **1807**, 1846, **1846**
  spirit photography 1931–2, **1932**
Evans, Caradoc 1831
extra-sensory perception (ESP)
  Ganzfeld state 1810–13, **1810–13**
  Sargent, Carl 1810–13, **1810**
  spontaneous 1810–13

F

Farmer, John S. 1931
Fatalvero, Jacinto 1893
feng-shui 1903
Findlay, J. Arthur 1830
Flamel, Nicolas
  Prieuré de Sion 1876
Flew, Prof. A. G. N. 1842
Fliess, Wilhelm 1828, 1829
flower remedies 1869
Flowerdew, Capt. 759
Fontaine, Franck 1801–5, 1854–7, **1854–7**
Forgione, Padre Pio 1937
Foyster, Lionel A. 1897, 1918–19, **1919**
Foyster, Marianne 1897, 1918–19, **1919**, 1920
Freitas, Lourival de 1838–40, **1838–40**
Fukurai, Tomokichi 1885

G

Galen, Claudius 1851
Ganzfeld state 1810–13, **1810–13**
Geiger, H. 1820
Geley, Dr Gustave 1847–8
Gell-Mann, Murray 1834, **1835**
geo-magnetic field 1828, 1829
geomancy 1926–7, 1969
  method of divination 1903–5, **1903–5**
Giotto **1821**
Gladstone, William 1847
Glanville, Helen 1844
Glanville, Sidney 1844, 1894, 1920
Glover, C. G. 1920
Goldney, K. M.
  Borley Rectory 1842, 1844, 1918–19, **1919**, 1920
Graves, Robert
  fertility goddess 1906, 1907, **1908**
  witchcraft 1876

Greatrakes, Valentine **1915**
Green-Price, Lady Jean 1844
Green-Price, Sir Robert 1844
Gregson, Capt. W. H. 1920
Guieu, Jimmy
  Cergy-Pontoise UFO 1803–4, **1803**, 1805, 1854, 1857
Guinevere 1874, 1908
Guppy, Mrs Samuel 1807

H

Hahnemann, Samuel 1866, **1867, 1868**
Hall, S. C. 303
Hall, Trevor H.
  Borley Rectory 1842–5, 1918–20
Harley, Trevor 1811
Harlow, Prof Harry 1814
Harper, Charles 1246
Hawker, Robert S. 1893, **1893**
healing, alternative
  acupuncture 1850
  Bible mysteries and 1889
  chiropractic 1916–17, **1917**
  effect of touch 1914–17, **1914–17**
  herbalism 1851–3, **1851–3**
  homoeopathy 1866–9, **1866–9**
  placebo effect 1915–16
  shiatsu 1916
Hennell, Percy 1879–80
Henning, Rev. A. C. 1919
Henry III 1875
Hersey, Dr Rexford 1827, **1827**
Higginson, Gordon 1815, **1816**
Hippocrates 1851
  homoeopathy 1866
Homer 1852
homoeopathy 1866–9, **1866–9**
Hope, Lord Charles 1842
Hope, William **1932**
Houdini, Harry **1847**
  direct voice mediums **1830**
Hubbell, Walter 1918
Hudson, Frederick 1933
Hudson, Henry 1891, 1893
Hugo, Victor 1823
Huxley, Sir Julian 1976
Hygeia 1851–2, **1852**
hypnosis
  alternative medicine and 1850

I

I Ching 1903, 1905, 1926–9, **1926–9**
Insall, G. S. M. 1849
Institut Mondial des Sciences Avancés 1803–4, 1857
Irving, James 1921–5, **1921–5**
Irving, Margaret 1921–5, **1921–5**
Irving, Voirrey 1921–5, **1921–5**
Isis
  and Osiris 1907

J

Jenkins, Michael 1868
Jesus
  Holy blood and the Holy Grail, The 1821–5
  possible descendants of 1821–5
  prediction 1887
Jinarajadasa, C. **1836**, 1837
Joad, C. E. M. **1842**, 1845
Joan of Arc
  ritual killing 1877

John XXIII, Pope 1792
   Prieuré de Sion **1824**, 1825
Joly, Fabrice 1855, 1857
Jones, Raynor 1868
Joynson-Hicks, William 1938–9, **1938**
Jupiter 1873
Jürgenson, Friedrich 398–400, **399**, 418, 419, 420, 734
Jussieu, Laurent de 901
Justinian, Emperor 55, 187

K

Kellar, Harry 1847
Kent, James Tyler 1866
Kettle, Police Constable 1910–11
Kluski, Franek 1847–8, **1847–8**
Knight, Constance 1844
Knights Templar
   Prieuré de Sion **1822**, 1823–5, 1874–6
Kollerstrom, Dr Jean 1867–8
Krippner, Stanley
   spontaneous ESP 1811

L

Lambert, R. S. 1925
laser
Lawton, Canon H. 1919
Leadbeater, Charles
   'ultimate physical atom' 1818–20, **1818–20**, 1834–7, **1834–7**
Ledsham, Cynthia 1920
Leeb, Gunther **1817**
Leonard, Gladys Osborne 1882–3
Lethbridge, C. 1911–13, **1911–12**
levitation
   Bible mysteries 1889
Lieber, Dr Arnold 1829
Lincoln, Abraham 1930, **1930**
Lincoln, Mary Todd 1930, **1930**
Lindsay, Capt. Lionel 1939
Lodge, Sir Oliver
   spirit photography 1883
Lonitzer, Adam **1850**
Lowen, Alexander 1914
Luce, Gay Gaer 1827
Lynn, T. 1809

M

McCarthy, Dr C. W. 1807
McElhoney, Paul 1806, **1806**
McKenzie, James Hewat
   Lynn, T. 1809
magnetism, terrestrial
   biorhythms and 1828–9
   sunspot activity 1870–73, **1870–73**
Malory, Sir Thomas 1822
Marsden, E. 1820
Mary of Agreda, Sister 1937
Mary of Bethany 1823
Mary Magdalene 1934–7
   Jesus and 1822–3, **1823**, 1909
materialisation
   physical mediums and 1846–9, **1846–9**
Mayhew, Henry 1851
Meares, Ainslie
   touch therapy 1915–16
medicine
   and mediumship 1848–9
medium
   apports 1806–9, **1806–9**
   Crandon, Mina ('Margery') 1830, 1832, 1833
   direct voice phenomenon 1830–33, **1830–33**
   Eglinton, William 1847, **1847**, 1849, 1930–31, **1931**
   Esperance, Madame d' 1806–7, **1807**, 1846, **1846**, 1931–2, **1932**
   Guppy, Mrs Samuel 1807
   Houdini and **1847**
   Kluski, Franek 1847–8, **1847–8**
   Leonard Gladys Osborne 1882–3
   McElhoney, Paul 1806, **1806**
   materialisation 1846–9, **1846–9**
   Monck, Rev. Francis Ward 1847

Northage, Isa 1848–9
physical mediums 1806–9, **1806–9**, 1830–33, **1830–33**, 1846–9, **1846–9**
Rhinehart, Keith Milton **1808**, 1809
Roy, William 1833
Sloan, John Campbell 1830
Spriggs, George 1848, **1848**
Valiantine, George 1831–2, **1831**, 1833
Webber, Jack 1809, **1809**, 1830, 1832
Williams, Margo
Wriedt, Etta 1831, **1832**
menstrual cycle 1826–9
Mercer, J. R. 1930
Mercury
   radio 'weather' 1873
merfolk 1890–93, **1890–93**
metal bending
micro-psi 1818–20, **1818–20**, 1834–7, **1834–7**
Miles, Dr Laughton E. M. 1828
Milton, Julie 1813
Minoan civilisation
Monck, Rev. Francis Ward 1847
mongoose, talking 1921–5, **1921–5**
Montagu, Ashley 1914
Moon
   biorhythms 1826, **1826**, 1828–9
   zodiac 1907, **1907**
Moon gods 1875–6, **1875**, 1906–9, **1906–9**
Moore, W. Usborne 1831
Mordred 1908, **1909**
Morgan, Steven 1939
Moses
   and burning bush **1863**
Moss, G. H. 1882–3, **1882–3**
Mowbray, Major C. 1809
Mumler, William 1881, 1930, **1930**, 1933
Munro, William 1891–3
Murray, Dr Margaret 1875, 1877

N

Napier, Dr John 1952, 1953
naturopathy 1850
Nelson, John
   effects of sunspot activity **1872–3**, 1873
neutrino
   detector 1900, **1900**
   reactions at Sun's core 1898–1900, **1898–1900**
   sunspot activity 1870
Newton, Isaac
   atom 1820
   Prieuré de Sion 1823
Northage, Isa, 1848–9
Nostradamus 1876

O

Ocholowicz, Col Norbert 1848
Odent, Michel 1915
Oehler, Pauline 1885
Order of the Garter 1874–7, **1874**
Osiris
   Moon worship 1907
osteopathy 1850
out-of-the-body experience
Oxley, William 1847

P

Panacea (goddess) 1851
Pearson, Mary 1897
Peretti, Cavaliere 1808
Perks, P. C. Colin 1880
Philippe II, King 1875
Philippe IV, King 1823
Philippines 1814–17
Phythian-Adams, Dr W. J. 1844
Piccardi, Prof Giorgio 1871
Piccin, Michel 1854
Pierce, Prof Benjamin 1783
placebo effect
   homoeopathy 1866
   psychic surgery 1816
   touch therapy 1915–16

Playfair, Guy Lyon 1806
Pliny
   mermaids 1890–91
Pluto
   radio 'weather' 1873
Pottier, Patrick **1856**
precognition 1811–12, 1887
   Bible mysteries 1865
prediction
   Bible mysteries 1887
Prévost, Jean-Pierre 1801–5, **1802**, 1854–7, **1856**
Price, Harry
   Borley Rectory 1841–5, **1841–5**, 1895–7, **1897**
Prince, Walter Franklin
   poltergeist activity 1918
prophecy
   divination and 1901–2
psi
   psi-mediated instrumental response 1864, 1888
psychic surgery
   Agpaoa, Tony 1814, 1815
   Dooley, Anne 1838–40, **1838–40**
   Elizalde, David and Helen 1814–15, **1815**, 1816
   Freitas, Lourival de 1838–40, **1838–40**
   Philippines 1816–17
psychical research
   mongoose, talking 1921–5, **1921–5**

Q

quantum mechanics 1820
quark 1834–7, **1834**

R

Rais, Gilles de
   ritual killing 1877
Randi, James
   psychic surgery 1815, **1816**
Ravitz, Leonard J. 1827
reflexology 1850
Reid, Dr H. A. 1930
Renoir, Pierre Auguste 1812, **1812**
Rhinehart, Keith Milton **1808**, 1809
Richard Lionheart 1875
Richardson, Dr Mark 1832
Richet, Charles **1849**
   and Kluski, Franek 1848
Robinson, W. Heath 1811, **1811**, 1813
Roll, William **1814**
Rosicrucian movement
   Prieuré de Sion 1825
Roux, Emile le 1884–5, **1884**
Rowse, A. L. 1901
Roy, William 1833, **1833**
Rugge-Price, Sir Charles 1844
Russell, Anthony 1878–80, **1878–80**

S

Sai Baba **1809**, 1889
Saint-Clair, Pierre Plantard de **1825**
Sargent, Dr Carl 1810–13, **1810**
Sargon II, King 1890
Sausse, Henry 1809
schizophrenia 1914
Schrenck-Nötzing, Baron
   spirit photography 1932–3
Scientific and Medical Network 1867
Scotto, Marquis Centurione 1832
seance
   direct voice phenomena 1830–33, **1830–33**
   materialisation 1846–9, **1846–9**
sensory deprivation
   Ganzfeld technique 1810–13
Serios, Ted 1885
Seurat, Georges 1813, **1813**
Shakespeare, William 1901–2
Sharp, Dr Robert P. 1858–9
Shaw, Duncan 1892
Silva, José 1816–17
Singh, Sadhu Sundar 1888
Skylab, 1870–71
   Project Chicken Little
Sloan, John Campbell 1830
Smith, E. Lester 1834

Smith, Rev. G. Eric 1895–6
speaking in tongues 1889
spirit photography 1881–5, **1881–5**, 1930–33, **1930–33**
Spiritualists' National Union 1814
spontaneous combustion
   Bible mysteries 1863, **1863**
spontaneous human combustion (SHC)
   Bible mysteries 1863
Spriggs, George 1848, **1848**
Stanford, Rex G.
   psi-mediated instrumental response 1864, 1888
Stanley, George M. 1858
Stead, Estelle 1882, **1882**
Stead, W. T.
   spirit photography 1882, **1882**
Stelter, Alfred 1816–17
Stinson, Walter **1830**, 1832–3
stones, moving
   Death Valley National Park, USA 1858–60, **1858–60**
   Nova Scotia 1860
Sun
   biorhythm theory 1828–9
   Earth activity and 1870–73, **1870–73**
   reaction at core of 1898–1900, **1898–1900**
   solar corona **1872**
   sunspot activity 1870–73, **1870–73**
Sutton, Charles 1841–2
Swoboda, Hermann 1829
Sydenham, Thomas 1866

T

Tabori, Dr Paul 1842
Takata, Dr Maki 1871
Tao, principle of 1926, **1927**
Tarot pack 1905
telepathy
   Ganzfeld experiments 1810–13, **1810–13**
   micro-psi 1818–20, **1818–20**
Thomas à Becket
   ritual murder **1876**, 1877
Thomson, J. J.
   concept of atom 1820
Thorogood, B. K. 1832
thoughtography 1885
Totty, Hilda 1815
touch therapy 1914–17, **1914–17**
transcendental meditation
Tree of Life 1835, **1835**
Trewhella, Mathy 1891
Trilha, Ivan **1814**, 1817
Trithemius, Abbot 1971
tumo 1690
Turin shroud 1824, 1937
Tweedale, Rev. Charles 1884
Tweedale, Margaret 1884

U

Underwood, Peter 1842, **1843**
UFO: close encounters of the first kind
   London (1966) 1878–80, **1878–80**
UFO: close encounters of the fourth kind 1801–5, **1801–5**, 1854–7, **1854–7**

V

Valiantine, George 1831–2, **1831**, 1833
Vinci, Leonardo da 1823
Vogh, James 1907

W

Wall, V. C. 1895–6
Warwick, Dowager Duchess of 1831, **1832**
Watson, Lyall
   psychic surgery 1816–17
Webber, Jack 1809, **1809**, 1830, 1832
White, Prof. Charles A. 1860, **1860**
Whitman, Walt **1932**
Whymant, Dr Neville 1831–2
Wickstead, Mrs **1881**, 1883–4
William Rufus 1877, **1877**

Willows, E. T. 1939
Wilson, Colin
  Borley Rectory 1842, 1845
Winder, R. H. B. 1879–80
witch, witchcraft
  Order of the Garter and 1874–7, **1874–7**
Wriedt, Etta 1831, **1832**
Wyllie, Edward 1930, **1931**, 1933, **1933**

Y

yang, principle of
  I Ching **660**, 1927, **1927**
yin, principle of
  I Ching 1927, **1927**
yoga
  alternative healing 1850
  knowledge of the small 1818

Z

Zeppelin, Count Ferdinand von 1911–12, **1912**
Zeus 1852
Zweig, George 1834

Three young Frenchmen hit the news headlines in early December 1979 with a tale about a UFO abduction at Cergy-Pontoise. But was their amazing story a fabrication? HILARY EVANS sorts out the facts from the fiction

'FRENCHMAN BACK TO EARTH with a bump' was the headline in the London *Times* – and across the world the media reported the news with the same uncertainty whether to take it seriously or not. But this much was certain: Franck Fontaine, who had allegedly been kidnapped by a UFO a week before, had been restored to friends, family, and a wondering world in the early hours of Monday, 3 December 1979.

Where had he spent those seven days? The world, hoping for a story that would make the Moon landing seem tame, was disappointed. Fontaine's recollections were few and confused. It seemed to him he had simply dropped off to sleep for half an hour: he was astonished and dismayed to find he had been away for a week. He attributed the strange images in his mind to dreams: he was bewildered to learn that he might have been abducted by extra-terrestrial aliens and carried to their distant world.

Police search a field in Cergy-Pontoise, France, for clues to the disappearance of Franck Fontaine, reported as having been abducted by a UFO. Fontaine's two friends, Jean-Pierre Prévost and Salomon N'Diaye, said they had witnessed the kidnapping early one morning in late November 1979. In the background is the block of flats in which Prévost and N'Diaye lived and near which the event occurred

Fontaine was no less dismayed to find himself the focus of the world's attention. During his seven-day absence, it had been his friends Salomon N'Diaye and Jean-Pierre Prévost, witnesses of his abduction, who had been the objects of attention. Ever since their first startling telephone call to the police – 'A friend of mine's just been carried off by a UFO!' – they had been subjected to interrogation by the police, by the press, and by UFO investigative groups ranging from the scientific to the bizarre. If Fontaine's return brought renewed publicity and fresh problems, at least it cleared them of the suspicion that they were responsible for their friend's disappearance – perhaps even his death.

The life-style of the three young men was not of a sort to dispel suspicion. All three – Prévost, aged 26, N'Diaye, 25, Fontaine, 18 – scraped an uncertain living by selling jeans in street markets. They drove an old car that was unlicensed and uninsured, none of them having a driving licence. Prévost was a self-declared anarchist. He and N'Diaye lived next door to each other in a modern block at Cergy-Pontoise on the outskirts of Paris. Fontaine lived 2 miles (3 kilometres) away.

According to their account, Fontaine had

Mystery of the lost week

Cergy-Pontoise affair

spent Sunday evening in Prévost's flat because they wanted to be up by 3.30 a.m. to travel the 35 miles (60 kilometres) to the street market at Gisors. The market didn't start until 8 a.m. but they wanted a good place. Besides, their Taunus estate car had been acting up lately, so they thought it prudent to allow extra time. At 3.30, after only about four hours' sleep, they were up and ready to load the car with clothes.

First, though, they gave the car a push-start to make sure the engine would function. Having got it going, they decided that Fontaine should stay in the car to make sure it didn't stop again while the other two got on with the loading. Fontaine had leisure to look about him, and so it was that he noticed a brilliant light in the sky some distance away. When his companions arrived with their next

load, he pointed the object out. It was cylindrical in shape, but otherwise unidentifiable. When it moved behind the block of flats, N'Diaye rushed upstairs to fetch a camera, thinking he might take a photograph of the object to sell to the newspapers. Prévost went in to get another load of clothing while Fontaine, hoping for another view of the mysterious object, drove up onto the main road that ran close by the flats.

Hearing the sound of the moving vehicle, his companions looked out of the windows of their respective flats. Both saw that Fontaine had stopped the car on the main road and noted that the engine was no longer running. Prévost, angry because they would probably have to push-start the car a second time, rushed downstairs again. He called to N'Diaye to forget about his camera because the UFO had vanished. N'Diaye came after him saying that in any case he had no film in his camera, and adding that from his window it had looked as though the car was surrounded by a great ball of light.

Outdoors again, the two young men stopped in amazement: the rear of their car was

Top: Franck Fontaine leaving the police station after being questioned upon his safe return. He said that his 'missing week' was a blank in his mind

Salomon N'Diaye (above) and Jean-Pierre Prévost (right) reported the UFO incident to the police at once – a fact that convinced many they were telling the truth

enveloped in a sharply defined sphere of glowing mist, near which a number of smaller balls of light were moving about. While they stood watching, they saw the larger globe absorb all but one of the smaller ones. Then a beam of light emerged, which grew in size until it was like the cylindrical shape they had seen earlier. The large sphere seemed to enter this cylinder, which shot up into the sky and disappeared from sight.

The two hurried to the car, but found no sign of Fontaine. He was not in the car, in the road, or in the cabbage field beside the road. Prévost insisted on calling the police immediately and N'Diaye went off to do so. Prévost, remaining near the car, was the only witness to the last phase of the incident: a ball of light, like those previously moving about

Cergy-Pontoise affair

the car, seemed to push the car door shut. Then it too vanished.

Such was the account that the two young men gave to the police on their arrival a few minutes later. Because UFO sightings are a military matter in France, the police instructed Prévost and N'Diaye to inform the gendarmerie, which comes under the Ministry of National Defence. The two spent most of the day with the gendarmes, telling and retelling the story. The interrogators stopped for lunch, during which time the witnesses telephoned the press with their story. Later, Commandant Courcoux of the Cergy gendarmerie told the press that there were no grounds for disbelieving the young men's story, that he had no doubt 'something' had occurred, and that he could give no indication of what that 'something' might be. In a later interview he admitted, 'We are swimming in fantasy.'

For a week, that was all the world knew. During that week, the young men were questioned over and over again. Some people accepted the UFO story as it stood. Others suspected it to be a smokescreen, perhaps a cunning plan to help Fontaine avoid doing his military service, perhaps something more sinister. But one fact stood out clearly: Prévost and N'Diaye had informed the police promptly and voluntarily. Given their backgrounds, wasn't this convincing proof of their sincerity?

When Fontaine gave his version of the story, there seemed no reason to question his sincerity either. He told how he had woken to find himself lying in the cabbage field. Getting to his feet, he realised he was just across the main road from the flats, close to where he had stopped the car to watch the UFO. But the car was no longer there. His first thought,

Jimmy Guieu, well-known science fiction writer and founder of a UFO group. The trio put themselves into his hands exclusively; other UFO investigators found them to be very unco-operative

as he hurried towards the still-darkened building, was that somebody had stolen their car and its valuable load of clothing. Neither Prévost nor N'Diaye was to be seen, so he rushed upstairs and rang the bell of Prévost's flat. When there was no reply, he went to N'Diaye's. A sleepy N'Diaye appeared, gawped at him in amazement, then flung his arms round him in delighted welcome. Fontaine, already surprised to find his friend in his night clothes, was even more amazed to learn that an entire week had gone by since the morning of the Gisors market.

He had little to tell the press or the police. The world's media reported his return but reserved judgement till they heard what the authorities had to say. But the police declared it was no longer their business: no crime had been committed. Apart from the inherent improbability of Fontaine's story, they had no reason to doubt his word or that of his friends.

Besieged by ufologists

So now it was up to the UFO organisations to see what further light could be thrown on the case. From the start, the witnesses had been besieged by the various French groups; there are dozens of these, most of them fiercely independent and reluctant to co-operate with the others. One of the most reputable of all is Control, to whom we owe most of what we now know of the inside story of the Cergy-Pontoise case.

But another group declared its interest before Control, while Fontaine was still missing: the *Institut Mondial des Sciences Avancés* (World Institute of Advanced Sciences). Its co-founder and spokesman was the well-known science fiction writer and author of two books about UFOs, Jimmy

Right: the cylinder-shaped UFO seen by the three friends appeared to have a diameter larger than that of the full Moon that night. It had a rounded front end and a tail that trailed off into a hazy cloud. It was when Fontaine went closer to the UFO – alone – that he disappeared

Cergy-Pontoise affair

Guieu. Before he had carried out an investigation, Guieu affirmed his belief in the story: 'No question of it, Franck Fontaine has been abducted on board a UFO,' he stated in an interview. 'Admittedly I haven't questioned the young man's two companions, but I hold their account to be true a priori.'

Delighted to have their story accepted without reservation by so eminent an authority, Fontaine's two friends agreed to cooperate with Guieu. When Fontaine returned, he too was taken under IMSA's wing. Guieu offered them a secret refuge in the south of France where they could work on a book together, Guieu writing it and all sharing the proceeds.

Guieu's book, *Cergy-Pontoise UFO contacts*, was rushed into print with astonishing speed, appearing a bare four months after Fontaine's return. Thanks to the combination of Guieu's name and the intense interest in the case, it was an instant best-seller. But readers hoping for a conclusive verdict were disappointed. The book was padded out by Guieu's journalistic style and digressive accounts of other cases, and there was an almost total absence of first-hand testimony from the principal witness – the abducted Fontaine – whose story the world wanted to hear. Such revelations as the book contained were of quite another nature.

Guieu had hoped that Fontaine would be able to recall more of his adventure if he were hypnotised, but the young man obstinately refused to submit to hypnosis. Then Prévost suggested that he should be hypnotised instead. What resulted was truly amazing. It now emerged that Prévost, not Fontaine, had been the true object of alien interest. Now, speaking through him, the aliens explained all. Fontaine had simply been the means to establish communication: Prévost was the channel through whom they could communicate to help save Earth from impending disaster. The aliens identified themselves as 'the intelligences from beyond' but gave no clearer clue to the whereabouts of 'beyond' than that it is 'a planet not like yours'. Their spokesman was Haurrio, a friendly if somewhat garrulous character.

In Guieu's book, Prévost becomes the hero of the story and the only evidence we have for the events is his word. His two companions seem to have become irrelevant.

Jimmy Guieu's book *Cergy-Pontoise UFO contacts* (top) and Jean-Pierre Prévost's book *The truth about the Cergy-Pontoise affair* (above). Both were published speedily after the alleged kidnapping of Franck Fontaine. Both were long on fantasy and short on facts, disappointing all who hoped for some clarification of what had really happened

This book having raised more questions than it answered, much was hoped for when Prévost announced that he was writing his own account of the event. But *The truth about the Cergy-Pontoise affair*, published later that same year, was even less satisfactory. It was a rambling, incoherent farrago in which great doses of alien 'philosophy' – transmitted by Prévost – show that pious platitudes about the need for more love and less science are not confined to planet Earth.

There is virtually no mention of Franck Fontaine's abduction: indeed, he and Salomon N'Diaye are scarcely referred to. But Prévost's visit to a secret alien base is described in some detail, and this gives us a good yardstick for evaluating the rest of the material. It seems that one morning soon

Above: a group of people anticipate a close encounter with aliens at Cergy-Pontoise on 15 August 1980. They gathered there when Fontaine revealed that he had made an arrangement to meet on that day with his abductors of the previous December

Left: a being named Haurrio allegedly contacted Prévost on behalf of the 'intelligences from beyond'. On one occasion Haurrio was dressed in a one-piece silver garment, looking decidedly 'like an alien'. On another he had long blond hair and looked like a masculine woman in a suit. He was said to be friendly and very talkative

after Fontaine's return, there was a ring at Prévost's door. The caller was a travelling salesman, a total stranger who said he had to make a trip to Bourg-de-Sirod and invited Prévost to come along. Now, Bourg-de-Sirod is a small village near the Swiss border some 225 miles (360 kilometres) from Cergy. On the face of it, there is no conceivable reason why a salesman should go there, nor why he should think that Prévost might wish to go there given that they were strangers in the first place.

However, there was a reason for interest by Prévost. Bourg-de-Sirod was a specially significant place for him because as a child he had gone to a summer camp nearby and had later worked there. More recently still, he and Fontaine had spent a camping holiday there. So Prévost, though surprised at the stranger's offer, cheerfully accepted it. The salesman dropped him off at the village and he set off up the hill towards a particular site that had always fascinated him – a railway tunnel containing an abandoned train carriage from the Second World War.

Arriving at the tunnel in late evening, Prévost found that other people were there before him: a group of young men gathered round a fire in the open. One of them called out his name; he was from the Sahara and had recently written to Prévost. It turned out that he and the others had come there from many parts of the world, thanks to the 'intelligences from beyond'. Each spoke his own language – but was understood by the rest.

When Haurrio, the alien representative, arrived, he informed them that they had been chosen to spread the philosophy of the 'intelligences' on Earth. A beautiful female alien then took them on a tour of the tunnel, now being used as a UFO base. They saw several spacecraft, similar to ones that Prévost had seen as a child. After their tour, the young men returned to their camp fire and went to sleep on the ground – which, on a December night in the mountains, must have been less than comfortable. Next morning Prévost found his friendly salesman waiting to chauffeur him back to Cergy.

Whether Jimmy Guieu and Jean-Pierre Prévost seriously expected their accounts to be believed, we may never know. But the more they provided in the way of checkable statements, the harder it became to accept the original account of the alleged abduction. Doubts grew even more when an investigative team from Control persisted in taking up the case without the co-operation of the witnesses – checking all the conflicting statements and fragmented testimony as best they could.

Was there ever an abduction by aliens at Cergy-Pontoise? See page 1854

Apports: a moving story

Flowers, fresh fruit, ornaments – even living animals – have been said to have materialised as 'apports' through the physical mediumship of some particularly gifted sensitives. ROY STEMMAN describes some examples of this controversial phenomenon

IN THE PRIVATE home circle of London medium Paul McElhoney, objects are frequently produced 'out of thin air'. These apparent materialisations are known to psychical researchers as 'apports'. Like other physical phenomena produced by mediums they usually occur in darkness and that rouses the suspicions of believers as well as sceptics. But doubts about the authenticity of apport mediumship frequently evaporate when one considers the conditions under which they are produced, or the type of object that materialises.

In the case of Paul McElhoney, several observers have reported that flowers are apported in his mouth. Spiritualist Michael Cleary told the weekly newspaper *Psychic News* (28 November 1981) of his experience at the medium's home circle a week earlier. He had searched the medium and the seance room before the proceedings began. During the seance the medium was entranced by a spirit called Ceros. 'When Ceros brought the first flowers the lights were on,' said Cleary. 'I looked into Paul's mouth. There was nothing there. Then a [fresh] flower began to fall from his mouth. Carnations are very significant in my family. I had previously asked my mother in the spirit world to bring that kind of flower. When Ceros apported a carnation for me he said it was a present from a woman in the spirit world.'

Another witness to this phenomenon was author and investigator Guy Lyon Playfair, who also received a carnation. When he got home he put it in his mouth and tried to talk as the medium had done. 'The stalk stuck in my throat. I nearly threw up. Paul talked easily and then produced the carnation.'

Flowers have been common apports for well over 150 years. One of the earliest investigators of this phenomenon was a Frenchman, Dr G. P. Billot, who witnessed the production of flower apports by a blind woman medium in October 1820.

One of the most extraordinary accounts of an apport concerns a famous English medium, Madame d'Esperance, in whose presence a materialised spirit named Yolande was said to appear. At a seance in 1880 Yolande took a glass carafe that had been half

Top: physical medium Paul McElhoney produces an apport of a fresh flower from his mouth. There were no signs that it had been regurgitated. Although flower apports (above) appear most often at his seances, other objects have materialised, such as this cast metal model of Cologne cathedral (right), which landed in the palm of SPR council member Anita Gregory – 'from nowhere'. Ceros, McElhoney's spirit guide, said it was a gift from her dead father. Mrs Gregory discovered later that her father had spent his honeymoon in a hotel overlooking Cologne cathedral

Physical mediums

filled with sand and water and placed it in the centre of the room, covering it with a thin piece of drapery. The sitters then watched in amazement as the drapery began rising and Yolande came out of the cabinet, in which Madame d'Esperance was seated, to inspect what was happening. When she removed the drapery it was seen that a perfect plant had grown in minutes.

Yolande told the sitters to sing quietly for a few minutes, and when they inspected the plant again they found it had burst into bloom, with a flower 5 inches (12.5 centimetres) in diameter. It had a thick woody stem, which filled the neck of the carafe, was 22 inches (56 centimetres) high and had 29 leaves. It was subsequently identified as a native of India, *Ixora crocata*, and was kept alive for three months by the gardener of one of the witnesses.

Living for the present
Ten years later, the same medium was responsible for an equally spectacular apport. This time – on 28 June 1890 – a beautiful golden lily with an overpowering perfume grew before the eyes of the sitters to a height of 7 feet (2 metres). Five of its 11 flowers were in full bloom, and in photographs taken at the time it was seen to tower above the medium. Yolande told the sitters, however, that it could not remain and became quite upset when she found she could not dematerialise it. She asked them to keep the plant in a darkened room until the next session, on 5 July, when it was placed in the centre of the room. Its presence was recorded at 9.23 p.m. but by 9.30 p.m. it had vanished. The only proof of its existence were the photographs that had been taken and a couple of the flowers.

Even with such large apports, the more hardened sceptics could probably suggest ways in which they might have been produced fraudulently. But fraud is difficult to accept in cases where mediums materialise items at the request of sitters, as did Agnes Nichols (later Mrs Samuel Guppy), one of the most gifted apport mediums during the 1860s and 1870s. It is recorded that one of her friends asked for a sunflower, and the medium complied with the immediate production, in a darkened seance room, of a 6-foot (1.6-metre) specimen, which arrived on a table with a mass of earth around its roots. At another seance each sitter was asked to name a fruit or vegetable; and the apports that were received were a banana, two oranges, a bunch of white grapes, a bunch of black grapes, a cluster of filberts, three walnuts, a dozen damsons, a slice of candied

Right: Madame d'Esperance, one of the foremost physical mediums of the late 19th century, with the golden lily that – through the agency of her materialised guide Yolande – literally grew in front of her sitters on 28 June 1890 to a height of 7 feet (2 metres). Exuding a strong fragrance and with 5 of its 11 flowers in bloom, it seemed solid enough – yet at her next seance Yolande dematerialised it in seven minutes. All that remained was this photograph and a couple of the flowers

pineapple, three figs, two apples, an onion, a peach, a few almonds, three dates, a potato, two large pears, a pomegranate, two crystallised greengages, a pile of dried currants, a lemon and a large bunch of raisins.

Doves and other birds are as popular with apport mediums as they are with magicians, but their materialisation is achieved under very different conditions. An Australian bootmaker, Charles Bailey, is credited with apporting an entire menagerie during his many years as a medium. To rule out trickery, he allowed himself to be stripped, searched and dressed in clothes supplied by investigators. Dr C. W. McCarthy, an eminent medical man in Sydney, imposed even more stringent test conditions. Having searched Bailey, he then placed the medium in a sack with holes for his hands, and tied him up.

On occasions the sitters were searched as well and the medium placed inside a cage

1807

Physical mediums

covered with mosquito netting. The door to the room was locked or sealed, the fireplace was blocked and paper pasted over the window. The only furniture allowed in the room was a table and chairs for the sitters. Yet, after a few minutes of darkness, when the lights were put on Bailey was found to be holding apports, such as two nests with a live bird in each. At other seances he produced a live, 18-inch (46-centimetre), shovel-nosed shark and a crab dripping in seaweed. Many of the live apports produced at his seances disappeared as mysteriously as they had arrived.

Later in his career, Bailey's mediumship was found to be far from convincing by a number of investigators who produced evidence to show that he had purchased the 'apports' from animal dealers. But others remained convinced that some of his phenomena were genuine.

Accessories and allegations

But where do apports come from? The 'spirit control' of a famous medium, Mrs Everitt, refused to produce them. 'I do not approve of bringing them,' she explained cryptically, 'for they are generally stolen.' There have been well-corroborated cases, however, where an apport has been an object that has been dematerialised from one place and rematerialised in another, sometimes at a sitter's request. This account was written by Ernesto Bozzano, an eminent Italian psychical researcher:

> In March, 1904, in a sitting in the house of Cavaliere Peretti, in which the medium was an intimate friend of ours, gifted with remarkable physical mediumship, and with whom apports could be obtained at command, I begged the communicating spirit to bring me a small block of pyrites which was lying on my writing table about two kilometres [1.2 miles] away. The spirit replied (through the entranced medium) that the power was almost exhausted but that all the same he

Above: the American medium Keith Milton Rhinehart, whose public demonstration in London in the 1960s provoked a guarded reaction from some members of the audience. He produced several objects (above right) from his mouth, including a prickly sea horse, but there is some evidence that he had merely regurgitated them

Below: two frames from one of the controversial films taken at Rolla, Missouri, USA, which allegedly show the paranormal movement of objects through the glass wall of the minilab. Despite several years of research, none of the minilab pioneers has managed to induce PK on the scale of the physical mediums

would make the attempt.

Soon after the medium sustained the usual spasmodic twitchings which signified the arrival of an apport, but without our hearing the fall of any object on the table or floor. We asked for an explanation from the spirit operator, who informed us that although he had managed to disintegrate a portion of the object desired, and had brought it into the room, there was not enough power for him to . . . re-integrate it.

He added, 'Light the light.' We did so, and found, to our great surprise, that the table, the clothes and hair of the sitters, as well as the furniture and carpets of the room, were covered with the thinnest layer of brilliant impalpable pyrites. When I returned home after the sitting I found the little block of pyrites lying on my writing table from which a large fragment, about one third of the whole piece, was missing.

Apport mediums seem to use different psychic techniques to produce the phenomenon, but with some the object seems to materialise

Physical mediums

out of their bodies. T. Lynn, a miner from the north of England, was photographed producing apports in this way. Small ectoplasmic shapes were often seen extending from his body, usually near the solar plexus, and Hewat McKenzie and Major C. Mowbray tested Lynn at the British College of Psychic Science, London, in 1928. The medium was put in a bag and his hands were tied to his knees with tapes. Flashlight photographs taken by the investigators showed luminous connections between his body and the apports.

Another miner, Jack Webber, was photographed some years later producing an apport in a similar way. Webber, a Welshman, was famous as a physical medium at whose seances trumpets would levitate and spirit voices would speak to those present. At a seance in 1938, Webber was searched thoroughly by a policeman in front of all the

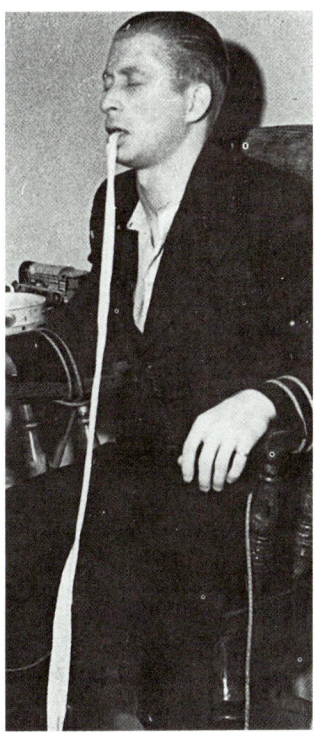

sitters, then tied to a chair. This account of the seance is taken from Harry Edwards's book, *The mediumship of Jack Webber* (1939):

> The red light was on, sufficiently bright for all to see the medium with his arms bound to the chair. Trumpets were in levitation ... one of these turned round, presenting its large opening to the solar plexus region and an object was heard to fall into it. It then came to the author who was asked to take out of the trumpet the article within – an Egyptian ornament. After a minute or two the trumpet again travelled to the solar plexus and another object was heard to fall into it.

In November of the same year, at a seance in Paddington, London, Webber's guide announced his intention of trying to materialise

Above left: Sai Baba, worshipped as a modern Hindu saint, holds one of his many apports

Above: the ex-miner Jack Webber produces a cord-like string of ectoplasm. On several occasions small ornaments (top) were seen to take shape in a white cloud over his solar plexus, but when handled they were perfectly solid

a brass ornament from an adjoining room. He asked for a photograph to be taken at a particular moment and said that this ought to record the production of the apport. The sitters then heard the sound of an object falling to the floor. When the plate was developed the small ornament – a bird weighing 2 ounces (57 grams) – could be seen apparently emerging in a white substance from the medium's solar plexus.

American medium Keith Milton Rhinehart demonstrated apport mediumship in London in the 1960s at the Caxton Hall. In a well-lit hall, before a capacity audience, he produced a number of items from his mouth, including a very prickly sea horse. Semiprecious stones were also 'apported' *through* his body: they were found embedded in his skin and were plucked out by witnesses. Some members of the audience, however, were distinctly unimpressed: the stones were never seen to emerge through his skin and looked as if they had been deliberately implanted in his flesh. Similarly, some witnesses thought some of his 'apports' to have been merely regurgitated.

But a comparison of the best apport mediums does provide some striking similarities, which indicate that it is a genuine phenomenon. At the turn of the century, Henry Sausse recorded many instances, in *Des preuves? en voilà*, of apports produced by an entranced woman medium. Her method was to form her hands into a cup, in full light, and a small cloud was seen to form inside. This would transform itself instantly into an apport, such as a spray of roses, complete with flowers, buds and leaves.

Although there are countless similar stories of physical mediumship in the literature, the fact remains that apports are rare today. But other, no less remarkable feats of mediumship are constantly reported.

Can spirits 'come through' and talk with their earthly voices? See page 1830

ESP unlimited

The Ganzfeld experiments, designed to encourage telepathy in special laboratory conditions, have had the unexpected result of producing spontaneous ESP. CARL SARGENT describes how this 'spin-off' happens

Left: Dr Carl Sargent, head of the Ganzfeld experiments at Cambridge. He himself participates in the tests, acting both as sender and receiver at various times

Below: a subject in the Ganzfeld state, ready to try to receive telepathic messages from a sender in another location. In the Ganzfeld environment, the subject is deprived of normal sight and sound

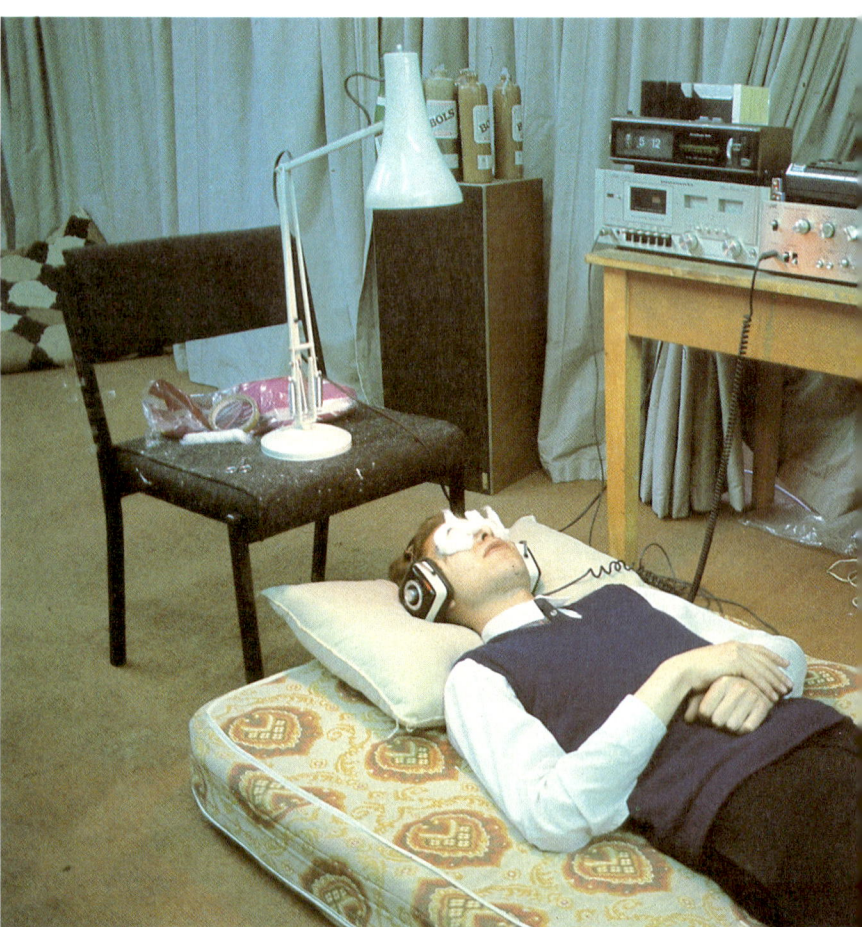

SPONTANEOUS ESP in the laboratory? It seems a contradiction in terms, but it occurs. Indeed, ESP experiments at the University of Cambridge have shown that the laboratory can even *stimulate* spontaneous ESP – a powerful rejoinder to those who object to scientific 'testing' of psi.

One particular kind of ESP experiment has dominated parapsychological work at Cambridge since 1978 – telepathy of subjects in the Ganzfeld state (see page 1430). Using pictures as targets, the 'receiver' in the experiment is kept in an environment of unchanging uniform light and sound for 30 minutes or so. For much of this time, a 'sender' at a distant location looks at one – and only one – randomly chosen target picture. This picture could be almost anything: a newspaper cutting, greeting card, art print or cartoon, for example. The receiver is asked to talk about his or her visual or auditory images, physical feelings, stray thoughts, everything, while the experimenter writes down everything said. At the end of the experiment the receiver is shown a set of four different pictures, one of which is a copy of the target picture viewed by the sender. Even the experimenter does not know which one it is. The receiver tries to pick it out on the basis of the impressions he or she had while in the Ganzfeld environment. The experiment is more sophisticated than this in detail, but this is the essence of it.

What the experimenters are looking for is a scoring rate that is well above the chance level. If chance alone operated, the correct picture would be chosen one time out of four, or 25 per cent of the time. In fact, the 'direct hit' rate from nearly 500 Ganzfeld test sessions at Cambridge is just over 39 per cent, notably higher than chance.

These simple and unobjectionable statistical tests give clear evidence of ESP in operation. But it is also clear that the statistics are not measuring all the ESP that occurs – after all, spontaneous ESP by definition cannot be detected with pre-designed statistical tests.

The receivers in the Ganzfeld tests often exhibit ESP unconnected to the target picture. For example, one receiver was plagued with a pain in his lower back during his session, although he typically did not suffer this. Later we learned that medical students had been listening to a lecture on rheumatism in a nearby lecture theatre. In another session filmed for television, an experimenter squashed a beetle that was crawling across the page on which he was writing down a receiver's comments. The receiver reported hearing The Beatles singing *Please please me* – an ironic verbal pun. Sometimes receivers pick up extraneous aspects of the feelings of other participants in experiments. Once, when I sat in my office fretting over a personal difficulty, a receiver experienced severe anxiety during her session. Such cases

ESP on test

Below: the lady of the lake, the legendary figure who was supposed to have given King Arthur the great sword Excalibur. In independent tests held on the same day, two Ganzfeld subjects received impressions of her – an example of 'crosstalk'

Below right: a cartoon of Noah's ark by W. Heath Robinson. This painting has assumed a special place in the Ganzfeld tests, having more than once been the focus of crosstalk

Two minds as one

The similarities – or correspondences – between two consecutive Ganzfeld experiments at Cambridge University on 25 August 1980 illustrate what is meant by 'crosstalk'. With no contact between them, Trevor Harley picked up on and described elements of Carl Sargent's responses in the earlier of the two tests. The remarks below are the exact words of the subjects.

Sargent's session
Cross shapes, crucifixes, floating.

A stag's head . . . very clear, or maybe a horse. Even a giraffe; the horse's head grew as I looked at it.
A huge variety of animals. It's like a bloody Noah's ark.

Harley's session
Someone being crucified.
Crucifix shapes and crosses.
A giraffe with its neck outstretched reaching up to a tree. Now its head turns into a horse's head.
The white dove hovering, branch in beak, looking at the ark. Noah is looking at it.

of ESP have been reported from other laboratories. Stanley Krippner of the Maimonides Medical Center in New York reported a dream telepathy session in which he, as sender, was preoccupied with a stomach pain that he feared might require an operation. The dreamer picked up the theme of the stomach operation in detail, but not the target picture Krippner was looking at. Indeed, in all these cases cited, the receivers were not successful in picking up the target. Perhaps only so much ESP can operate at any one time.

Receivers may even 'crosstalk' – that is, detect and report elements from another receiver's session. In the Cambridge files are two transcripts in which the theme of 'the lady of the lake' – and more specifically, of her hand holding Arthur's sword aloft – is described. They were collected on the same day from two subjects who had no contact with each other.

This kind of crosstalk may be put down to common features in the environment – maybe the newspaper both receivers read that day contained something on Arthurian legends. But another example shows this cannot be the whole explanation. On 25 August 1980 I myself acted as a subject in a precognition experiment starting at 12.16 p.m. I scored a direct hit on a W. Heath Robinson picture of Noah's ark, called *Spring cleaning on the ark*. At 2.15 p.m. another subject, Trevor Harley, started his session in the same experiment. I had been careful to say absolutely nothing about my session to him, but the correspondences between his experiences and mine are really remarkable (see box). Incidentally, Harley had scored badly on the target picture. His ESP had been distracted by going through my memories rather than concentrated on receiving the target picture.

Receivers may also demonstrate precognition as well as ESP in their sessions. One student subject confided before a session that

1811

ESP on test

exactly which part of the picture he had detected first. It was as if he had sent that information to me to be recognised when I saw the target.

A more dramatic example of a receiver-turned-sender occurred in a session on 27 March 1979 when the target picture was Renoir's *Le moulin de la galette*. This picture shows a group of people at a French outdoor café, with a bottle and glasses on a table. In Ashton's mind these objects became a ouija board and he became a physical medium. (Anyone doubting that the Ganzfeld procedure can induce a genuinely altered state of consciousness should have heard his respiration rate treble.) As sender in that session, I had the most bizarre mental sensations I have ever experienced. I found it impossible to concentrate and 'send' the picture. It was like the mental equivalent of trying to walk through water, and in my session notes I specifically wrote, 'It feels as if I'm being hypnotised at a distance.' It is intriguing that I should have had this sensation at the time that Ashton imagined he was a medium.

Senders have also frequently and correctly noted impressions about what the receiver is experiencing and feeling – for example, being very anxious, feeling physically disorientated, experiencing floating sensations. But the senders could logically, if unconsciously, infer that anyone in the artificial Ganzfeld state might have such feelings.

Sometimes crosstalk occurs between experiments. In the course of one dream precognition experiment, the subject dreamed that the next two targets would be a B and a D picture. These were wrong for this experiment – but correct for another test going on at the same time.

The most striking cases of spontaneous ESP are the extended correspondences, of which two instances can be given. Hugh Ashton again figures in one. In a session run

he had a very strong impression that the target was going to show a Highland stag, because he had dreamed about such an animal being in the laboratory the night before. An antlered buck deer was a prominent feature of the target picture, and only two of the 220 potential targets then available contained such an animal.

Hugh Ashton, one of the regular receivers in the Cambridge Ganzfeld tests, has the strange facility of turning into a sender during his sessions. Ashton is a 25-year-old statistician who doubles as bass and keyboards player in a Cambridge band. He has made several outstanding ESP hits on targets. In the first session undertaken with this receiver, I acted as sender. When I opened the sealed envelope containing the randomly selected target picture for that session, it was a piece of feminist art. I knew at once, with complete certainty, – and correctly as it turned out – that Ashton had already identified the target and I knew

1812

ESP on test

on 27 November 1981 he acted as the receiver. I was the sender and a student, Julie Milton, was the experimenter. His first comment was that I had an envelope on which the number 39 was marked. Then he said that the picture was W. Heath Robinson's cartoon of Noah's ark. Now, this target (is there something significant about this particular picture?) had been used for a session on 20 November 1981 with me as receiver, Julie as sender, and another student, Sheila Bennett, as experimenter. Hugh knew nothing of the previous test and had no idea that this cartoon was in our pool of possible targets, by now expanded to over 340 pictures. He had exactly specified the target of the earlier test. The number 39 was the number of the set of pictures used in the next session involving myself, Julie and Sheila, but not Hugh. He seems to have picked up information from the past and future, with a startling exactness.

The second example is also intriguing. On 14 June 1981 a student subject tested by two other students gave as a first impression of the target a picture by the French artist Seurat. It must be said that such specific impressions are rather rare. Four days later, on the morning of 18 June 1981, a student experimenter, who knew nothing of the earlier session, woke and gazed at Seurat's picture of *The bathers*, which hung on her wall. That would make a nice target for the day's session, she said to herself. And it did so happen that it was the target picture that day. As was the practice, it was selected at random. The fourth student experimenter who picked picture set number 17 by chance had no idea that picture 17A was Seurat's *The bathers*. This ESP concentrated on Seurat continued: on 20 June yet another subject reported an impression of – indeed, the same

Left: Hugh Ashton, a regular participant in the Ganzfeld experiments. Ashton has made several outstanding hits on ESP targets and has been known to turn into a sender during sessions when he is receiving

Below: Georges Seurat's *The bathers*, another of the target pictures for the Ganzfeld tests. During a four-day period in 1981, this particular picture sparked off a series of telepathic impressions from such unrelated sources that the events could only be described as spontaneous extra-sensory perception

Below left: *Le moulin de la galette*, a painting by the French Impressionist Renoir. This picture was a target on one of the occasions that Ashton reversed roles from subject to sender

painting. Apart from the two mentions on the 14th and 20th, sandwiching the test session in which *The bathers* was the actual target, I have only one other specific citing of Seurat from nearly 500 transcripts.

In my final illustration of spontaneous ESP in the laboratory, I cannot give full details because the sender wishes to remain anonymous. On the occasion in question, I was acting as experimenter. The sender reported seeing quite clearly an apparitional figure of me walk through the locked door of the room in which she was sitting, and look around.

What are we to make of all this – the receiver crosstalk, the receivers acting as senders, timeslips and even apparitions in the laboratory? As with anything spontaneous, it is impossible to prove paranormality. But to demand such proof is to miss the point. What is important is that spontaneous events do occur in the laboratory and that they are common to many experimenters. The laboratory is not after all hostile to spontaneous ESP. Indeed, the atmosphere of the experimental laboratory may even spark it. And perhaps we should not lament the fact that scientists cannot trap all the possible ESP in experiments with pre-planned statistical measurements. Although recent successful lines of experiments, such as the tests for altered states of consciousness, have a better repeatability record than anything previously reported in parapsychology, it is oddly satisfying to know that ESP still remains somewhat erratic and unpredictable. It may be of interest to know that my experience in the session with Hugh Ashton on that March night in 1979, when I felt my mental processes paralysed, did more to convince me of the reality of psi than any number of statistics. As far as I am concerned, ESP certainly exists – I literally felt it.

1813

Theatre of blood

Psychic surgeons have been widely criticised by those who allege that their methods are fraudulent. Nevertheless, many of them seem genuinely able to heal their patients. Why does psychic surgery work? DAVID HARVEY ponders this puzzling question

BELIEVERS IN THE REALITY of psychic surgery must have been surprised to read reports that Antonio 'Doctor Tony' Agpaoa resorted to the surgeon's knife when he was suffering from appendicitis in 1979. The man who had built up a reputation for his bare-hand surgery entered hospital under an assumed name in preference to undergoing treatment at the hands of his fellow Filipino miracle workers. He is reported to have confided to the surgeon who operated on him, 'You know, doc, physicians can't heal themselves.'

Here is one more mystery in the saga of the psychic surgeons through which are woven claims of miracles, allegations of fraud, and evidence that is confusingly contradictory.

The visit to the UK in 1978 of the Elizaldes, a husband-and-wife team practising psychic surgery, roused considerable interest because it appeared to offer scientists an opportunity to study the phenomenon closely at first hand. Perhaps, at last, they would be able to find a definitive answer to the many questions that the reports of psychic surgery had raised. In the event, the scandal the Elizaldes were to leave in their wake simply served to deepen the conviction of the cynics that the whole business was based on fraud, an explanation that, for many people, rang all too true.

David and Helen Elizalde's first UK visit in 1978 was sponsored by the Spiritualists' National Union (SNU). Although they live in Australia, David Elizalde is Filipino by birth and his wife is English of Cypriot parentage. They claim to be able to penetrate the human body with their hands, in the same way as the native Filipino psychic surgeons, leaving the patient's body unblemished and free from scars. After the visit there were several testimonies to the effectiveness of their work, including reports of cures and improvements.

In 1979 they returned to give treatment to the sick at the SNU's headquarters at Stansted Hall, Essex. The operations were carried out in conditions screened from public gaze. Patients were required to make a prior appointment, and the literature put out by the SNU stressed that no 'unauthorised' people would be allowed to be present. If patients wished to be accompanied by another person, a special request had to be made on

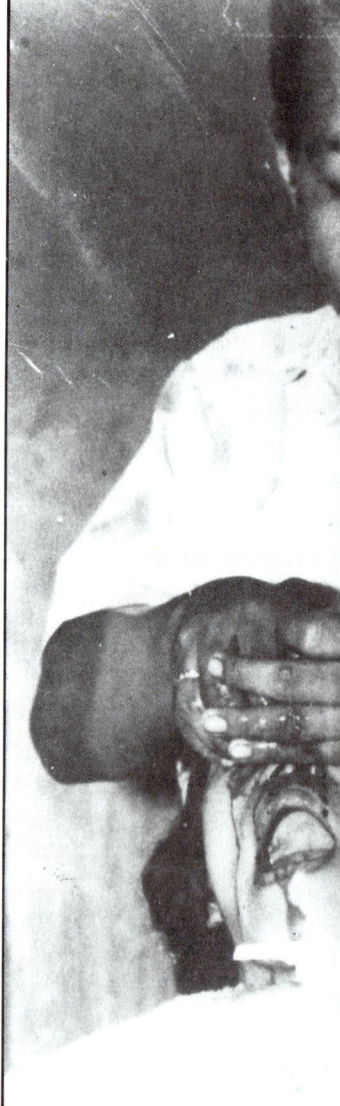

Below left: the Paraguayan psychic surgeon Ivan Trilha demonstrates a leg operation in Mexico City in 1979, under the watchful eyes of parapsychologists Bill Roll (left) and Hans Bender (right, next to cameraman)

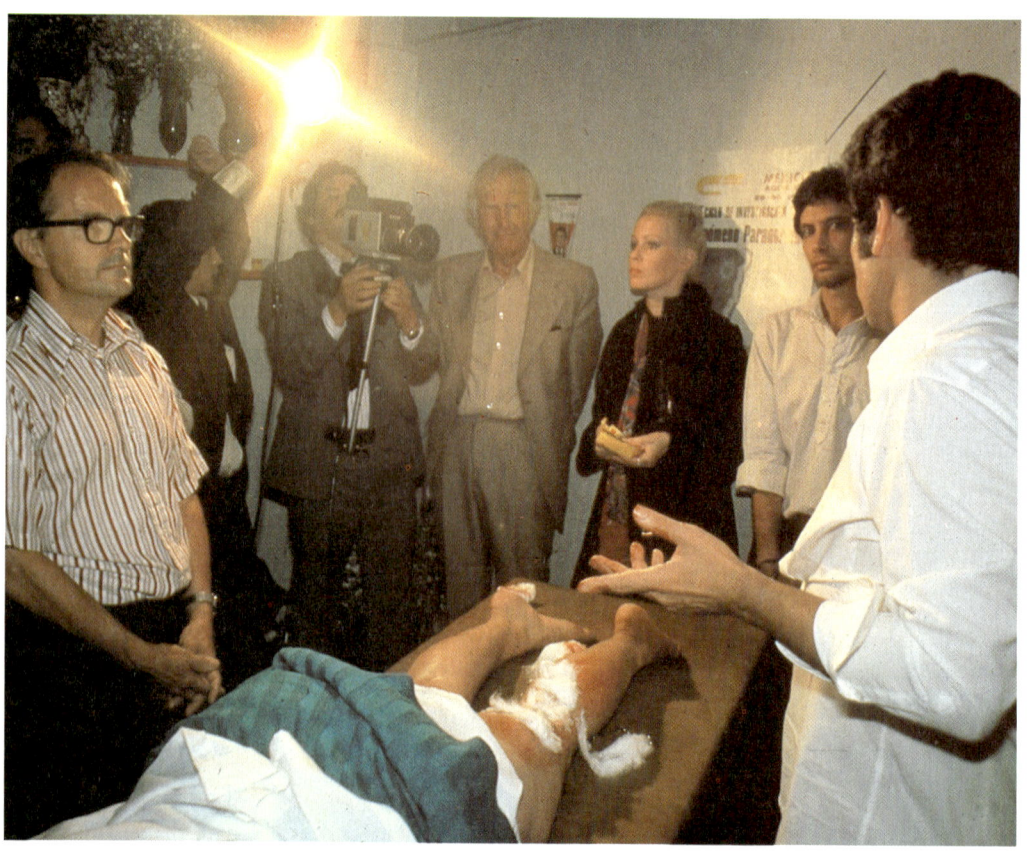

Psychic surgery

Right: David and Helen Elizalde perform an operation using bare-hand surgery. On one of their visits to Britain, in 1979, their work was subjected to close scrutiny by the BBC television programme *Nationwide* – whose investigators concluded that they were frauds. Nevertheless, many of the Elizaldes' patients swear that they have been effectively cured

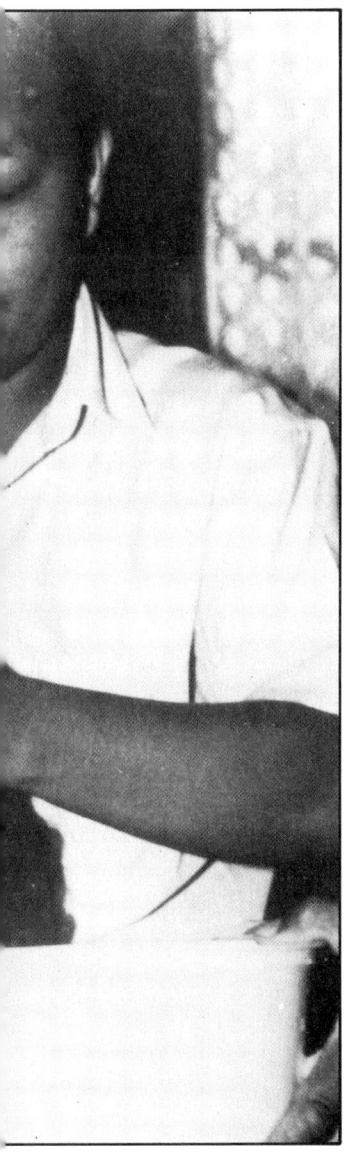

Below: the Brazilian psychic surgeon Tony Agpaoa. Agpaoa notched up an impressive record of successes – and yet, when he became ill with appendicitis in 1979, he went to hospital for treatment by orthodox doctors rather than seek the help of his fellow psychic surgeons

the application form. Were these precautions simply designed to make for better operating conditions? It seems unlikely – for they do not seem to be necessary for other psychic surgeons, who regularly carry out their work in front of observers. Or were they designed to keep out the prying eyes of critical observers? Suspicions that this might have been so were strengthened by the forthright and scathing condemnation made by BBC-TV's *Nationwide* programme in May 1979.

The *Nationwide* evidence was made up of several elements: a film of the Elizaldes at work, and a critical commentary on it by the arch-sceptic and conjurer James Randi, interviews with patients and forensic reports on some of the blood and other substances produced during the operations.

While the *Nationwide* film looked impressive at first sight, Randi was able to point out, in a frame-by-frame analysis, that what was going on was almost certainly faked. He pointed to a number of sequences that, he maintained, were standard sleight-of-hand tricks. The surgeons did not have their fingers buried deeply inside their patients, but simply folded them, pressing down on the flesh with their knuckles. This is all very well – but where does the blood and gore come from? It was obvious to Randi. He showed how they could have been 'palmed' during the operation by the non-operating partner, who was ostensibly there simply to pass swabs and lend assistance to the other. Randi claimed that at one stage David Elizalde held his hand 'exactly as a conjurer would if he had concealed something in his hand'. He was able to give a fair imitation of a bare-hand operation incorporating the ploys he had noted on the film.

Unacceptable evidence?

The case for fraud was reinforced by forensic tests carried out on samples of blood retrieved from an operation on Gordon Higginson, then president of the SNU. Unknown to the psychic surgeons, members of the *Nationwide* team were present incognito, and assisted during the operation. One of them held the bowl into which bloodstained cotton wool and blood clots were dropped. Analysis at a forensic laboratory showed that it was pig's blood. Bloodspattered clothing belonging to Higginson and another patient was also tested, and the same finding was made. Confronted by the evidence, Higginson simply refused to accept the report. 'I think that this is just put up. I think they [the forensic experts] are telling an untruth. I know that it is genuine.' Helen Elizalde had another line. 'Well, I think it is very strange, although I have heard that the structure of the blood does change.'

Nationwide reporter Roger Cook drew attention to this refusal to accept what seemed to be clinching proof:

despite this overwhelming scientific evidence, the SNU won't admit that they've bought a pig in a poke, and that they've brought to this country, at great expense, two confidence tricksters, because that's what the Elizaldes are: unscrupulous, frauds and liars, exploiting the chronically sick. If they dispute this then they're of course quite at liberty to take us to court. I doubt very much that they will because they know full well that what they're doing won't stand up to any properly conducted investigation.

The matter did not rest there. After they had left the country, the Elizaldes became the subject of an investigation by the Director of Public Prosecutions who, in September 1981, announced that if the Elizaldes returned to the UK, they would be arrested and held for questioning and would face possible prosecution. Despite the allegations, however, there were still a number of people who claimed they had been helped by the Elizaldes, and jumped to their defence.

A retired nurse and midwife, Hilda Totty, who had acted as assistant to the Elizaldes on scores of occasions, had herself been operated on twice for sinus trouble, with complete success. 'I am free from discomfort,' she told *Psychic News*. 'Before my sinuses were blocked which caused headaches and eye pain. Now it's gone. I can taste food; before, I could not.' Others have come forward and vouched for the benefit that they received. But if we accept this evidence for the moment, does it mean that psychic surgery may still be a reality? Perhaps.

Doctors know the value of suggestion. A persuasive bedside manner has always been suspected to be a powerful force in promoting improvement in the condition of patients. Formal confirmation by medical

Psychic surgery

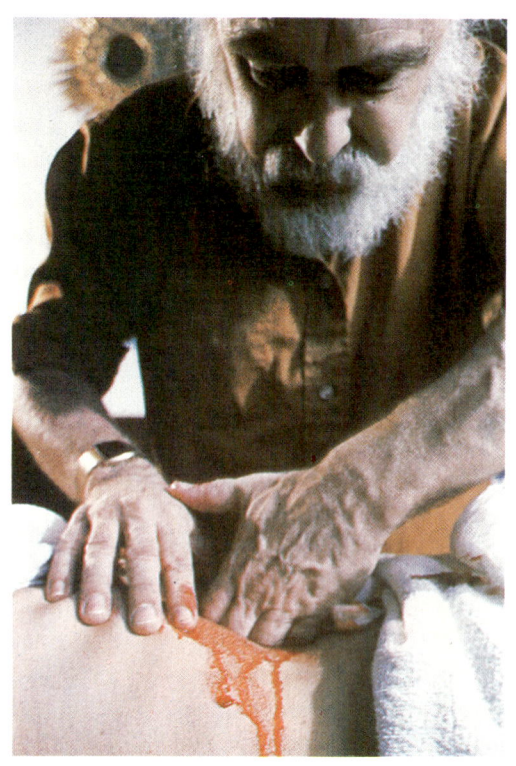

Left: conjurer James Randi simulates psychic surgery. In the investigation of the Elizaldes by the BBC television programme *Nationwide*, Randi was able to demonstrate that every single effect produced by the Elizaldes could be duplicated by conjurers' tricks

Below: Gordon Higginson, president of the SNU, who was treated by the Elizaldes during their 1979 visit. Blood that had appeared to come from Higginson's body was analysed after the operation – and turned out to be pig's blood.
Nationwide reporter Roger Cook (bottom) concluded that the Elizaldes were 'unscrupulous, frauds and liars, exploiting the chronically sick'

science of the placebo effect – the fact that, with enough faith in their doctors, patients will improve markedly even if they are administered sugar pills instead of real drugs – showed that there was definitely something in this belief. Confidence in the treatment and an expectation of results can be enough for physical changes to occur. Could the performance of a sham operation, with impressive blood-and-gore props, have the same effect? It seems quite possible that it could. In this case, the psychic surgeon would be manipulating the patient's propensity to believe in the authenticity of the psychic operation to bring about improvements. Of course, the psychic surgeon would have to protest the authenticity of his operation for the mind cure to work.

José Silva, founder of the Silva Mind Control system, a method of dynamic meditation, self-healing and related techniques, studied a wide range of phenomena including the potential of mind power. What he saw carried out in the name of psychic surgery was, he found, a sham, but it could nonetheless be dramatically beneficial for the patient. Someone complaining of pains in the head, for example, would lie down while the surgeon wielded a knife with which, he assured the patient, he would cut out the cause of the discomfort. The knife was lunged at the patient's head and buried in the pillow, which had been stuffed with chickens' entrails. The surgeon triumphantly showed the patient the offending growth he had cut out, and the patient went away believing that he had been treated successfully. It was, of course, the mind that did the real healing work. That puts a rather different complexion on the practice of psychic surgery. On one point Silva and the *Nationwide* team were in agreement: they both observed what they believed was an elaborate theatrical performance. In the respective cases of the psychic surgeons they investigated, they reached totally different conclusions about their motivation. Where Silva found a genuine desire to heal, *Nationwide* identified merely a desire for financial gain.

That the Elizaldes did benefit from their 14-day trip was confirmed by a subsequent statement by the SNU. In addition to paying for their trip and other costs, the £10 charged per patient generated fees of £2500 for the couple.

If *Nationwide*'s conclusion was correct, is it reasonable to assume that all other psychic surgeons are necessarily concerned only with profit? Lyall Watson attempts to put the problem of fraud into context in *The Romeo error*, written in 1973, when there had already been allegations that exploitation and fraud were the realities behind psychic surgery:

> During the last three years there has been a great deal of publicity, both good and bad, concerning the Philippine healers. Tens of thousands of foreign patients have been attracted to Manila. Where there is such a demand, accompanied as it is by the offer of considerable sums of money from desperate people, there will be those who will do anything to meet that demand and obtain the proffered rewards. . . . But it is sad that the commotion should be allowed to obscure the fact that something very extraordinary still happens in the Philippines.

Suspicion of fraud

It is tempting to use examples of fraud to provide a universal explanation for psychic surgery. After all, that way there is no need to ponder the staggering implications of the practice if it were ever proved genuine. But what if it is – in some cases: despite extensive investigations of the Brazilian José Arigo, for example, his rusty-knife surgery was never exposed as fraud (see page 378).

The real problem arises when we come to explain psychic surgery as a real phenomenon. Alfred Stelter, the German investigator who made his own on-the-spot study of Agpaoa and other psychic surgeons (see page 1770), thoroughly investigated the contradictory evidence that has been advanced variously to support and demolish the claims for their authenticity. He points out the difficulty that the materialistic mind has in accepting evidence that defies any attempt to be measured by the yardstick of scientific appraisal. His book *Psi-healing* contains many examples of failures or partial successes of psychic surgery, along with remarkable cures. There are also several telling case studies of attempts to investigate psychic surgery in which the evidence has been

Psychic surgery

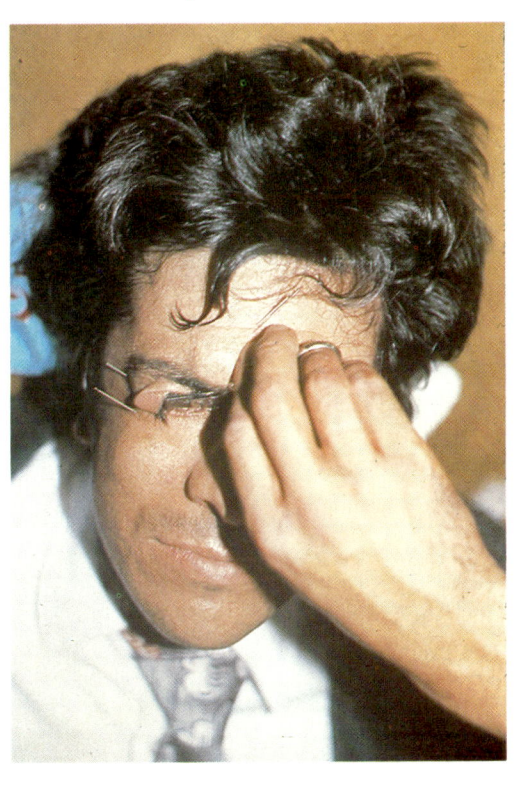

Left: Ivan Trilha performs an eye operation

Below: a Filipino psychic surgeon known as Marcello conducts a stomach operation in this photograph, taken by the German journalist Gunther Leeb. Leeb spent three weeks on a filming mission in the Philippines in 1971, during which time he himself underwent psychic surgery for a chronic ailment of the lower abdomen, at the hands of Marcello and another psychic surgeon. Their treatment apparently effected a complete cure

sufferer who could not be helped in Europe, but in the fact that the surgery goes beyond the frame of reference of Western science; given further research, this will lead to new spiritual and scientific territory tending to revolutionize our whole picture of man.

Stelter's is a challenging conclusion that clashes with the more brutal findings of investigations such as *Nationwide*'s of the Elizaldes. It is certainly far more difficult to grasp than the bold accusation that the psychic surgeons were no more than liars and frauds who set out to exploit the sick in an unscrupulously heartless way. Stelter's seems both an exciting and a reasonable conclusion – and yet there are snags. What of Agpaoa? If, as Stelter suggests, he was a miracle worker, why did he turn to orthodox medicine for help when he was ill? There is no simple answer that resolves all the facts and, despite the desire for neatly packaged, definitive solutions to mysteries such as this one, perhaps there never can be.

On page 1838: a first-hand account of treatment at the hands of a psychic surgeon

loaded in the final report to fit the conclusion that the authors want to reach. Like Lyall Watson, Stelter comes to the conclusion that there is something behind the claims, although he does not pretend to have fathomed the secrets of psychic surgery. Doctor Tony does, he concedes, sometimes work miracles.

What may be involved, he speculates, is a kind of temporary suspension of physical reality in which there is some subtle interplay between spiritual and physical energies, manipulated by the psychic surgeon. Matter materialises in odd and unpredictable ways but, according to the cases Stelter has investigated, it is not through trickery.

Ultimately, it does seem that there is a spectrum of explanations for what is claimed to be psychic surgery. At one extreme there are outright frauds and deceptions intended to exploit the tragic plight of the sick. Somewhere in the middle there are the theatrical performances that Silva observed, intended to trigger psychogenic, or mind, cures. Both are comprehensible in the light of Western beliefs and values. But Western understanding fails before José Arigo's rusty-knife surgery and bare-hand operations.

Confronted by the inexplicable, many researchers feel that all they can do is acknowledge the problem and try to live with it. Stelter felt that he could deny neither his own experience of psychic surgery nor the corroborative evidence he and other scientists unearthed, notwithstanding the perplexing problems it raised for Western minds.

The Philippine healers bring about astonishing results, but there is no way yet to quantify their success. The significance of psychic surgery, in my view, lies less in the cure of one or another

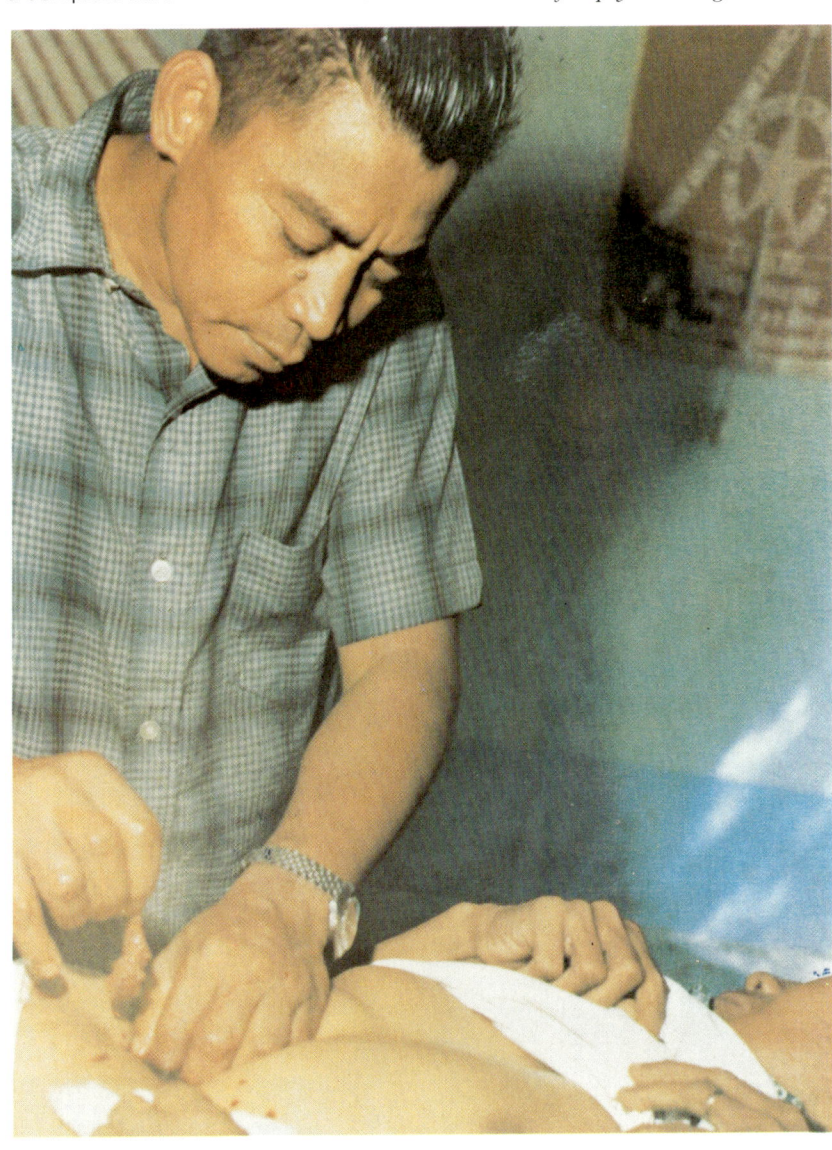

A penetrating vision

Modern physicists are probing ever deeper into the structure of matter, using costly and sophisticated technology. However, STEPHEN M. PHILLIPS asks whether some of their discoveries have been made before — by means of ancient Indian yoga techniques

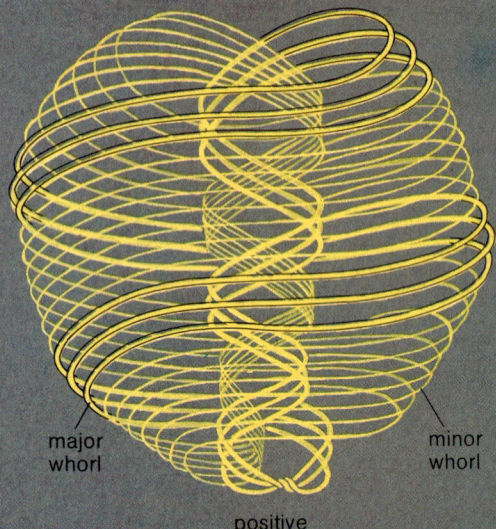

major whorl — minor whorl
positive

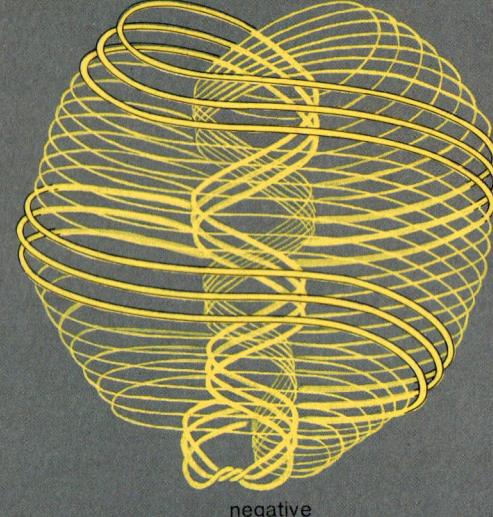

negative

Left: the two kinds of 'ultimate physical atom' seen clairvoyantly by Annie Besant and C.W. Leadbeater. The 'atoms' consisted of currents of energy forming spiral whorls. Colours constantly flashed out, changing according to which spiral was most active. The 'atoms' spun incessantly

THE TWO FIGURES WHO DOMINATED the Theosophical Society at the end of the 19th century, Annie Besant and Charles W. Leadbeater, began in 1895 a series of researches that was to last nearly 40 years. They were studying the ultimate structure of matter, using methods that orthodox science did not countenance: they were attempting to view atoms by extra-sensory perception. The vast amounts of information they produced seemed to bear no relationship to the findings of chemists and physicists during those four decades. Only in the 1980s were resemblances noticed between their descriptions and the modern theory of the structure of fundamental particles. It now seems possible that Besant and Leadbeater saw by occult means the 'quarks' that physicists postulate as the building blocks of matter.

The power of viewing the very small is one of the *siddhis*, or psychic faculties, that, according to Eastern tradition, can be cultivated by yoga meditation. In the ancient *Yoga sutras* the semi-legendary sage Patanjali lists the *siddhis*: one of them is the power to gain 'knowledge of the small, the hidden, or the distant by directing the light of a superphysical faculty'. This ability to acquire 'knowledge of the small' will be called 'micro-psi' in this article. Besant and Leadbeater claimed to have gained their micro-psi abilities under the tutelage of their Indian gurus.

To acquire knowledge paranormally that is confirmed by conventional science only

Below: Annie Besant with Charles Leadbeater. They divided their work while clairvoyantly viewing matter on the small scale, the highest magnifications being achieved by Mrs Besant. Their observations were in conflict with the science of their time

many years later is perhaps the most convincing type of ESP. In such cases there is no possibility that the psychic has access to normal sources of information. Whether or not the ESP was exercised under controlled laboratory conditions, it is impossible in principle to gain information by fraud or by means of the normal senses.

In 1895 Annie Besant and Charles Leadbeater published pictures of what they

Occult chemistry

Window on the whorls

The diagrams drawn from the descriptions provided by the two Theosophists Annie Besant and Charles Leadbeater give only a faint impression of the spectacle they witnessed. What they saw was confirmed by later clairvoyants using micro-psi (the faculty of viewing the very small) in the late 1950s. Initially a mist or haze of light appeared when they observed matter on the microscopic scale. With greater magnification the mist was resolved into myriad points of light, scintillating and moving chaotically. Some moved in regular orbits, forming the seven minor and three major whorls of the 'atoms'. Some cascaded, like showers of meteors. The motions of the 'atoms' were confined to well-defined volumes of space, in any one of seven different geometric forms.

Each 'ultimate physical atom' was enclosed in a 'bubble', as if some transparent membrane surrounded it. The Theosophists spoke of space itself being pushed back by the dynamic activity of the matter in the 'atom'. This accorded with the complex theories of Theosophy, in which what we normally regard as a vacuum was only one of the seven states of matter.

claimed were hydrogen, nitrogen and oxygen atoms present in the air. According to their description a hydrogen atom was

> seen to consist of six small bodies, contained in an egg-like form.... It rotated with great rapidity on its own axis, vibrating at the same time, the internal bodies performing similar gyrations. The whole atom spins and quivers and has to be steadied before exact observation is possible. The six little bodies are arranged in two sets of three, forming two triangles that are not interchangeable.

Below left: the atom of hydrogen, according to Besant and Leadbeater. It was a transparent egg-shaped body containing smaller globes arranged in two interlinked triangles. Each one of the globes contained three of the 'ultimate physical atoms'

Below right: the seven geometrical forms of the micro-psi 'atoms'

But the 'six little bodies' were not the most basic units of matter. The psychics could magnify the images of them and found that each was composed of a globe enclosing three 'points of light'. When these in turn were highly magnified, they appeared as particles of definite size. Besant and Leadbeater called them 'ultimate physical atoms'.

Each of these 'ultimate' particles was seen to be made up of 10 convoluted spiral curves, or whorls, three of which (the 'major' whorls) appeared thicker or brighter than the other seven ('minor') whorls. The overall form of the whorls was that of a heart, with

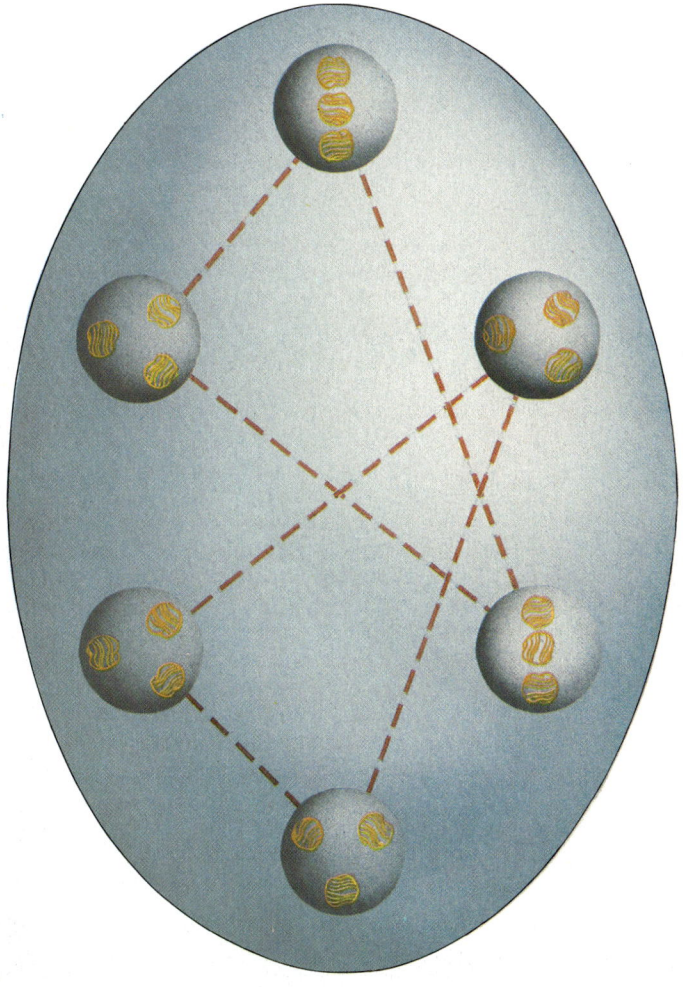

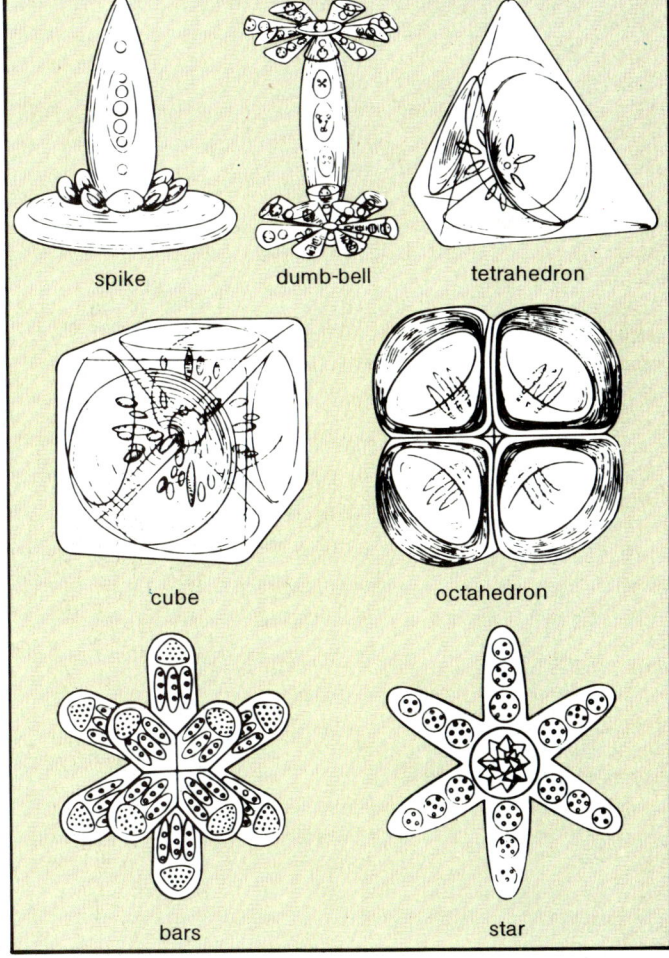

spike dumb-bell tetrahedron

cube octahedron

bars star

1819

Occult chemistry

one end slightly concave and the other end pointed.

The Theosophists' description of matter differed greatly from the contemporary scientific notions of the atom. Two centuries earlier Sir Isaac Newton had conjectured that atoms were 'solid, massy, impenetrable'. In 1895 it was suspected that atoms in fact had a structure and that they were composed of smaller electrically charged particles. One of these was the electron, a hypothetical negatively charged particle much lighter than an atom. Electric currents were thought to consist of electrons in motion. In 1897 the electron's existence was demonstrated by the English physicist J. J. Thomson. Various models of the structure of the atom were then proposed. But the theory that finally won acceptance, as the result of the experimental and theoretical analyses of the physicists H. Geiger, E. Marsden and Lord Rutherford, was that of the 'nuclear' atom. They showed that the electrons in an atom orbited a tiny nucleus in which all the atom's positive charge and most of its mass were concentrated. When this was first demonstrated, from 1909 onwards, the electrons were supposed to move in well-defined orbits like those of the planets. They whirled around the nucleus millions of times per second, in a volume with a ten-millionth of the breadth of a pinhead. In the 1920s, with the advent of quantum mechanics, the electrons and their orbits came to be regarded as 'fuzzy' and ill-defined in position (see page 856).

Ahead of the scientists

As each scientific picture of the atom was discarded and replaced by the next, Besant and Leadbeater continued to produce remarkably consistent descriptions of their 'micro-psi atoms', which at no time bore any resemblance to those of the scientists.

The two Theosophists observed that in certain elements – for example, the gases neon, argon, krypton and xenon and the metal platinum – the atoms were not all identical. This anticipated the scientific realisation that chemically indistinguishable variants of an element could exist, having atoms of different masses. These variants came to be called 'isotopes'.

One of the most important tools of orthodox chemistry is the periodic table. This is a classification of the elements in terms of their chemical properties and their atomic weights – the relative weights of their atoms, as determined chemically. The atomic weights of the elements increase as one reads across the table from left to right and down it from top to bottom. Chemical properties change systematically along each row of the table and down each column. Besant and Leadbeater found that the complex shape of the micro-psi 'atom' corresponded to the column of the periodic table in which that element lay.

When the two psychics began their

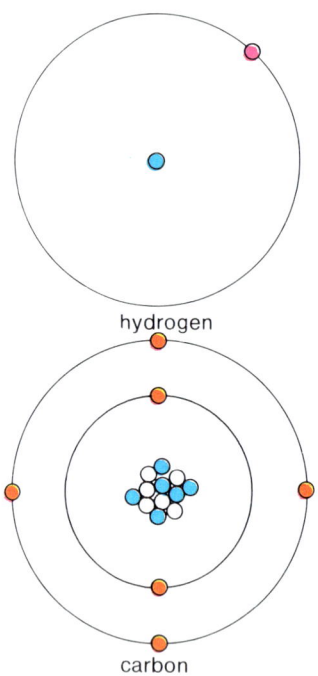

Above: in the scientific picture, the nucleus of hydrogen is a single positively charged particle, the proton. The nuclei of heavier atoms, such as carbon, consist of protons and neutral particles called neutrons. Negatively charged electrons circle the nucleus

Below: isotopes of an element such as neon have equal numbers of protons, but different numbers of neutrons

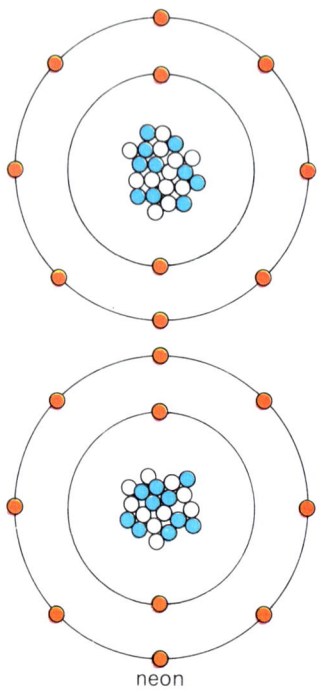

research, between 60 and 70 elements were known (of the 90 or so that occur in nature) and there were many gaps in the periodic table. Besant and Leadbeater described a number of types of micro-psi 'atom' that corresponded, they believed, to gaps in the periodic table. The existence of these elements, and many of their properties, could be predicted by conventional science, but they had not yet been observed.

The two psychics discovered that the number of 'ultimate' particles in the micro-psi 'atoms' was very nearly equal to 18 times the atomic weight of the corresponding element. (The atomic weight of an element is the average weight of the atoms of its various isotopes. Scientists at that time took their unit to be the weight of the hydrogen atom.) Thus hydrogen, with the atomic weight 1, had 18 'ultimate' particles; carbon, with an atomic weight of 12, had 216.

The 'atoms' that the two psychics described were sometimes seen to be combined into larger units, just as the corresponding chemical atoms combined into larger groupings, called molecules. The micro-psi 'atoms' were combined in the same numbers as the atoms known to science. But, in total violation of all that was known to chemistry, micro-psi 'atoms' were observed to be broken up and their constituent particles mixed with those of other atoms. Sceptics felt that this discredited Besant and Leadbeater's claims, since chemical atoms do not split up and mix with each other wholesale when they combine, though they share or transfer some outer electrons.

Other problems emerged. For example, Leadbeater described the micro-psi molecule of the compound benzene as being octahedral – that is, as having the overall shape of an eight-faced solid. But chemists already knew that the chemical molecule of benzene was flat and hexagonal. And the psychics described micro-psi 'atoms' of several supposed elements for which there was no room whatever in the periodic table.

Such problems as these add up to overwhelming evidence against the two Theosophists' interpretation of the micro-psi 'atoms' as being the atoms studied by the chemist. Neither could they have been the nuclei of atoms, which do not split up in chemical reactions. What, then, were they? If they were merely hallucinations, why should the number of 'ultimate' constituents, of which there could be several thousand, always have been 18 times the correct atomic weight? Why should the forms described by Besant and Leadbeater have correlated with the position of the element in the periodic table? How could the two workers have 'guessed' that some atoms exist in different forms five years before scientists suspected the existence of isotopes?

On page 1834: how the quark theory ties in with the occult chemists' descriptions

Christ's suffering and death are at the very centre of Christian belief. But what if he did not die on the cross, but married and had children – whose descendants are alive today? STAN GOOCH examines the evidence

THE DISCOVERY OF secret documents, and possibly a hoard of treasure, and perhaps, some have suggested, mummified relics of Christ, in the small village of Rennes-le-Château in south-west France, made a poor village priest into a millionaire (see page 162). But it also set in motion a chain of events that led to the discovery of a secret that, if it is true, is the most disturbing revelation in the history of Christianity.

The story of the clues that led them to their amazing conclusion is related by Michael Baigent, Richard Leigh and Henry Lincoln, in their bestseller *The holy blood and the Holy Grail*. The book has aroused the extremes of either instant enthusiasm or instant antagonism in its readers. Establishment critics, fairly predictably, have tended to dismiss the book as a wild romance based on the flimsiest evidence. Nevertheless, such comment is both unfair and demonstrably untrue. No one can simply sweep aside the mass of evidence assembled by the authors, and their presentation of it is admirably cautious. This series of articles, far from describing the authors of *The holy blood and the Holy Grail* as incautious, will show that they have seriously *under*estimated the extent and implications of the material they have gathered, and that there is much more they have overlooked. A still greater mystery lies behind the secrets that they document.

The authors of *The holy blood and the Holy Grail* present evidence of a powerful and ancient international mystery, and of a many layered secret society whose widespread

The crucifixion, here depicted by Giotto (*c*.1266-1337), has been a source of inspiration for countless artists. But did Christ actually *die* on the cross? The authors of a powerfully argued book, *The holy blood and the Holy Grail* (1982), believe he did not – and put forward a completely new interpretation

The royal house of Jesus

1821

Holy blood, Holy Grail

Left: Richard Leigh, Henry Lincoln and Michael Baigent (left to right), authors of *The holy blood and the Holy Grail*, in which they put forward the startling theory that a secret society, the Priory of Sion, guards the interests of the blood descendants of Christ. They claim these descendants are ready, when the occasion arises, to assume a leading role in the government of Europe – and perhaps the world

influence extends right to the present. The starting point of the authors' investigation of the mystery concerned a massive buried treasure; their final conclusion is an astonishing claim that Jesus Christ married Mary Magdalene and produced children. Descendants of these children, they believe, intermarried with other kings and rulers of ancient times, notably with the Merovingians, the first dynasty of Frankish kings in Gaul; and direct descendants of these are alive and well, awaiting the call – or opportunity – to assume a leading role in the politics of Europe, and possibly of the world. That, at least, is where the authors' evidence leads them.

The connection between the holy blood and the Holy Grail of the title of Baigent, Leigh and Lincoln's book is made through an ingenious wordplay. The Holy Grail is a complex and mysterious concept. For some authors it is a stone, for others a repository for saintly relics. But most often it is the cup used by Jesus at the Last Supper, in which his blood was caught as he hung upon the cross. In many of the early Grail manuscripts, it is referred to as the Sangraal; and even in the later version by Malory, it is the Sangreal. Baigent, Leigh and Lincoln argue that some such form – Sangraal or Sangreal – must have been close to the original. And, dividing this into two words in a way that seems entirely reasonable, they conclude that the word may not originally have been 'San Graal' or 'San Greal' – from which the English translation 'Holy Grail' comes – but 'Sang Raal' or 'Sang Réal'. 'Or,' as they triumphantly conclude, 'to employ the modern spelling, Sang Royal. Royal blood.' That is, the legend of the transportation of the Holy Grail from Judea to Europe is not the legend of the bringing of an artefact – but the true history of the arrival of the descendants of Jesus and Mary Magdalene, carriers of the royal blood or 'Sang Réal', in France.

It is, to say the least, an impressive hypothesis. But the claim for the existence of these living descendants of Christ is a weak link in Baigent, Leigh and Lincoln's argument, a less than convincing interpretation of the evidence. It seems improbable, for instance, that in all the dozens and dozens of generations that have elapsed since the time of Christ one or other descendant would not have succumbed to the temptation to announce 'I am the lineal Son of Christ.' We find no whisper of any such announcement in

Right: a Knight Templar. The authors of *The holy blood and the Holy Grail* argue that the Knights Templar, an immensely powerful order of warrior monks that flourished from 1124 to 1307, were only the military arm of a yet more powerful organisation, the Priory of Sion – the guardians of the interests of Christ's descendants

Holy blood, Holy Grail

the whole of 2000 years; nor, indeed, any really solid evidence of any actual progeny. Instead we have a mass of evidence and stories referring obliquely to a central mystery, and to specifics like a Holy Grail (see page 1314), to talking skulls and severed heads, to blood as a substance and as a symbol, to alchemical wonders, and to some kind of guiding society of elders or initiates. Yet, even if Baigent, Leigh and Lincoln are correct in their belief in the survival of the descendants of Christ, the central mystery, on their own evidence, is something still wider and older. The Christ story and the events that surround it are but one piece (an important piece, certainly) of a still larger mosaic.

Warrior monks
Baigent, Leigh and Lincoln allege that the Knights Templar were among the major custodians of the secret. This band of warrior monks was formed around 1120 for the purpose of protecting pilgrims to the Holy Land. With astonishing rapidity, they became both a powerful military force and, effectively, the bankers of Europe (see page 188). Their ascendancy came to an abrupt end, however, on the night of Friday, 13 October 1307, when, on the orders of King Philippe IV, all the Templars in France were arrested. Trials and punishments followed, and the order was finally suppressed, by order of the Pope, in 1312.

The authors of *The holy blood and the Holy Grail* have uncovered documents that suggest that the Templars were the military wing of an older mystical alliance called the Priory of Sion – an alliance that, they claim, was created and continues to exist for the purpose of protecting and promoting the interests of the direct descendants of Christ. The list of the leaders of the Priory of Sion through the ages includes Leonardo da Vinci, Sandro Filipepi – better known as Botticelli – Isaac Newton, Victor Hugo and Claude Debussy, as well as a number of seemingly unimportant French aristocratic figures.

During the trials of the French Templars in 1308, one member of the order testified that on his induction he was shown a crucifix

Bride of Christ?

Was Jesus married? According to Michael Baigent, Richard Leigh and Henry Lincoln, in their book *The holy blood and the Holy Grail*, the gospels themselves suggest he was.

They cite, in particular, Jesus's first major miracle, the transmutation of water into wine at the wedding feast at Cana (John 2:1-13). According to the familiar story, Jesus and his mother, Mary, are invited – or 'called' – to a country wedding feast. For reasons not explained in the text of the gospel, Mary calls on Jesus to replenish the wine – something that would normally be the responsibility of the host, or bridegroom's family. Why should she do this – unless the wedding was, in fact, Jesus's own? More direct evidence comes immediately after the miracle has been performed when 'the governor of the feast called *the bridegroom*, and saith unto him, Every man at the beginning doth set forth good wine; and when men have well drunk, then that which is worse: but *thou* hast kept the good wine until now.' (Editorial italics.) The implication is clear: the wedding is Christ's own.

If this surmise is correct, the obvious question is: who was Christ's wife? Again, Baigent, Leigh and Lincoln have their answers ready. The two obvious candidates, from a reading of the synoptic gospels, are Mary Magdalene and Mary of Bethany. The authors contend that these two characters are actually one woman, and that she was indeed the wife of Christ.

Christ meets Mary Magdalene in the garden after his resurrection. Is this a meeting between husband and wife?

Additional support for this theory comes from some of the apocryphal gospels, suppressed early in the history of the Church. In the gospel of Mary, for example, Peter speaks to Mary Magdalene in these words: 'Sister, we know that the Saviour loved you more than the rest of women. Tell us the words of the Saviour which you remember – which you know but we do not.' Subsequently Peter complains to the other disciples, 'Did he really speak privately with a woman and not openly to us? Are we to turn about and all listen to her? Did he prefer her to us?' Later one of the other disciples consoles him: 'Surely the Saviour knows her very well. That is why he loved her more than us.'

The gospel of Philip is still more emphatic: 'And the companion of the Saviour is Mary Magdalene. But Christ loved her more than all the disciples and used to kiss her often on her mouth. The rest of the disciples were offended by it and expressed disapproval. They said to him, "Why do you love her more than all of us?" The Saviour answered and said to them, "Why do I not love you like her?"'

Towards the end of the same gospel, Baigent, Leigh and Lincoln point out, there is one more relevant passage – which, to those prepared to admit it as valid evidence, clinches the argument: 'There is the Son of man and there is the son of the Son of man. The Lord is the Son of man, and the son of the Son of man is he who is created through the Son of man.'

Holy blood, Holy Grail

and told, 'Set not much faith in this, for it is too young.' Another was told, 'Christ is a false prophet,' and a third, 'Do not believe that the man Jesus whom the Jews crucified in Outremer [Palestine] is God and that he can save you.' Apart from specific charges, the Templars were accused in general of denying, trampling and spitting on the cross. In the light of this it is perhaps significant that, in his decorations of the church of Notre Dame de France in London, executed in 1960, Jean Cocteau, who allegedly succeeded Debussy as the leader of the Priory of Sion, depicts himself standing with his back to the cross. What is more, at the foot of the cross he paints a gigantic rose – an extremely ancient mystical symbol.

Baigent, Leigh and Lincoln admit that no satisfactory explanation has been advanced for the Templars' rejection of the cross and the crucifixion. Yet they fail to acknowledge the serious weakness this rejection creates in their own line of reasoning. If the Templars and their associates reject the cross and the crucifixion (for whatever reason), why should they be dedicated to preserving the secret of Jesus's physical descendants and restoring them to power? One possible explanation, advanced later by the authors themselves, is that a fake Jesus died on the cross – and that the real one escaped. Yet this does not at all seem to be the tenor of the Templars' remarks – 'Christ is a false prophet' not 'that was a false Christ'. And what in any case of the remark that the crucifix is 'too young' to be an object of veneration? There is, in fact, much other evidence to show that the Templar concerns were quite other, much older – and much more mysterious.

The Templars were also charged, both by the Catholic Church and by persistent popular rumour, that they believed the bearded heads and skulls they worshipped in secret could 'make the trees flower and the land

A detail from an anonymous 15th-century painting of the Last Supper, from the monastery of St Neophytos in Cyprus. The mysterious object known as the Holy Grail is often identified as the cup used at the Last Supper – a vessel that was also used, so the legend goes, to catch Christ's blood as he hung upon the cross. But the authors of *The holy blood and the Holy Grail* argue that the legends surrounding the Holy Grail refer to something quite different – the holy bloodline, or family, of Christ

Right: Pope John XXIII (1881-1963), who used the same papal name as a 15th-century antipope (below). It has been argued that Pope John XXIII was sympathetic to, or even a member of, the Priory of Sion

germinate'. This last charge may seem innocuous enough at first sight. But in fact it links Templar practice and tradition firmly with ancient and pre-Christian fertility religions, with that which was not 'too young' to have real occult powers. There is much else besides that Baigent, Leigh and Lincoln do not consider – for example, the fact that the Templars shouted 'Selah' and other 'meaningless' words when prostrating themselves before the heads. 'Selah' appears occasionally at the ends of verses of the Psalms, and it has been conjectured by scholars that it is a musical direction to choirmasters. But there is another possible explanation: could Selah be a corruption of Shiloh? Shiloh is an ancient site in the mountains near Jerusalem – and Jerusalem was where the Templars originated – that was regarded by the ancient Jews as a holy place and whose name was often used in the Old Testament to indicate the 'Messiah'. Nevertheless, like Jerusalem itself and the Jewish Sabbath, Shiloh was considered by the Jews to be a woman, something that may be highly significant.

Betrayal and downfall

The Knights Templar were betrayed to the Inquisition and all simultaneously arrested on Friday the thirteenth – of October, 1307. Given the preoccupation of the medieval mind with numerology, perhaps this is significant. And even if the attackers of the Templars took no account of such superstitious trifles, perhaps someone else did. For on the arguments of Baigent, Leigh and Lincoln, someone not only engineered the Templars' downfall, but gave them advance warning of it, enabling them to destroy most of their records and remove to safety their vast treasure and their sacred relics (including perhaps the shroud of Turin [see page

Holy blood, Holy Grail

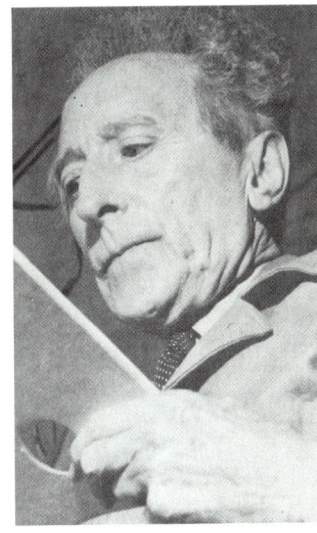

In his mural (right) for the church of Notre Dame de France in London, Jean Cocteau (above) – allegedly Grand Master of the Priory of Sion from 1918 to 1963 – shows himself, significantly, looking *away* from the cross

287] and the mummified head of Christ) – for none of these items were ever found. Perhaps the Priory of Sion itself wanted to curb its military arm – but certainly not to have the central mystery, the treasure, or its own long-term purpose destroyed.

The number 13 plays a significant role in the mystery unfolded by Baigent, Leigh and Lincoln. From their own text, let us consider one of the many hints that cast light upon this recurrent number. Records state that the Grand Master of the Priory of Sion from 1637 to 1654 was J. Valentin Andrea. Around the beginning of the same century, the Rosicrucian movement – a mysterious fraternity claiming to possess certain 'spiritual truths' – had announced its existence in Europe, and Andrea was himself a dedicated Rosicrucian. Despite his knowledge that all heresies had for some 200 years been strictly punished by the Church, Andrea set up in Europe a network of semi-secret societies, the Christian Unions, to preserve 'knowledge' that was bound to be regarded by the orthodox church as heretical. Each of these unions was headed by an anonymous 'prince' assisted by 12 followers. This grouping is, of course, strongly reminiscent of witches' covens – the 12 men or women led by a familiar or initiate – or, of course, of the group formed by Jesus and his 12 disciples.

A particularly fascinating piece of evidence produced by Baigent, Leigh and Lincoln concerns Pope John XXIII. His choice, on his election in 1959, of the name John is a surprising one in view of the fact that a 15th-century antipope, or contestant for the papacy, had also carried the name John XXIII. After the modern Pope John's death

Pierre Plantard de Saint-Clair, who was allegedly elected Grand Master of the Priory of Sion on 17 January 1981 – and is also said to be a direct descendant of Christ

there were those who suggested that he was a member of the Rosicrucians and of the Priory of Sion. Had he adopted the name John because it was also the Christian name of Jean Cocteau, then the Grand Master of Sion? The coincidence becomes significant on consideration of a further fact: this modern Pope John decreed that Catholics now had permission to be Freemasons – a complete reversal of the Vatican's previous policy. Freemasons claim direct descent, ultimately, from the Knights Templar themselves, but also from such organisations as the Christian Unions. Moreover, Pope John proclaimed that the most important item of the whole crucifixion was not the resurrection, but the shedding of Christ's blood. This strange proclamation already turns our thoughts to the Holy Grail – the receptacle usually understood to have captured the blood Christ shed while on the cross. For Baigent, Leigh and Lincoln, however, the blood of Christ means specifically the blood*line* – the descendants – of Christ. Yet in fact, as we shall see, the implications of blood are far older and broader than these authors imagine. It will startle most Christians to learn, for instance, that the word 'sabbath' (from Akkadian *shabattu* or *shapattu*) originally means 'the festival of the menstruating Moon goddess'.

It is such seemingly unrelated themes as these that we must begin to examine. We shall discover a web of interconnecting societies, secret and public, in which one mystery is solved only to reveal another.

On page 1874: alchemists, qabalists, witches and their connection with the Holy Grail

Since the mid 1960s the biorhythm theory has caught the popular imagination – and there is no doubt that people are indeed affected by natural cycles. But are they the same as biorhythmic cycles? GUY LYON PLAYFAIR sums up

ALL FORMS OF LIFE ON EARTH are affected by rhythms or cycles and we humans are no exception. The most important cycle in our lives is the day, to which we have given the time measure of 24 hours. Our hearts, lungs, temperature and blood pressure show periodicities that are locked into the 24-hour cycle. Indeed, some of our bodily functions will maintain their regular cycles even when we are deprived of visible time cues, as experiments in underground bunkers and in the constant sunlight of the Arctic summer have shown.

Cycles taking a period of more than one day are called ultradian. The most important ultradian cycle is the month – or rather months, for the changing orbit of our satellite, the Moon, creates five different cycles ranging in length from 27.21 to 29.53 days.

Right: the changing seasons, in a painting by Walter Crane. The year is one of the most important and obvious cycles in human life

Below: the full Moon has long held a special place in folklore as an influence on human behaviour. Once dismissed by science, this view has begun to come back into favour

A tide in the affairs of men

The former is the time between full Moons or one orbit of the Moon with respect to the Sun. The latter is equal to a lunar orbit in relation to the Earth–Sun orbital plane.

Of special interest is the month of 27.55 days, which marks the time between lunar perigees – the point at which the Moon is closest to the Earth. This full Moon has a visible gravitational effect on the tides in our waters and, as we shall see, there is evidence that it also affects 'tides' in human behaviour.

The female menstrual cycle is a clear example of the ultradian periods, and its connection with the Moon has long been taken for granted although the precise cause and effect relationship remains unestablished. It now appears that the average length of the menstrual cycle is closest to that of the 29.53-day month. In his clinic in the United States, Dr Edmond Dewan has reported remarkable success in regulating his patients' cycles by doing no more than having them sleep with a light on during the fourteenth to seventeenth nights after their menstrual period starts. He was, in effect, providing them with an artificial full Moon.

The menstrual cycle, however, is rarely linked to that of the Moon nowadays. So, if there is a 28-day emotional biorhythmic cycle, something else must be causing it. It cannot be the Moon, because none of its months is of exactly 28 days. The same objection applies to the 23-day physical and the 33-day intellectual biorhythms identified by the first biorhythm theorists (see page 1790). What could cause them?

While body cycles can be seen to

Biorhythms

conform to the 24-hour period, there is no obvious natural driving force for any cycle of 23, 28 or 33 days. Some ascribe such supposed ultradian cycles to unspecified actions of cells or glands, but this is no explanation. Moreover, the menstrual cycle – that 28-day emotional one – varies widely among individuals, as do many of the ultradian and circadian (24-hour) cycles. It would therefore be surprising if all humans contained three in-built rhythm regulators that remained unaffected throughout the life span by any external stimulus.

Where is the proof?

Proof of the biorhythm theory requires precise measurements of many variables over long periods, and few attempts have been made to do them. One of the first was made by Dr Rexford Hersey of the University of Pennsylvania. His work is often cited in support of the biorhythm theory, but in fact actually provides good evidence against it. In 1931 Hersey published the results of a year-long study of the emotional moods of 25 industrial workers selected for their apparent emotional stability. Emotional cycles did indeed appear, but they ranged in length from 16 to 63 days with the average being about 35 days.

A similar spread of personal biocycles was revealed in a 1977 survey of 200 subjects by the Biocron Systems Co. of California. Members of this group were tested for all three biorhythms and were found to have them, but the cycles proved to be anywhere from 2 to 54 days in duration.

In 1974 a team of researchers from Wyoming University studied hospitalised psychotics to test the 'critical days' hypothesis. They found that it 'was not shown to be a meaningful concept' and that it had 'no predictive value beyond chance'.

An investigative approach of a different kind is to take instrumental readings of measurable states of the body and examine them for signs of periodicity. Two such surveys, both published in 1962, give good reason to suppose that at least one of the three biorhythms may not be far from the mark.

In one of these surveys, psychiatrist Leonard J. Ravitz took 30,000 electrical readings from about 500 American university students. He found that they had several cycles, of which one of the most pronounced was of 28 to 29 days. It is surprising that this promising lead does not seem to have been followed up.

This is also the case with the other 1962 report, by Dr Robert O. Becker of the State University of New York. He and two colleagues took readings of direct-current electrical potentials on four subjects over a two-month period, and reported 'a definite cyclic pattern' with a period of approximately 28 days. This was a very small sample, but it lent some support to Dr Ravitz's more thorough survey. However, both reports identified the cycle as being only approximately, and not exactly, 28 days. Still, it can be said that there is some evidence in support of a biorhythm of about 28 days, which could in theory have its roots in one of the lunar cycles. But there is as yet no kind of case for, or any obvious natural cause of, the other two biorhythms of 23 and 33 days.

Is the biorhythm theory just a crank idea then? Gay Gaer Luce, in her definitive study of the natural rhythms of the human

Above: Dr Rexford Hersey, who made one of the few long-term studies of human cyclical rhythms while working at the University of Pennsylvania. His results did little to support the biorhythm theory

Right: the setting Sun marks the end of another day. The Sun has a profound effect on the rhythms of our lives

Biorhythms

body, deplores the biorhythm pioneer Wilhelm Fliess as 'a blatantly unsophisticated' mathematician. But she readily admits that 'the underlying idea may not be so farfetched.' It may be that we can expect our minds and bodies to obey cyclic patterns. But can we expect that all of us will obey the same three biorhythms all the time?

The most obvious cycles in our lives are a day and a year, which come about by the motions of the Earth with respect to the Sun. But the Sun has cycles of its own. For reasons unknown, its rotation period is not uniform and ranges from 25 Earth days at the equator to 34 days at the poles, averaging one cycle every 27 days. Its overall output of all radiation is also cyclic, ebbing and flowing in an average period of just over 11 years. This 11-year solar cycle is also called the sunspot cycle, because of the appearance of dark blobs on the Sun's surface that are associated with extra bursts of radiation. The causes of both the cycle and the spots have yet to be fully explained, but it does seem that a number of events on Earth come and go in time with the sunspot cycle.

By the light of the Moon

To the cycles of the Sun we must add those of our satellite the Moon. Some living creatures display precise responses to lunar cycles. The Californian grunion fish, for example, lays its eggs only in the few hours following the peak of a spring tide. The eggs then wait in the sand to be hatched on immersion at the following spring tide. At least 50 other varieties of fish and some crabs also spawn like clockwork, with the Moon acting as the pendulum. Lunar alignment has also been identified in at least one large animal, the African gnu. In a well-known experiment, biologist Professor Frank A. Brown Jr, then of Northwestern University at Evanston, Illinois, showed that Connecticut oysters opened their shells at the time of high tide in his laboratory – hundreds of miles from their home beds and with no Moon in sight. Crabs and hamsters have shown similar linkage to an invisible Moon.

So have humans. In 1977 Dr Laughton E. M. Miles of Stanford University reported that a blind hospital patient of his had many of his daily body cycles phased-locked with the *lunar* day of 24.84 hours, the time it takes the Moon to go once round the Earth. Miles also noted a 'remarkable coincidence' between the time the man went to sleep and the local low tide. Freed from the need to conform to a schedule dictated by the daily Sun cycle, the blind man seemed to have instinctively fallen into step with the less obvious but no less influential cycle of the Moon.

Top: the life of the grunion, a fish of the Californian coastal waters, is synchronised with the phases of the Moon. For example, it lays its eggs precisely during the first three hours after the peak of a spring tide

Above: the timing of the African gnu's mating season is related to the lunar cycle, according to A.R.E. Sinclair in an article written in 1977

Solar and lunar cycles affect us not only directly, but also indirectly through the natural magnetic field of Earth, or the geomagnetic field (GMF). The GMF does far more than make compass needles indicate north, says Soviet Academician Dr Aleksandr P. Dubrov. In 1974 he stated that 'the GMF has an effect on absolutely all organisms and on all processes taking place in living organisms' – a claim he has supported with abundant evidence.

Of special interest are the GMF's sudden sharp fluctuations known as magnetic storms, which are caused by charged particles from the Sun. They are said to have any number of effects on us, from causing delayed reactions – and hence increased susceptibility to accidents – to the onset of mental disorders and even heart attacks. Magnetic storms have a 27-day cycle linked to the Sun's rotation. They also have an

Biorhythms

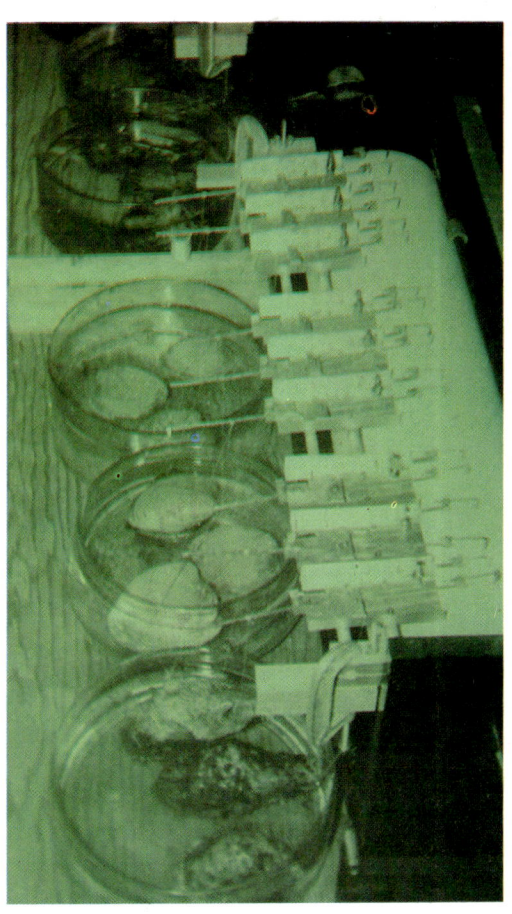

Left: in a now classic experiment, Connecticut oysters opened their shells at the time of the high tide in their natural habitat – though they were hundreds of miles away in a laboratory at an Illinois university

Right: Apollo, the Greek god of reason and order, might be said to be symbolic of the logical left brain. The occult belief that the left brain is the logical one and the right brain the intuitive one has been taken up by Dr Arnold Lieber, a Florida psychiatrist. The left brain, Lieber says, seems to be affected by the Sun – and, curiously enough, Apollo was identified with the Sun

annual one in which there is an increase in storms at the equinoxes in March and September and a decrease during the solstices of June and December. But searching for universal cycles in the GMF is complicated by the facts that some storms are only local in effect and that magnetic activity is significantly affected by latitude. Moreover, the GMF is not uniform to start with. It is, for example, three times stronger in the region of Kursk in the USSR than it is in Rio de Janeiro in Brazil.

Since the Moon and the Sun have different cycles, it seems that we must lock in to two unequal cycles at once. Miami psychiatrist Dr Arnold Lieber has gathered considerable evidence in support of the folk belief that the Moon affects human behaviour, usually for the worse. He also speculates that the two cycles of the Sun and Moon are reflected in the dual nature of the human brain, with its left and right hemispheres responding in different ways to different external stimuli. In a statement reminiscent of the work of some occult writers, he says that the 'logical' left brain seems to take its cue from the Sun and the 'intuitive' right from the Moon. We have, it seems, made a forced adjustment of our schedules to the Sun.

Yet, as Dr Lieber points out, not everybody is influenced equally by the cosmic cycles. Healthy and well-balanced people order their own lives regardless of where the Moon is in its cycle. But in the case of the emotionally unstable, an awareness of cyclical influences could help reduce the effects of probable critical days or times of the year. He suggests adopting a solar-lunar calendar by means of which policemen, firemen and hospital staff might predict periods of likely increase in their work loads. He even recommends holding events such as rock concerts during the quarters of the Moon rather than at new or full Moon to avoid the possible adverse effect on behaviour. Just as there are tides in the oceans, he says, there may be biological tides in the body. After all, our body is more than three quarters water.

On the whole, the evidence indicates that all living beings experience the effects of innumerable cycles, almost all of them caused by the Sun, Moon or the magnetic field of the Earth. These range in length from a few hours to several years. There is a plausible case for a biorhythm of *approximately* 28 days, but there is no supporting evidence for the other two biorhythmic cycles of 23 and 33 days. All God's children certainly have biorhythm, but it has not yet been established that they have it in the form that Fliess, Swoboda and their heirs would have us believe. A better awareness of the known natural cycles that affect our lives would probably be more helpful than adherence to the unsupported dogma of biorhythm – for all its popular appeal.

Further reading
A. P. Dubrov, *The geomagnetic field and life*, Plenum 1978
M. Gauquelin, *The cosmic clock*, Avon (New York) 1969
R. S. Hersey, *Zest for work*, Harper (New York) 1955
A. L. Lieber and J. Agel, *The lunar effect*, Anchor Press/Doubleday (Garden City, New York) 1978
G. G. Luce, *Body time*, Paladin 1977
G. L. Playfair and S. Hill, *The cycles of heaven*, Pan 1979
George Thommen, *Is this your day?*, Crown (New York) 1964

A word to the wise

The voice of the Chinese philosopher Confucius was heard over 2000 years after his death, speaking in old Chinese – but was this just a medium's clever ventriloquism? ROY STEMMAN investigates this and other claims made for 'direct voice' phenomena

JOHN CAMPBELL SLOAN could have made a small fortune had he exploited his direct voice mediumship commercially. For in his presence the dead were said to speak in their own voices and hold long, characteristic conversations with their living relatives and friends. But Sloan, a kindly, ill-educated Scotsman, chose to be a non-professional medium. For 50 years he gave seances for which he never charged, working instead as a tailor, a Post Office employee, a packer, garagehand and newsagent.

Many of the astonishing direct voice seances that Sloan gave were recorded in a best-selling book written by Spiritualist author J. Arthur Findlay, *On the edge of the etheric*. In this, Findlay gives an account of the very first seance he attended with Sloan, on 20 September 1918. It took place, as is often the case with direct voice phenomena, in a darkened room:

Suddenly a voice spoke in front of me. I felt scared. A man sitting next to me said, 'Someone wants to speak to you, friend,' so I said, 'Yes, who are you?' 'Your father, Robert Downie Findlay,' the voice replied, and then went on to refer to something that only he and I and one other ever knew on earth, and that other, like my father, was some years dead. I was therefore the only living person with any knowledge of what the voice was referring to.

That was extraordinary enough, but my surprise was heightened when, after my father had finished, another voice gave the name David Kidston, the name of the other person who on earth knew about the subject, and he continued the conversation which my father had begun.

How do sceptics explain such occurrences? Perhaps the medium was a ventriloquist and had chanced upon the information that Findlay thought was known to no one else. He dismisses such 'normal' explanations with this answer:

No spy system, however thorough, no impersonation by the medium or by any accomplices could be responsible for this, and, moreover, I was an entire stranger to everyone present. I did not give my name when I entered the room, I knew no one in that room and no one knew me or anything about me.

Sloan was sometimes able to produce two or three spirit voices simultaneously. On occasions he went into trance at the start of a seance, on others he remained conscious and held conversations with the spirit communicators.

One of the most gifted direct voice

Margery Crandon, a Boston medium of the 1920s, was exposed as a fraud by Harry Houdini (left), who demonstrated her tricks as part of his stage act. The medium's 'spirit guide', her dead brother Walter, allegedly left his thumb print (bottom, left) after a seance, but this was later proved to be that of a previous sitter (bottom, right). The whorls and ridges (numbered) match exactly. But was Margery always a fraud?

Below: Jack Webber produces ectoplasm. He was said to produce ectoplasmic 'voice boxes' so the dead could speak through them

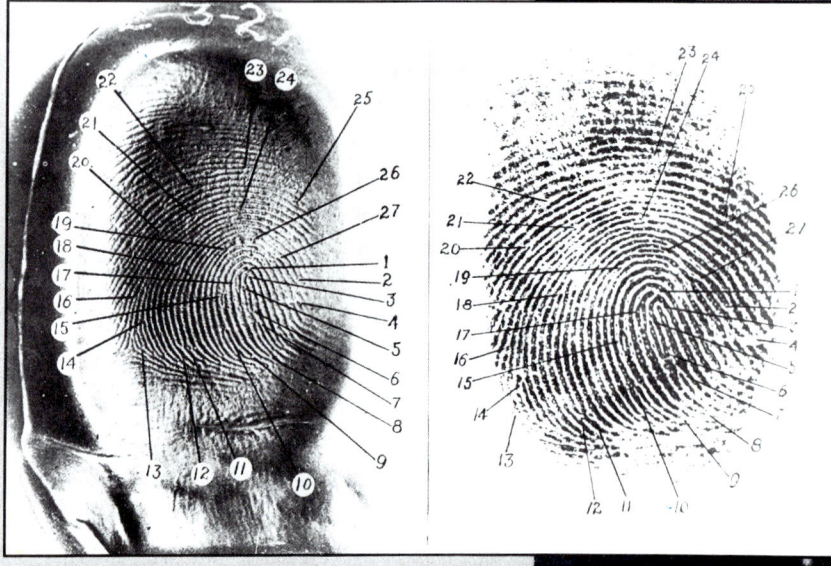

Physical mediums

mediums of all time was Mrs Etta Wriedt of Detroit, Michigan, USA. She never went into a trance, nor separated herself from the other sitters by using a cabinet – as many mediums do. Instead, she would sit with the sitters and join in the conversations they had with the spirits. If, however, a foreign language 'came through' she would get out her knitting. She could speak only English.

A British vice-admiral, W. Usborne Moore, also had the opportunity of sitting with Mrs Wriedt when she visited England in the 1920s and testified: 'Frequently two, sometimes three, voices spoke at the same moment in different parts of the circle. It was somewhat confusing.' And at an American seance with the same medium, 'I have heard three voices talking at once, one in each ear and one through the trumpet; sometimes two in the trumpet.' These conversations were so realistic, said Usborne Moore, that he sometimes forgot that he was talking with 'those whom we ignorantly speak of as "the dead"'.

Another testimony to Mrs Wriedt's direct voice mediumship came from the Dowager Duchess of Warwick, who had been one of King Edward VII's mistresses. She first invited the medium to her home because it had been plagued with strange phenomena. On her arrival at Warwick Castle, Mrs Wriedt was shown to her room; some of her belongings, including a seance trumpet, were left in the hall outside her door. Lady Warwick, while waiting for her guest to appear, picked up the trumpet and placed it against her ear. Immediately she heard the characteristic voice of King Edward speaking to her and she was able to carry on a conversation with him, partly in German.

The king became a regular and persistent communicator at subsequent direct voice seances held at the castle – to such an extent that other communicators could hardly get a word in. In view of her former lover's apparent possessiveness from beyond the grave, Lady Warwick decided to terminate the seances with Mrs Wriedt.

A New York medium, George Valiantine, was psychically speaking a late developer. He did not discover his mediumistic powers until he was 43, but soon made an impact, particularly with direct voice seances. In 1924, English author Dennis Bradley brought Valiantine to England, where he gave seances almost every day for five weeks. The invited guests included 50 prominent people, and 100 different spirit voices were said to have communicated. Caradoc Evans, the novelist, spoke to his father in idiomatic Welsh and other spirits spoke in Russian, German and Spanish.

Above: George Valiantine, American 'trumpet medium' – and accomplished fraud

Confucius, he say

The most impressive communication, however, came at a seance in New York in the late 1920s. Strange and unintelligible voices had been heard previously and so Dr Neville Whymant, an authority on Chinese history, philosophy and ancient literature, agreed to attend. Dr Whymant did not remain a sceptic for long. First he heard the sound of a flute played in a characteristically Chinese way, then a quiet, almost inaudible voice said 'K'ung-fu-T'Zu', which is the Chinese version of the name Confucius. Few people, except the Chinese, can pronounce it properly. Even so, Dr Whymant did not believe it was the famous philosopher who was communicating – perhaps it was just someone else speaking his name. But when Dr Whymant began to refer to a passage from Confucius that he believed had been transcribed wrongly, and quoted the first line:

> At once, the words were taken out of my mouth, and the whole passage was recited in Chinese, exactly as it is recorded in the standard works of reference. After a pause of about 15 seconds the passage was again repeated, this time with certain alterations which gave it new meaning. 'Thus read,' said the voice, 'does not its meaning become plain?'

Subsequently, after having the opportunity of speaking to the voice again, Dr Whymant declared that there were only six Chinese scholars in the world capable of displaying

Physical mediums

Left: Etta Wriedt, one of the most powerful direct voice mediums of all time. Often two or more voices spoke together; men, women and children 'came through' and spoke clearly, sometimes in foreign languages. When they did so, Mrs Wriedt, who understood only English, got out her knitting. On a visit to England she was invited to Warwick Castle where the Dowager Duchess (below) was experiencing strange phenomena. While showing her to her room, the Duchess picked up Mrs Wriedt's seance trumpet and was astonished to hear her ex-lover, King Edward VII, speaking to her, partly in German. He later became so persistent that the Duchess gave up her seances with Mrs Wriedt

such knowledge of the language and of Confucius, none of whom was in the United States at the time. Dr Whymant also testified to hearing a Sicilian chant at one of Valiantine's seances and he conversed in Italian with another communicator.

The man who brought him to England, Dennis Bradley, claimed that Valiantine had apparently passed on his direct voice powers to him, and another regular sitter, an Italian, the Marquis Centurione Scotto, also developed direct voice mediumship.

One of the last great British mediums to demonstrate direct voice phenomena was a Welsh miner, Jack Webber, whose powers gradually developed at weekly seances run by his in-laws. He refused to use a cabinet because he knew it would be regarded with suspicion. Instead, he allowed himself to be tied to a chair and a red light to be turned on at intervals throughout the seance to allow the sitters to confirm that he was still bound. He also allowed infra-red photographs to be taken at some of his seances, to record a number of physical phenomena including levitation, partial materialisation, and the sessions demonstrating direct voice through trumpets.

His powers were recorded by famous healer Harry Edwards in his book *The mediumship of Jack Webber*, which tells of events recorded over the 14-month period leading up to December 1939, when Webber suddenly died. In that time more than 4000 people witnessed Webber's mediumship.

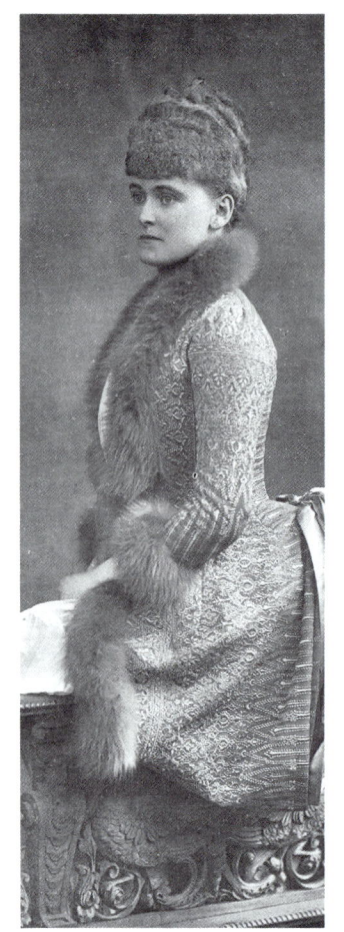

Edwards heard men, women and children communicating through Webber's seance trumpets, some speaking in foreign tongues, their messages frequently containing intimate personal information. He also testified to hearing two spirit voices singing simultaneously through a single trumpet.

The photographs taken at Webber's seances seem to throw some light on the apparent mechanism of direct voice mediumship. Ectoplasmic shapes are seen to connect the medium with the levitated trumpet and in some of the pictures small round shapes, about the size of a human heart, are seen to be attached to the small end. These are said to be 'voice boxes' through which the dead are able to speak.

Off to a good start

In the United States, one of the most famous physical mediums, Margery (whose real name was Mina) Crandon, allowed some ingenious devices to be used during the investigation of her direct voice mediumship. Margery Crandon was married to Dr L. R. G. Crandon, who was for 16 years professor of surgery at Harvard Medical School. Their seances began in 1923 and a variety of physical phenomena soon developed.

One piece of apparatus used to test her powers was developed by Dr Mark Richardson and consisted of a U-shaped tube containing water, with floats placed on the surface. Margery had to blow into this through a flexible tube, causing one column of water to rise, then keep her tongue and lips over the mouthpiece throughout the seance to prevent the water returning to its original level. (Sitters could verify this in the dark because the floats were luminous.) She did as she was asked, the water level remained as it should, and yet her regular 'spirit' communicator – her dead brother, Walter Stinson – spoke as loudly as ever.

An even more ingenious piece of equipment was invented by B. K. Thorogood: a box consisting of seven layers of different materials containing a large and sensitive microphone. This was closed, padlocked and placed in the seance room to record spirit voices. Two wires ran from it to a loudspeaker in another room. People in the adjoining room were able to hear Walter's voice coming out of the loudspeaker while those in the seance room could hear nothing being spoken into the microphone.

Not all these mediums were above suspicion, however. George Valiantine was accused of fraud on a number of occasions, and when both he and Mrs Crandon allowed themselves to be investigated by the *Scientific American* – a publication that offered $2500 for a demonstration of objective psychic phenomena – they failed to convince the magazine's committee.

Physical mediums

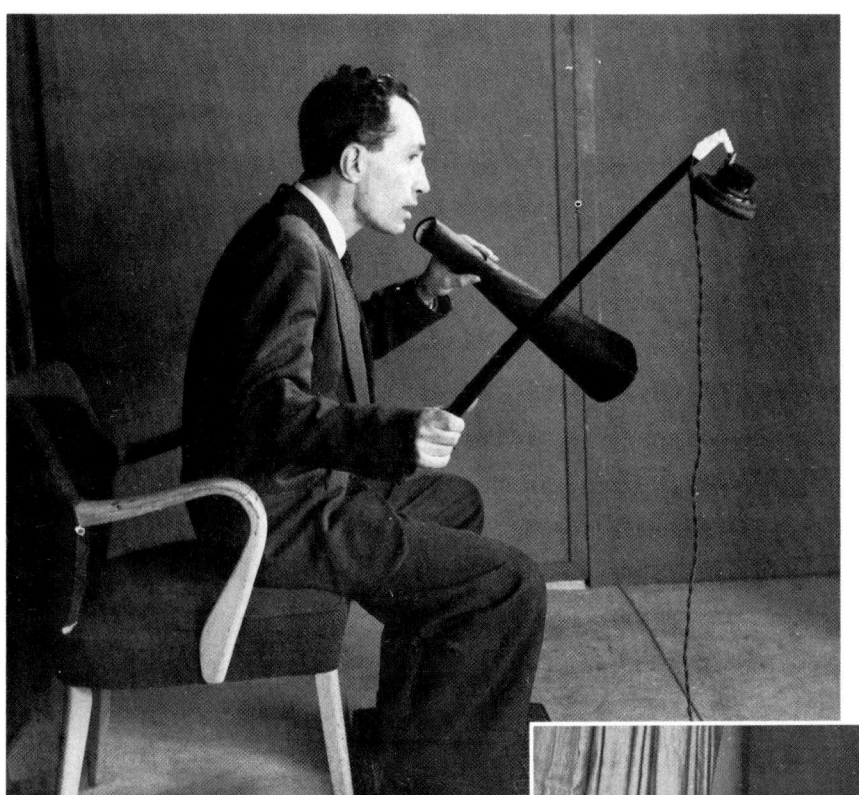

routine to make money out of gullible people. He claimed to have made a total of £50,000 from his 'direct voice' seances.

His technique was simple. He used a confederate who searched people's coats, wallets and handbags after they were safely settled in the seance room. He then conveyed any information thus gleaned to the medium via a sophisticated communications system that came into operation when William Roy placed metal plates on the soles of his shoes to tacks in the floor that were apparently holding down the carpet. The 'medium' then used a small receiver in his ear. The same device could be clipped to the end of a trumpet so that the confederate could produce one 'spirit voice' while Roy produced another, simultaneously, using a telescopic rod to levitate the trumpet.

Roy was exposed as a fraud in 1955 and sold his confession to the *Sunday Pictorial* (now the *Sunday Mirror*) in 1960. Despite being a self-confessed fraud, Roy (who had left the country) returned to Britain in the late 1960s and began giving seances once

But it was not their direct voice mediumship that was challenged. Valiantine had produced a series of wax impressions that were said to be the actual thumb prints of famous dead people. He was exposed by Dennis Bradley – the man who had championed him in two previous books – and the damning evidence was published in a third book, *And after*, in which Bradley said the prints 'were produced by Valiantine's big toes, fingers and elbows'.

Margery Crandon also ran into trouble with a thumb print, which was said to have been produced when her dead brother Walter's materialised hand left an impression in wax. In the early 1930s the Boston Society for Psychical Research showed that the thumb print was identical to that of Mrs Crandon's dentist, who had been a sitter at her early seances.

Sceptics believe that if these mediums did produce some of their phenomena fraudulently then it is more than likely that it was *all* phoney, though how they produced some of their most startling direct voice effects is difficult to imagine.

One man who did find a way, and performed successfully for many years, was William Roy – one of the most brilliant and ruthless frauds in Spiritualism's history. His real name was William George Holroyd Plowright and he was a small-time crook before he devised a fraudulent mediumistic

Top: William Roy, self-confessed fake, who claimed to have made £50,000 from his 'direct voice' seances. His confession in 1960 included an exposé of his tricks, such as the use of a confederate in the next room (above). Even so, he later claimed that the confession had been 'a pack of lies' and he set himself up as a medium once more under the name Bill Silver

more, using the name Bill Silver. His sitters included some of The Beatles.

It transpired that many people who were now attending 'Bill Silver's' seances knew he was William Roy, the self-confessed cheat. Yet they now believed he was genuine. And when challenged by a Sunday newspaper he claimed that his earlier published confession was 'a pack of lies', published for the money. His days of swindling the public ended in 1977 when he died.

Can materialised spirits go shopping – and perform operations? See page 1846

The hunting of the quark

In the early 20th century two leading Theosophists claimed to have probed the atom by clairvoyant vision. STEPHEN M. PHILLIPS describes the parallels between their account and modern scientific theories

TODAY, WHEN PEOPLE OSTENSIBLY bend spoons without touching them and leather rings link themselves together of their own accord on film (see page 1252), the claims of Annie Besant and Charles W. Leadbeater that they observed fundamental particles by psychic means seem less fantastic than they did in the early 1900s. But both prejudice and well-founded criticism have until recently made the two Theosophists' claims seem false and absurd to most scientists. Chemists as distinguished as E. Lester Smith, co-discoverer of vitamin B$_{12}$, pointed out the discrepancies between the descriptions of micro-psi 'atoms' and the current knowledge of chemical atoms. Sympathetic scientists lost any hope of reconciling Besant and Leadbeater's work with orthodox science.

What, then, were Besant and Leadbeater 'seeing'? In the 1970s the present author pointed out a solution to this problem. The two psychics' description of what they believed to be the hydrogen atom provides the vital clue to the puzzle.

In its normal state hydrogen does not consist of single atoms. It consists of pairs of atoms, tightly bound together. This pair is the 'molecule' of hydrogen – the smallest quantity of hydrogen that exists under ordinary conditions. This much was well-known even when Besant and Leadbeater began their work. Then it was discovered that each hydrogen atom consisted of a single proton – a positively charged particle – around which an electron – a negatively charged particle, much lighter than a proton – revolved in an orbit.

In 1964 the quark theory was proposed by the American physicists Murray Gell-Mann and George Zweig, working independently. They proposed that protons and neutrons – neutral particles of approximately the same mass as protons, occurring in all nuclei except the simplest, that of hydrogen – are made up of three fundamental particles called 'quarks'. So too are other relatively heavy particles studied by physicists. Several scientists, including this author, have gone further and have suggested the existence of 'subquarks' of which the quarks are supposedly composed.

Compare this picture with the micro-psi 'atom' of hydrogen, as described by Besant and Leadbeater. It consists of two intersecting triangular arrays, each consisting of three bodies. Each of these bodies in turn consists of three particles that the psychics named 'ultimate physical atoms'. They also referred to them as *anu*, a Sanskrit word, meaning 'atoms'. Can we identify these with subquarks? If we can, then three of them form a quark, which we can identify with the body lying at each corner of one of the triangular

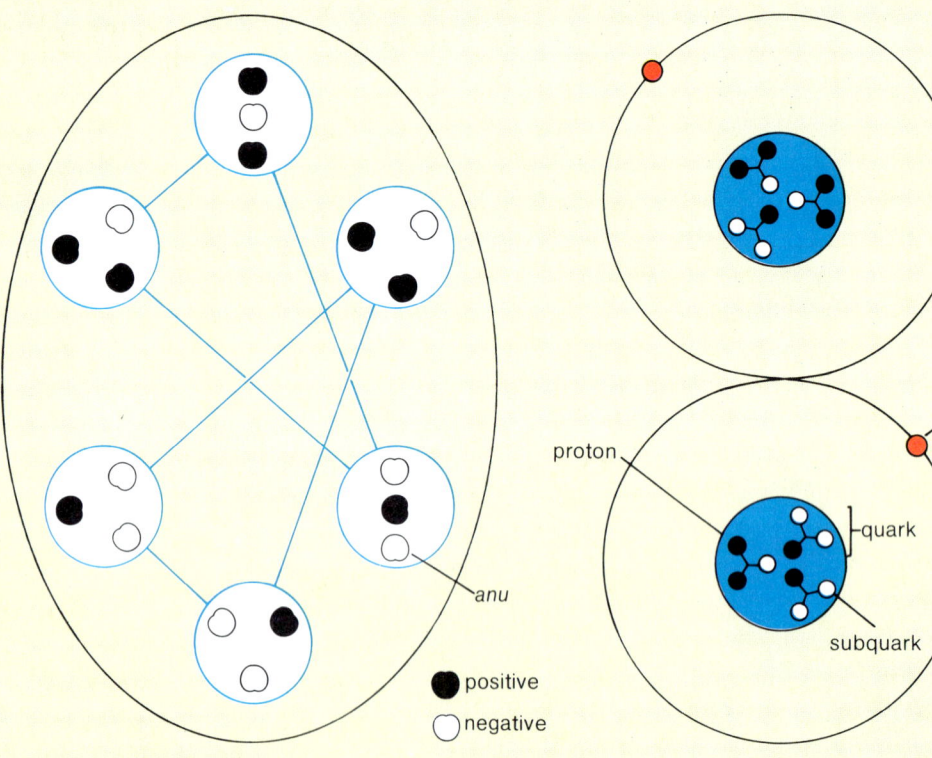

- positive
- negative

anu

proton — electron — quark — subquark

The structure (far left) believed by Annie Besant and C.W. Leadbeater to be the hydrogen atom may have been derived from a *pair* of atoms, linked to form a molecule (left). The fundamental *anu* would then correspond to hypothetical particles called subquarks. Three subquarks make up a quark, while the *anu* likewise occurred in triplets. Furthermore, subquarks come in two varieties, just as the *anu* did. Three quarks make up each atom's central proton, corresponding to each of the two triangular arrays 'seen' by the psychics. It seems that the hydrogen atoms must have been disrupted and intermixed when observed psychically; furthermore, the two electrons did not appear

Occult chemistry

Murray Gell-Mann shared a Nobel prize for proposing the theory that certain types of fundamental particle are composed of yet smaller 'quarks'

arrays. And each triangular array is a proton. The micro-psi hydrogen 'atom' is actually a structure derived from the hydrogen *molecule* with its two protons.

This interpretation explains why micro-psi 'atoms' of hydrogen were never observed in pairs, as would be expected if they were chemical atoms. But as observed by the two Theosophists, the protons appeared to be much closer together than we now know them to be in the hydrogen molecule – 100,000 times closer, in fact. To explain this it is necessary to suppose that the two atomic nuclei disintegrated and their constituent quarks recombined, at least for the period during which they were being observed by micro-psi.

The atomic weight of an element is defined as the weight of one of its atoms relative to the weight of one atom of hydrogen. Thus carbon, for example, has an atomic weight of 12 because its atom is 12 times as heavy as hydrogen's. But since a hydrogen atom weighs almost the same as a proton, which in turn is very close in weight to a neutron, the atomic weight of an element is almost exactly equal to the number of protons and neutrons in its atomic nucleus. Different isotopes of an element have different numbers of neutrons in the atomic nucleus, and their atomic weights differ accordingly. Furthermore, on the theory we are here considering, the number of subquarks very nearly equals nine times the atomic weight (because there are three subquarks per quark, and three quarks per proton or neutron).

The number of subquarks in any *pair* of nuclei of a given element is therefore close to 18 times the atomic weight of that element. And Besant and Leadbeater found that the number of *anu* in each micro-psi 'atom' was about 18 times the atomic weight of that element. So it seems that the two researchers were observing pairs of nuclei that had disintegrated and recombined, and they were succeeding in distinguishing the subquarks that made them up.

Usually the number of *anu* in an atom was not exactly equal to 18 times the atomic weight of the element. Now, Besant and Leadbeater had to estimate the number of *anu* in the more complex micro-psi atoms by

In his own image

Besant and Leadbeater related the structure of the *anu* to the ancient Jewish mystical doctrine of the Tree of Life. This is a kind of chart of reality, including the material Universe and its microcosm, the human body. The Tree is based on 10 *sephiroth* ('emanations') – the 10 stages in which God manifested himself in creation. Masculine qualities are placed on the right, feminine ones on the left. They are combined and reconciled in the central *sephiroth*. The highest is Kether (Crown, or godhead), giving rise to Chokmah (divine Wisdom) and Binah (divine Intelligence). A gulf separates this 'supernal triad' from the lower *sephiroth*. Chesed (Mercy) is a constructive, loving principle, contrasted with Geburah (Severity), which is associated with destruction and war. These two are united in Tiphereth (Beauty), representing the life force and symbolised by the Sun and by the heart. Next come Netzagh (Victory), representing instinct, the passions and forces of attraction, and Hod (Glory), standing for imagination, and also for reason, which is viewed as a negative quality. Yesod (Foundation) is linked with growth and decay, the Moon – which links the Sun and the Earth – and the genitals. Malkuth (Kingdom) is matter, the Earth, the body. To Besant and Leadbeater the three major whorls of the *anu* corresponded to the supernal triad and the remainder to the lower seven *sephiroth*.

Occult chemistry

counting them in individual 'spikes' or 'bars' and then multiplying by the number of such spikes or bars in the whole 'atom'. For example, the micro-psi 'atom' of one of the isotopes of neon is star-shaped. It consists of a central globe containing 120 *anu*, and six arms, each containing 46 *anu*. Besant and Leadbeater apparently counted 47 *anu* in one of these arms and thus overestimated the total number in the 'atom' by six. Almost all of the discrepancies in the numbers of *anu* reported by the psychics can be accounted for as the results of miscounting by one or two in one part of the structure they were observing – a structure that was complex and shifting, and could contain thousands of *anu*, so that such small errors are only to be expected.

Besant and Leadbeater commented on the difficulties they had in stopping the motion of the constituent particles by psychokinesis. Leadbeater once said:

> The molecule is spinning. You have to hold it still and then you have to be careful that you do not spoil its shape. I am always afraid of disturbing the things because I must stop their motion in order to give an idea of them.

What of the 'atoms' described by Besant and Leadbeater for which there are no places in the periodic table? These could have been formed from the nuclei of two different elements, with micro-psi 'atoms' of the same shape. The numbers of *anu* support this conjecture. One such anomalous object contained 2646 *anu*, equivalent to an atomic weight of 147. This is the average of 102 and 192, the atomic weights of the most common isotopes of ruthenium and osmium, which had micro-psi 'atoms' of the same shape. Further 'impossible' structures could be formed by the combination of different isotopes of a single element.

Further confirmation of the objective character of the Theosophists' observations is provided by their descriptions of the forces binding the *anu* together. They support the 'string model', which accounts for the forces between quarks.

This theory was developed because free quarks have never been detected, despite extensive searches over the years. Physicists concluded that these particles cannot escape from one another. The string model explains this by regarding quarks as resembling the ends of a piece of string. If the model is correct, then we can no more hope to find a free quark than we can hope to find a piece of string with a single end. The quark is regarded as a magnetic 'monopole' – a single source of magnetic field. The magnetic field can be visualised in terms of 'lines of force',

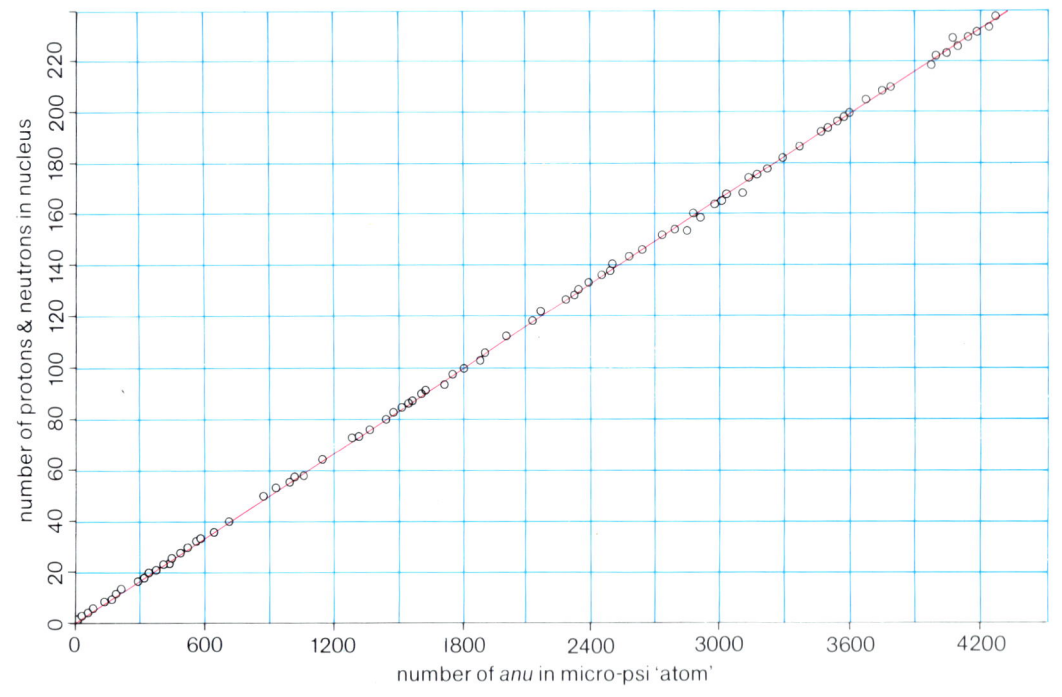

Opposite: Annie Besant and Charles Leadbeater conducted their research into the constitution of matter over four decades, while also controlling the affairs of the Theosophical Society. Another of their shared concerns was a belief in reincarnation

Above: a graph of the number of particles in each atomic nucleus – a number approximately equal to the atomic weight – against the number of anu seen in the atom by Besant and Leadbeater. If there were exactly 18 anu for each particle, all the points would lie on the red line. Small departures from the line could be due to small, plausible errors in counting by the psychics. The graph is impressive evidence that they were observing something objectively real

Right: structures (above) described by Besant and Leadbeater. They strikingly resemble modern 'string model' theories (below) in which quarks (or subquarks) are the ends of 'strings' of magnetic lines of force

Below: the collaborator and amanuensis of Besant and Leadbeater, C. Jinarajadasa, who took down their descriptions as they made their psychic observations

Occult chemistry

or field lines, like those traced out by iron filings shaken onto a piece of paper held over a bar magnet. The field lines from a quark form a narrow tube or string – the physicist thinks of the lines as being squeezed together by surrounding space. A quark and its corresponding antiquark (which is its antimatter equivalent – see page 857) lying at the end of a single string form one of a number of short-lived particles called mesons. Three quarks lying at the ends of a Y-shaped string form other types of particles, including protons and neutrons. If a string breaks, new quarks appear at the severed ends.

If quarks are regarded as themselves composite particles, then they consist of triplets of subquarks, and it is these that lie at the ends of Y-shaped strings.

Compare this picture with the diagrams of pairs and triplets of *anu* observed by Besant and Leadbeater. Some pairs were joined by single 'lines of force'. Sometimes three lines of force formed a Y-shaped configuration, each line ending on an *anu*. Such diagrams are, essentially, identical to depictions of subatomic particles appearing in the scientific journals of today.

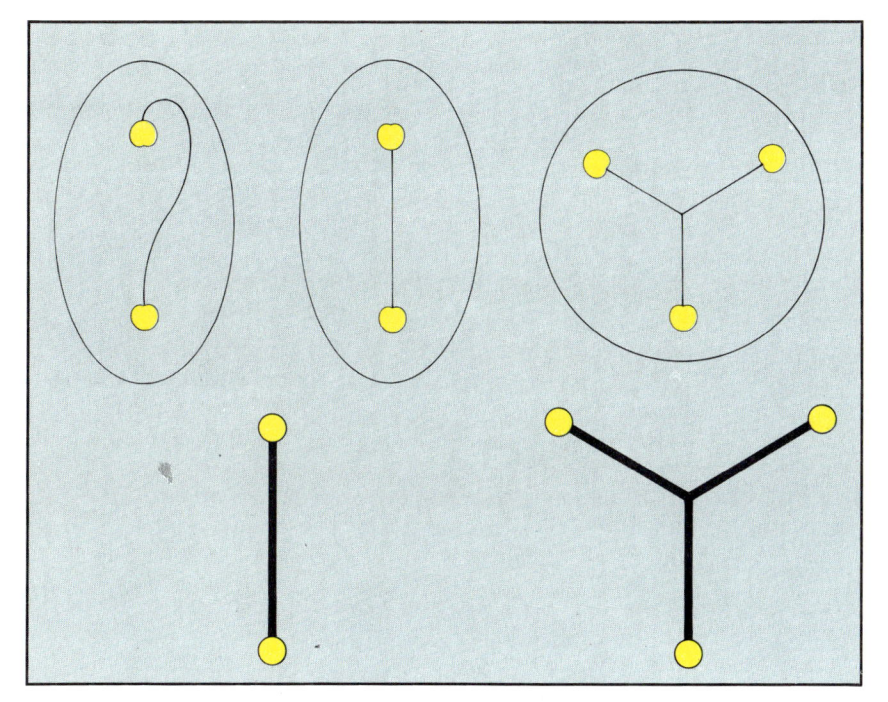

Annie Besant took responsibility for observing how the *anu* were bound together, whereas Leadbeater was concerned with the larger-scale structures, requiring less magnification. Besant depicted many string configurations, in addition to the single strings and Y-shaped strings. Together they add up to further evidence that the *anu* were single magnetic poles bound by string-like lines of force. Her observations give support from an unexpected direction to a modern scientific theory of the strong forces acting between fundamental particles.

The two Theosophists were assisted in their work by their friend C. Jinarajadasa who wrote down their descriptions as they dictated them. At the end of the third edition of *Occult chemistry*, he remarked:

> With the information revealed in *Occult chemistry*, a great expansion of our knowledge of Chemistry lies in front of us. It is just because this expansion is inevitable, that our clairvoyant investigators have toiled patiently for thirty years. They have claimed no recognition from chemists and physicists, because truth accepted or rejected is truth still, and any fact of nature seen and stated clearly will sooner or later be woven into the whole fabric of truth. The fact that this generation of scientists hardly knows anything at all of an extraordinary work of research extending for thirty years matters little, when we contemplate the long vistas of scientific investigation which the imagination sees awaiting mankind.

Today the 'extraordinary piece of research' by Besant and Leadbeater has at last shown its intrinsic scientific merit by revealing a remarkably high degree of consistency with ideas and well-established facts of nuclear and particle physics. Without knowing what they were observing, they described the subatomic world 70 years ago in a way that agrees with important areas of modern research. Scientists and lay people alike may find their claims difficult to believe. But they cannot dismiss the Theosophists' claims as fraudulent because their work was completed many years before pertinent scientific knowledge and theories became available to make a hoax possible even in principle. Nor can they honestly reject these claims as unsupported by scientific thought, for the very opposite is true. How, therefore, can one account for Besant and Leadbeater's remarkable anticipations of modern physics except by admitting that they did indeed observe the microphysical world by means of extra-sensory perception?

Further reading
Annie Besant and Charles W. Leadbeater, *Occult chemistry*, Theosophical Publishing House (Adyar, India) 1952
Stephen M. Phillips, *Extra-sensory perception of quarks*, Theosophical Publishing House (Wheaton USA) 1980
J.C. Polkinghorne, *The particle play*, W.H. Freeman 1979

The kindest cut of all

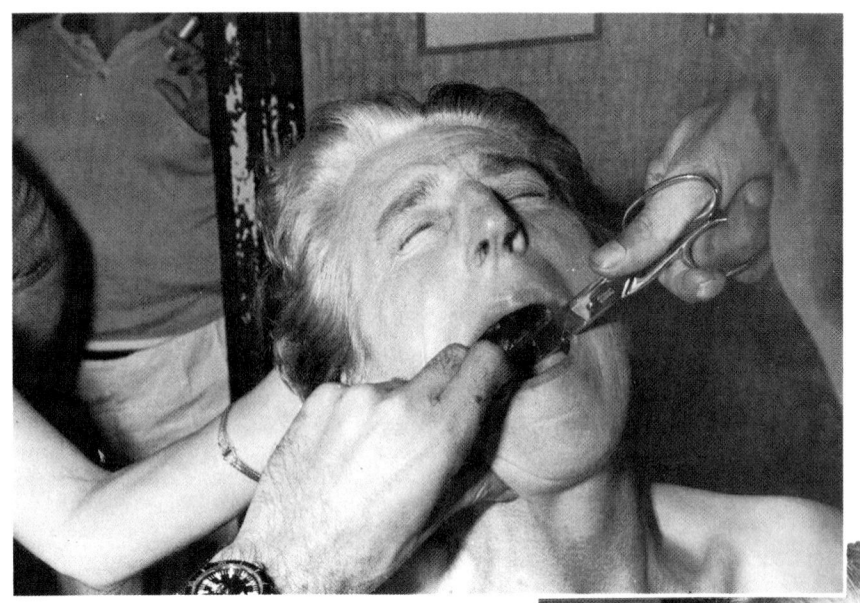

Claims and counterclaims for the merits of psychic surgery in general – and the superiority of the Brazilian over the Filipino methods in particular – have depended largely on eyewitness reports. Now ANNE DOOLEY tells it from the patient's point of view

HOW DOES IT FEEL to undergo psychic surgery of the Brazilian variety? No anaesthesia or sterilisation. No medical equipment or life-saving apparatus. And a medically untrained medium who does the operation in a trance under the control of a spirit guide. Is it any wonder that before my own 35-minute ordeal it was touch and go whether I stayed or fled? But I stayed that day in 1966 – and I'm glad for it.

I shall always be grateful to Lourival de Freitas who, rejecting payment, risked arrest to carry out an illegal operation. What made me decide to take the risk on my side?

In February 1946 I had a lung haemorrhage and ended up as an emergency patient at St Bartholomew's hospital in London. The subsequent 14 days of medical observation led to two possible diagnoses: tuberculosis or lung abscess. The former was a probability so strongly favoured by my own doctor that she notified the local authority to disinfect my flat. The hospital doctor laid his bets on a lung abscess.

Neither proved to be right. Eventually I was told that I was suffering from an inoperable lung condition called bronchiectasis. I was warned to stop smoking and told hectoringly that I would have to carry out postural drainage twice daily for the rest of my life. (Postural drainage involves hanging upside down for as long as one can bear the indignity and the resulting blinding headache.) I made three or four attempts to give up smoking but was totally unsuccessful and decided to take whatever physical risks were involved.

Again in 1959 I was told that my condition was inoperable by a chest specialist, who also gave a pessimistic view of my future. He said that I would have to take antibiotics for ever to ward off acute bronchial attacks, and that I might not be able to work full-time again.

That is why, after 20 years of suffering, I decided to undergo psychic surgery. I chose Lourival because I had met him and been impressed with him in the course of my journalistic work. In fact, on the first day we met, I witnessed an operation by him on a delicate six-year-old girl who also had bronchiectasis. By cupping a glass and slowly revolving it on her back, he 'drew out' some evilly discoloured tissue. Nine months later, when I saw her again after my own operation, she was like a different child.

Once in Brazil, preparation for my unorthodox operation began in a suitably unorthodox way. On a sightseeing trip to a beautiful waterfall, Lourival waded into a river and pulled up a large sharp-edged reed. With it he notched an oblique scar under my right shoulder blade. He then pronounced with satisfaction that 'the way the cut had taken' ensured that it would be possible to carry out the same kind of glass-cupping operation he had performed in London, for I did not want to go under the knife. The surgery was supposed to bring about a 40 to 70 per cent improvement in my condition.

In the intervening six days I had herbal treatment. Daily I drank four glasses of a

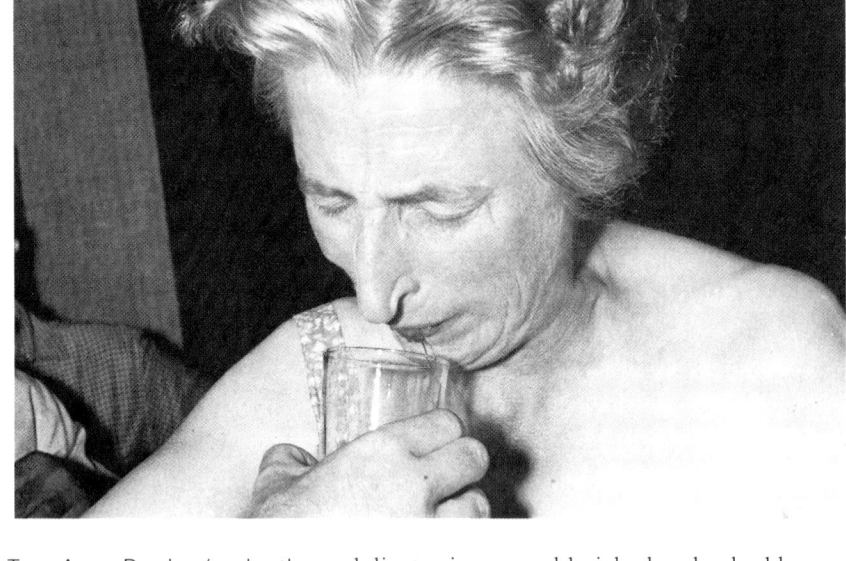

Top: Anne Dooley 'under the knife' – in this case, a pair of unsterilised scissors – during an unscheduled tonsilectomy at the hands of psychic surgeon Lourival de Freitas. The London journalist went to a secret location in Brazil in 1966 for an operation to improve a chronic lung condition. Secrecy was necessary because psychic surgery was illegal

Above: the patient spits into a tumbler after the surgery on her tonsils

1838

Psychic surgery

I was also nervous about the possible use of the knife, having banked on the glass-cupping method.

'Nero' proceeded to give a long, angry tirade which, I gathered from occasional words here and there, included criticism of me. I became increasingly depressed and tense. I again walked out of the room and stood in dejected indecision at the top of a flight of stone stairs leading to the garden below. I wanted to leave, but realised I couldn't. I was doubly committed: personally I had gratefully agreed to the proposed surgery; professionally I had a story to do and had travelled thousands of miles to study a man who, in my view, had been unjustly accused of trickery in England. And perhaps most important of all, here was Lourival bravely risking his freedom to give unrecompensed help where it was badly needed. I couldn't insult him by running away.

When it came to my turn I discovered that pleasant tasting lemon-mint mixture, which lessened my normally profuse bronchial catarrh noticeably. I also had to drink several tumblers of a nauseating herbal tea every day, to clear excess liquid from the kidneys.

Again I was told to stop smoking and I rashly cut it out altogether. This abrupt cessation of my normal daily intake of from 30 to 35 cigarettes undoubtedly contributed to the bouts of depression I had immediately prior to the operation. Subconscious fear was probably a subsidiary cause.

Then the night of the operation came. During the whole session, the healer worked in the harsh light of unshaded electric bulbs and an additional portable standard lamp. Other patients and observers varied from 12 to 15 in number throughout the evening. One of these spectators was a Brazilian journalist who wrote an eyewitness account for my book *Every wall a door* (1973). Lourival himself never left the site, which consisted of two large adjoining rooms linked by a wide arch.

Having been told that the session, due to start at 8 p.m., would be devoted solely to my bronchus operation, I was a little disturbed to see the others and to learn that there would be additional operations. Indeed the first one was not on me, but on an old man who had been Lourival's patient previously. Lourival's chief control that night was 'Nero', who removed a growth from the old man's right eye. During the second operation – on a child – a neck incision proved necessary. The child cried out piteously, but only during the actual cutting and subsequent sucking out of tissue. I turned away and walked out of the open door because momentarily I couldn't bear the child's apparent suffering. I had also learned earlier that 'Nero' didn't want me to look at any of the operations. I imagine that my mounting nervousness was known to the spirit control.

Top: Anne Dooley displays the tumbler containing ejected blood and tissue

Above: Lourival, under the guidance of his spirit control 'Nero', makes a razor incision for the planned lung operation

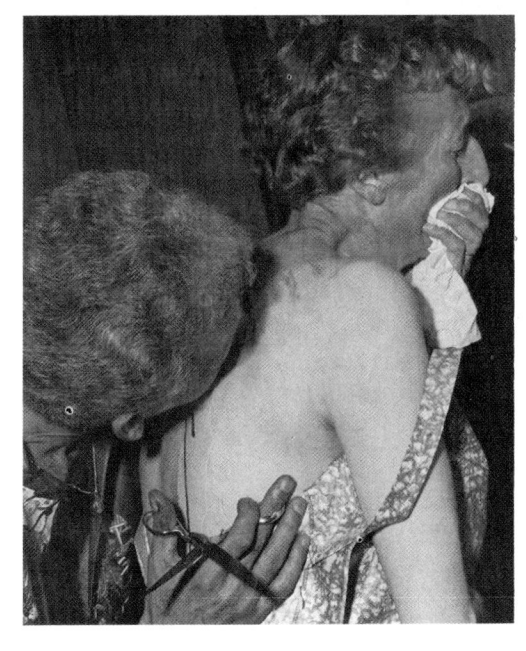

Right: the psychic surgeon sucks out the coagulated blood said to contain the lung virus that caused Anne Dooley so much suffering

1839

Psychic surgery

Further reading
Anne Dooley, *Every wall a door*, Corgi 1975
Harold Sherman, *Wonder healers of the Philippines*, Psychic Press 1967
Alfred Stelter, *Psi healing*, Bantam 1976
T. Valentine, *Psychic surgery*, Henry Regnery (Chicago) 1973
Lyall Watson, *The Romeo error*, Coronet 1976

Left: the healer shows the patient the clot he removed

Below: the stitching process begins as Anne Dooley clings to a helping hand

Bottom: the stretched flesh is pulled up by the stitching threads to 'enable full blood flow in the area'. Anne Dooley said the pain stopped at once

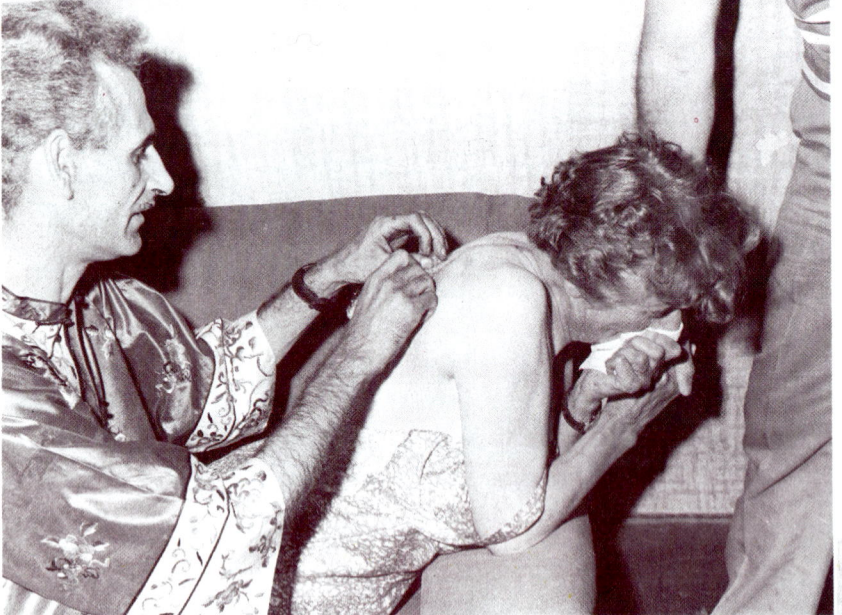

I was to have my tonsils removed – something not originally scheduled. The ensuing operation inside my throat was grim. I found it difficult to breathe when large scissors began digging into my back palate, particularly as I was simultaneously being semi-dragged across the room to enable the medium to get better light.

Then I found myself being handed a tumbler and being told: 'Don't cough. Just spit with all your might.' After I did, the tumbler contained some nasty stuff indeed: it was about a third full of a mixture of tissue and blood.

The second part of the operation began with my being asked to stand up again. I felt a razor blade cut lightly into my flesh at right angles to the earlier mark made with the reed. Then I could feel Lourival's teeth grip and squeeze my flesh and I worried inwardly over how long I would be able to bear the pressure if it got much worse. But it was quickly over. Next I found myself being handed a large clot of what looked like coagulated 'black' blood about the size of an elongated coin.

I lay face down as I was stitched up – about 9 to 12 stitches according to my confused counting. It was unpleasant each time the sewing needle plunged through the lips of the cut. Yet, incredibly, those stitches were cut after only about an hour. I felt very little pain and there was no bleeding. The sizeable scar was then latticed over with strip bandaging.

I never felt any further pain or the slightest discomfort from the scar on my back, but I had a bad 36 hours with my throat. Soon after the operation I began to spit up tiny pieces of torn flesh from where the scissors had apparently dug into the palate. Was this due to the operation on the tonsils or had the 'dematerialisation' process of some of the ejected tissue been incomplete? I found it excruciating to swallow, but within 24 hours, after being given salt gargles and an antibiotic tablet, I was drinking my first welcome cup of tea and healing tissue was already forming.

I was told to take things easy for 10 days, during which time I was given eight vitamin B injections and some calcium tablets. I felt well and the depth of my breathing was substantially increased. I no longer woke up feeling as if I was breathing over the top of a wall – as I had done for so many years prior to the operation.

And 16 years later I am still doing all right – near the age of 70 at that. The orthodox doctors were surprised by my improvement, admitting that the best they could have done was to 'keep me going' for as long as possible. Indeed I myself don't think I would be here if I hadn't volunteered for psychic surgery.

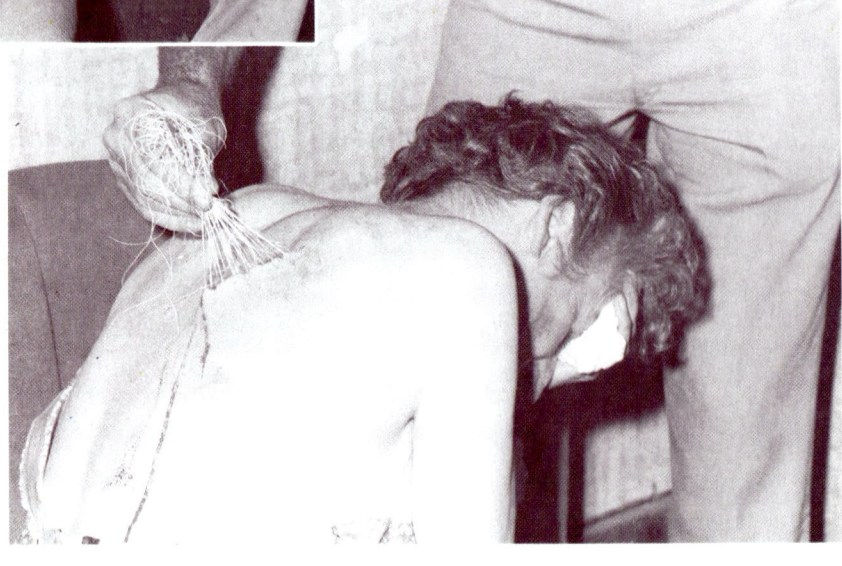

Was Borley Rectory really 'the most haunted house in England' – or was its fame built on a great publicity stunt by ghost hunter Harry Price? Indeed, was Price a headline-seeking fraud? FRANK SMYTH investigates

BORLEY PARISH CHURCH stands on a hillside overlooking the valley of the river Stour, which marks the boundary between the counties of Essex and Suffolk in England. Borley can hardly even be called a village: the hundred or so inhabitants of this Essex parish, mainly agricultural workers and weekend cottagers, do their shopping and socialising in Long Melford or Sudbury, the two nearest small towns on the Suffolk side; for more important business they travel from Borley Green to Bury St Edmunds, about 25 miles (40 kilometres) away.

But in 1940 the publication of a book entitled *The most haunted house in England* made the community world famous, and in 1946 a further volume, *The end of Borley Rectory*, set the seal on its fame. Both were written by the flamboyant ghost hunter Harry Price, who made psychical research headlines in his day. The two books claimed that Borley Rectory, a gloomy Victorian house that had burned down in 1939, was the centre of remarkably varied paranormal phenomena. These included a phantom coach, a headless monk, a ghostly nun who may or may not have been the monk's lover, the spirit of a former vicar, eerie lights, water that turned into ink, mysterious bells, and a multifarious cascade of things that went bump in the night.

'One of the events of the year 1940' was how the first book was described by *Time and Tide* in its glowing review, while the *Church Times* said that it would 'remain among the most remarkable contributions ever made to the study of the paranormal'. Price, who professed to have devoted 10 years to his study of Borley's ghosts, continued to lecture, broadcast and write on the subject until his death on 29 March 1948. An obituary in *The Times* the following day summed him up as a psychical researcher with 'a singularly honest and clear mind on a subject that by its very nature lends itself to all manner of trickery and chicanery'.

Not everyone who knew or worked with Price agreed with this glowing testimonial, however. Some months after his death, and with the danger of libel safely out of the way, an article by Charles Sutton of the *Daily Mail* appeared in the *Inky way annual*, a World's Press News publication. Writing of a visit he had paid to Borley in 1929, in the

Borley Church, whose vicars lived in the reputedly haunted Borley Rectory not far away. Harry Price, ghost hunter, psychical researcher and author, put the parish of Borley 'on the map' when he wrote a book about the rectory hauntings in 1940

Borley: a haunting tale

Borley Rectory

middle of Price's first investigation with another colleague, Sutton said that he had discovered what might be fraud on Price's part. After a large pebble had hit Sutton on the head, he found that Price had 'bricks and pebbles' in his pockets.

On a more careful investigation, two members of the Society for Psychical Research (SPR) – Lord Charles Hope and Major the Hon. Henry Douglas-Home – had had serious doubts about 'phenomena' they had witnessed at the rectory in the late 1920s. Both of them filed testimony with the SPR stating that they had grave suspicions. Douglas-Home went as far as to accuse Price of having a 'complete disregard for the truth in this matter'. He told how, on one occasion, he was accompanying Price around the rectory in the darkness when they heard a rustling that reminded him of cellophane being crumpled. Later, he sneaked a look into Price's suitcase and found a roll of cellophane with a torn edge.

It was as a result of this testimony that the Council of the SPR invited three of their members, Dr Eric J. Dingwall, Mrs K. M. Goldney and Mr Trevor H. Hall, to undertake a new survey of the evidence. The three were given access to Price's private papers and correspondence by his literary executor, Dr Paul Tabori. They also had access to documents in the Harry Price Collection, which Price had placed on permanent loan to the University of London in 1938 and bequeathed to that institution on his death. This survey took five years to prepare and was published in 1956 under the title *The haunting of Borley rectory*.

The reviews of this book were as enthusiastic as those of Price's two volumes in the 1940s, although for diametrically different reasons. The *Sunday Times* said that the Borley legend had been demolished 'with clinical thoroughness and aseptic objectivity', while Professor A.G.N. Flew in the *Spectator* commented that the 'shattering

Price in action: on the radio direct from a haunted house in Meopham, Kent, in 1936 (above) and on a much-publicised trip to Germany with C.E.M. Joad to re-create a magical scene on the Brocken in the Harz mountains in 1932 (below)

and fascinating document' had proved that Borley had been 'a house of cards built by the late Harry Price out of little more than a pack of lies'.

There, perhaps, the matter should have rested, but due to a combination of factors it did not. The principal reason may have been that Borley had made sensational copy for the world's popular newspapers for over a quarter of a century, and even the most objective of reporters dislikes seeing a good source dry up. Newspapers and television programmes glossed over the painstaking evidence of Dingwall, Goldney and Hall, one referring to them as 'the scoffers who accused Harry Price, the greatest of ghost seekers, of rigging the whole legend'. And once more, the events described by Price were said to be 'puzzling, frightening, and inexplicable'. Peter Underwood, the president of the Ghost Club, and the late Dr Tabori returned to Price's defence in 1973 with a book entitled *The ghosts of Borley: annals of the haunted rectory*. They dedicated it to 'the memory of Harry Price, the man who put Borley on the map'.

In his book *The occult*, published in 1971, Colin Wilson made a fair and scrupulously unbiased summing up of the evidence for and against the Borley case. His conclusion was that 'a hundred other similar cases could be extracted [from SPR records]. . . . Unless someone can produce a book proving that Price was a pathological liar with a craving for publicity, it is necessary to suspend judgement.'

And, indeed, in 1978 SPR investigator Trevor H. Hall set out to prove Price 'a pathological liar with a craving for publicity'. The title of his book, Search for Harry Price, was a pun based on Price's own autobiography Search for truth (1942).

Had it been less carefully documented, Hall's book could have been fairly described as a piece of muckraking. He revealed, for instance, that Price's father was a London grocer who had seduced and married Price's mother when she was 14 and he was over 40. Price himself, in his autobiography, had claimed to be the son of a wealthy paper manufacturer who came of 'an old Shropshire family'.

Price stated that his childhood had been spent between the London stockbroker suburb of Brockley and the family's country home in an unnamed part of Shropshire. He said that he usually 'broke his journey' there on the way to and from school, implying that he was educated at a boarding school in the country. Hall's researches clearly showed the family home to have been in New Cross, not far from, but far less salubrious than, Brockley. Price, said Hall, attended a local secondary school, Haberdasher's Aske's Hatcham Boys' School, a perfectly respectable lower middle class establishment, but not a public boarding school. The only family connection with Shropshire was that Price's grandfather had once been landlord of the Bull's Head at Rodington.

According to Price, he had held a directorship in his father's paper manufacturing company after leaving school, spending the 10 years between the end of his schooldays and his marriage in 1908 pleasantly as an amateur coin collector and archaeologist. In fact, according to Hall, Price earned his living in New Cross in a variety of odd ways. He took photographs of local shopfronts for advertising purposes; hired out his portable gramophone and records for dances, parties and other functions; performed conjuring tricks at concerts – a skill that he was later accused of using during his Borley investigation – and peddled glue, paste and a cure for footrot in sheep from door to door in the Kent countryside. Price had an indubitable flair for writing, as the impressive sales of his books – some 17 in all – testify.

In 1902 Price wrote an article for his old school magazine, *The Askean*, about the excavation of a Roman villa in Greenwich Park, quoting as his source a book written by the director of the project. By 1942, in *Search for truth*, he was claiming that he had actually helped to excavate the site. He also contributed a series of articles to the *Kentish Mercury* on coins and tokens of the county, following this up with another series for Shropshire's *Wellington Journal* on 'Shropshire tokens and mints'.

Hall asked the Reverend Charles Ellison, Archdeacon of Leeds and a leading authority

Above: Peter Underwood, the president of the Ghost Club, who came down on the side of Price in the controversy over the latter's integrity

Below: the ruins of Borley Rectory four years after it was completely destroyed by a mysterious fire. This did not end the speculation over its haunting

Borley Rectory

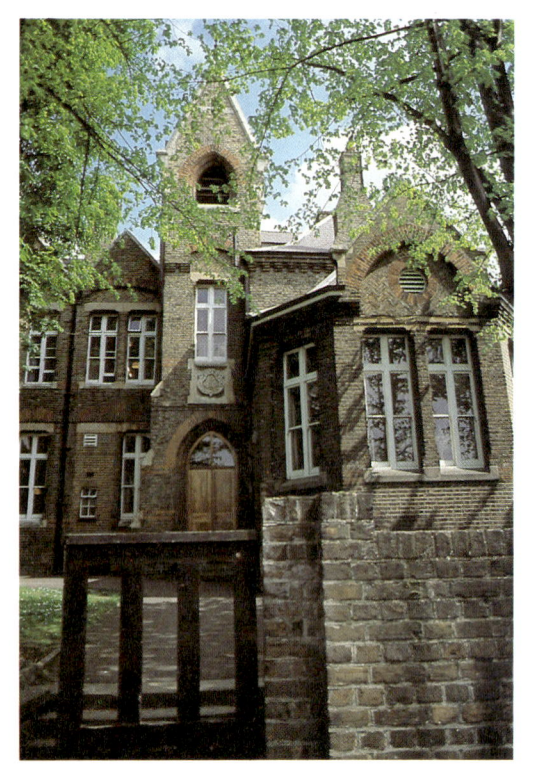

Left: Haberdasher's Aske's Hatcham Boys School, where Price had his education, as it looks today. According to Price's detractor, Trevor H. Hall, Price hinted in his autobiography that he had attended a public school

Below: the Harry Price Library in the Senate House at London University. Price bequeathed to the university his outstanding collection of thousands of books on magic and the occult – which Hall characterises as Price's 'most useful achievement'. Price also tried to get the university to establish a psychical research department, but failed. Some say that the institution was scared off by his flamboyant approach to scientific investigation

on numismatics, to examine Price's writings on coins. The archdeacon found them to be straight plagiarisms from two obscure works on the subject. 'It is unsafe to rely on any statement made by Harry Price which lacks independent confirmation,' he concluded.

Hall reported that Price's financial independence came from his marriage to Constance Knight, who inherited a comfortable fortune from her father. It was her means, and not family wealth as claimed, that gave him the leisure to put his days of door-to-door peddling behind him and embark on his career as psychical researcher and book collector. The assembling of a library of occult and magical books running into several thousand volumes was, said Hall, 'Price's most useful achievement during his life'.

Even the library seemed to offer opportunities for chicanery, however. In the collection Hall found several valuable books clearly marked with the imprint of the SPR. Price had catalogued them as his own, even attaching his own book plate.

Price's book plates were a source of interest and amusement for Hall, as well as another example of Price's covertness. Price used two crested plates. One featured a lion rampant and proved on investigation to be the family crest of Sir Charles Rugge-Price of Richmond, with whom Harry Price had no connection. The other, bearing a crest and coat of arms, carried the name 'Robert Ditcher-Price' and the address 'Norton Manor, Radnor'. Hall's investigations revealed that the crest and arms were those of Parr of Parr, Lancashire, and that Norton Manor belonged to Sir Robert Green-Price, Baronet, whose family had lived there since the 17th century. A letter from Lady Jean Green-Price unequivocally stated that she had never heard of Robert Ditcher-Price and that she was 'quite certain that he never resided at Norton Manor'.

In his first book on Borley Rectory in 1940 Price used a version of the 'nun's tale' supplied by the Glanville family – father Sydney, son Roger and daughter Helen. While holding a seance with a planchette at their home, Helen Glanville elicited the information that a nun had indeed been murdered at Borley and that she was a Frenchwoman called Marie Lairre. On the subject of this and subsequent seances he held, Sydney Glanville was almost apologetic to SPR researchers Dingwall, Goldney and Hall, admitting that suggestion had played a part: all three Glanvilles had studied the history of the Borley hauntings.

After the story of the French nun's ghost appeared in *The most haunted house in England*, Price received an elaborate theory from Dr W. J. Phythian-Adams, Canon of Carlisle, to the effect that Marie Lairre had been induced to leave her convent and marry one of the local landowners. She had been strangled by her husband and buried in a

Borley Rectory

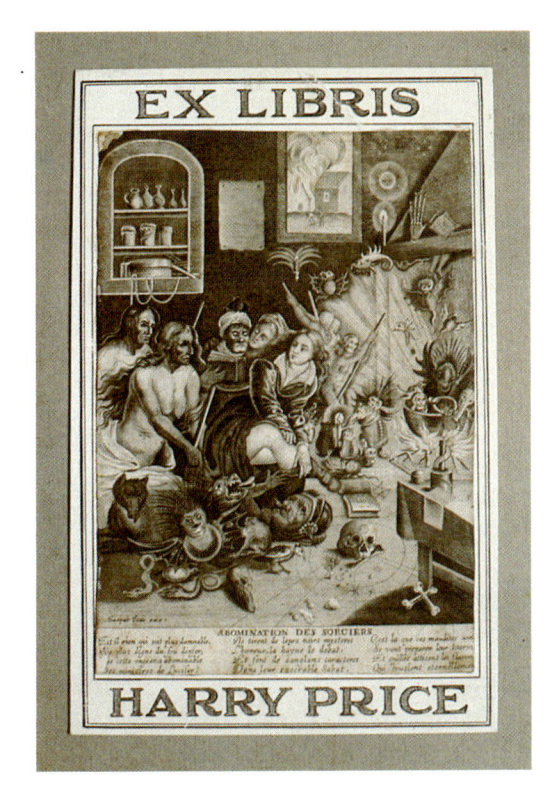

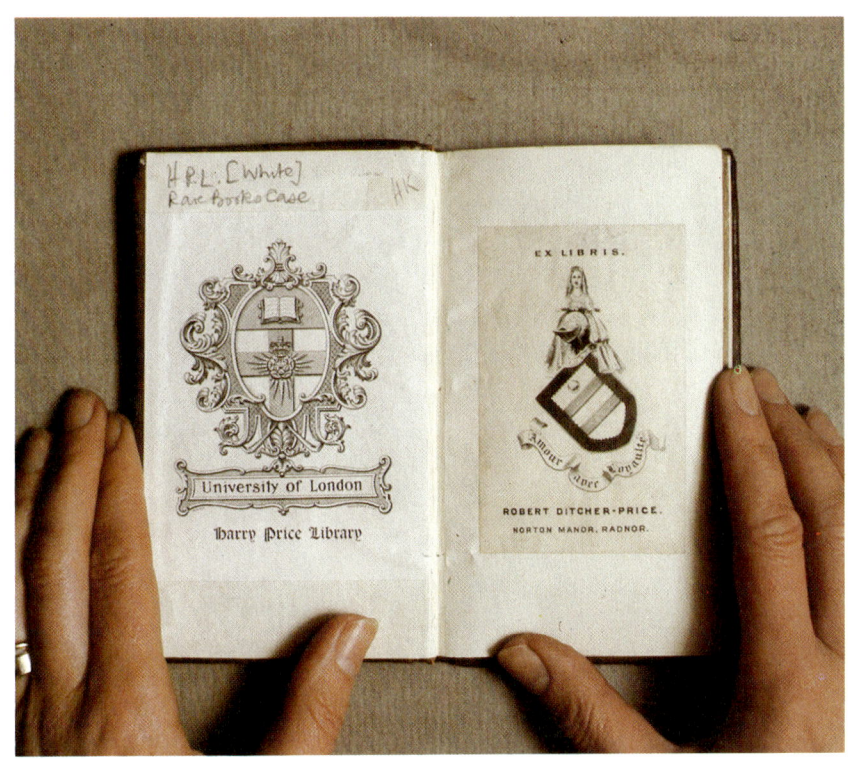

well on the site of the rectory. The canon suggested that the ghost of the former nun stole a French dictionary from the residents of Borley Rectory in the 19th century so that she could brush up on her English in order to communicate with them.

Despite some other preposterous twists in the canon's theory, Price seized on it eagerly. Hall accuses him of manufacturing and planting evidence to back it up. Part of this evidence was two French medals that Price claimed had appeared as 'apports' during his first visit to the rectory in 1929. One was a Roman Catholic confirmation medal and the other a badge or pass issued to members of the National Assembly after the revolution. Yet previously, Price had said that there was one apported medal and that it was a 'Loyola' medal. Price's faithful secretary stated that the Loyola medal was the only one she had ever seen.

Puzzling finds

Further to this case, Hall recounts how Price had excavated what he called a well in the ruined cellars of Borley Rectory in 1943, discovering a human jawbone in the soft earth. The excavation was made by lamplight. The well turned out to be a modern concrete basin. And during the demolition of the ruins, a switch and lengths of wire were found in the cellar, though the house had never been supplied with electricity. Had Price used this equipment with a portable battery to light the cellars as he secretly buried the jawbone for later discovery?

And so Trevor Hall's book goes on, each damning fact backed by documentary evidence, much of which is from Price's own unpublished notes and correspondence.

Three of Harry Price's book plates. The one on the far right, bearing the name of 'Robert Ditcher-Price' and the address 'Norton Manor, Radnor', was investigated by Hall. He says that the titled family residing at Norton Hall, the Green-Prices, had never heard of a Robert Ditcher-Price

Price's accounts of psychical research projects are shown time and again to be inaccurate, or almost entirely invented, or presented over the years in different versions with contradictory details. *Search for Harry Price* certainly fulfills Colin Wilson's criterion: it shows Price as a confirmed liar and publicity seeker. The absurd experiment in which Price and Professor C. E. M. Joad conducted a magical ceremony in the Harz mountains in Germany for a regiment of press photographers more than proves the latter. But even more, the revelations indicate that he was a fraud.

But does the tarnishing of Price's character necessarily mean that the haunting of Borley Rectory was fraudulent? From the year the rectory was built in 1863 until 1929, when Price first became interested in it, stories circulating in the area had seemed to suggest paranormal happenings. Furthermore, from 1930 to 1937 Price visited Borley only once, and yet at least 2000 allegedly paranormal incidents were recorded during that time. In a year straddling 1937 and 1938, when Price rented the empty rectory and recruited a team of independent witnesses through an advertisement in *The Times* to live there with him, several incidents were reported in Price's absence. Finally, between Price's residency and 27 February 1939, when the rectory was 'mysteriously' destroyed by fire at midnight, odd events occurred.

So, regardless of Price's role, was Borley Rectory in fact the 'most haunted house in England?'

A phantom nun, flying keys, raps and mystery lights: phenomena or fraud? See page 1894

This too, too solid flesh

Can the dead materialise in their physical bodies in the presence of unusually gifted mediums? ROY STEMMAN cites some of the rare cases of materialisation where fraud could apparently be ruled out

YOLANDE WAS A 15-year-old Arab girl. She was also, allegedly, a spirit, which meant she could appear and disappear at will, in the presence of a famous English materialisation medium, Madame Elizabeth d'Esperance. Visitors to Madame d'Esperance's seances often claimed to have seen both the materialisation and the medium simultaneously. The way in which Yolande departed from the seance left the witnesses in no doubt that she was a genuine paranormal manifestation, even though she appeared to be a normal, living person while she was materialised.

Being 'only human', Yolande took a liking to a certain brilliantly coloured scarf that a sitter was wearing, and 'borrowed' it. When she dematerialised the scarf disappeared with her, but she was seen to be wearing it at her next seance appearance. She made it clear, however, that she did not wish to part with it.

Sometimes Yolande's spirit form would gradually dissolve into a mist, on occasions in front of 20 witnesses, and only the scarf would be left lying on the ground. 'At last she has forgotten it,' a sitter would remark. But then the scarf, too, would slowly vanish in the same manner.

Madame d'Esperance was one of the earliest English materialisation mediums and she readily co-operated with investigators who wanted to prove the spirits were not produced by fraud – even to the extent of allowing photographs to be taken. But one particular seance experience suggests that materialisation is not a straightforward phenomenon.

At a seance in Newcastle in 1880 one of the sitters became suspicious because another of Madame d'Esperance's materialisations – known as 'the French lady' – looked uncannily like the medium. He made a grab for the spirit, which promptly vanished. But the medium suffered a lung haemorrhage and was ill for a long time after the seance. On two other occasions similar incidents occurred, but Madame d'Esperance was never found to be producing the strange manifestations fraudulently.

Spiritualists say that touching a materialisation (unless permission has been granted by the 'spirits') or putting a light on during a seance can do untold damage to mediums because it causes the 'ectoplasm' – from which the spirit forms are made – to return to

Above: Yolande, alleged spirit guide of Madame d'Esperance

Right: illustration by Tissot, depicting the two materialised spirits he encountered at a seance given by London medium William Eglinton (top right) in the 1880s. It seems logical that a genuine materialised spirit would still be wearing a shroud; but the voluminous clothing would also make an ideal disguise for fake 'spirits'

Physical mediums

the medium's body at too great a speed. Nevertheless, there have been cases where materialisations are said to have been produced in daylight.

It was London medium William Eglinton who was responsible for convincing many sceptics. After attending one of his seances, the famous conjurer Harry Kellar declared: 'I must own that I came away utterly unable to explain, by any natural means, the phenomena that I witnessed.' At one point during this seance both Kellar and Eglinton were levitated.

One of the alleged spirits who regularly appeared at Eglinton's seances was Abd-u-lah who had only one arm and was adorned with jewels, rings, crosses and clusters of rubies that were apparently worth a fortune. But another materialisation, a bearded man in a long robe, allowed one of the sitters to cut a piece of material from his clothes and a part of his beard. These were later said to match holes in a piece of muslin and a false beard found in a trunk belonging to Eglinton.

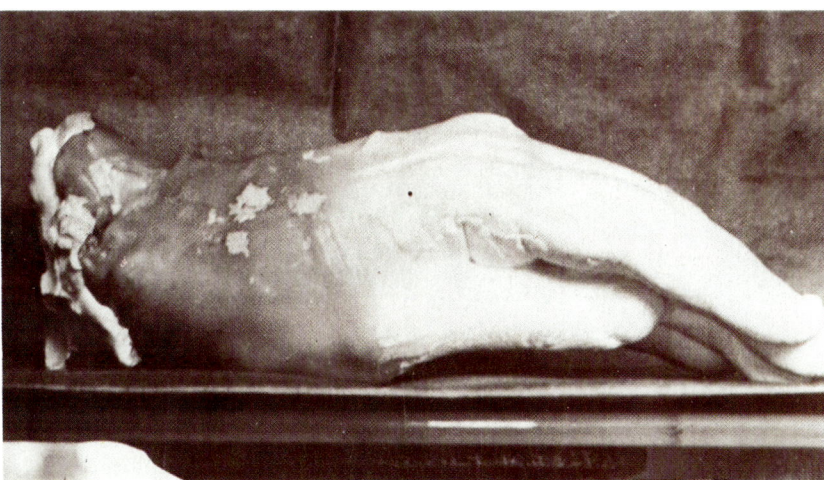

Despite this particular accusation of fraud – which was made by Archdeacon Thomas Colley – Eglinton continued to give seances and impressed many eminent people. He developed slate-writing powers: the spirits were said to write answers to questions on small black slates. William Gladstone visited him on 29 October 1884, and wrote down confidential questions in Spanish, Greek and French. The answers were given in those languages. The prime minister was so impressed that he became a member of the Society for Psychical Research.

The man who claimed to have exposed Eglinton was, ironically, no sceptic: Archdeacon Colley of Natal and Rector of Stockton, England, was a staunch supporter of another materialisation medium, an English clergyman-turned-medium, the Reverend Francis Ward Monck. Monck was not only accused of being a fraud but was sentenced to three months' imprisonment on the evidence of 'props' found in *his* room after a seance in Huddersfield in November 1876. Archdeacon Colley was in South Africa at the time but he was adamant that Monck was genuine.

The problem with materialisations is that they leave no tangible evidence of their reality. Investigator William Oxley, however, came up with an ingenious method of 'recording' the presence of Monck's materialised spirits (one that has been used successfully with other mediums). At a seance in Manchester in 1876 Oxley was able to make excellent paraffin moulds of the hands and feet of materialisations.

Waxing and waning

To make a paraffin mould, warm wax is poured onto the surface of a bowl of water and the materialisation is asked to plunge its hand into it. The spirit form then immerses its hand in a bowl of cold water, causing the wax to harden. The form then dematerialises leaving a glove-like wax cast – often with a very narrow wrist opening from which it would have been impossible for a human hand to withdraw without splitting the mould.

A Polish intellectual, Franek Kluski, was a very powerful physical medium who produced wax impressions in this way. He was never a professional medium, but he offered his services to Dr Gustave Geley and the Institut Métapsychique, Paris, in 1920. This eminent psychical researcher, and other investigators, testified that in Kluski's presence phantom limbs materialised, luminous forms glided around the seance room and brilliant lights suddenly appeared. Under strict controls they were even able to produce photographs of a phantom. And both Dr

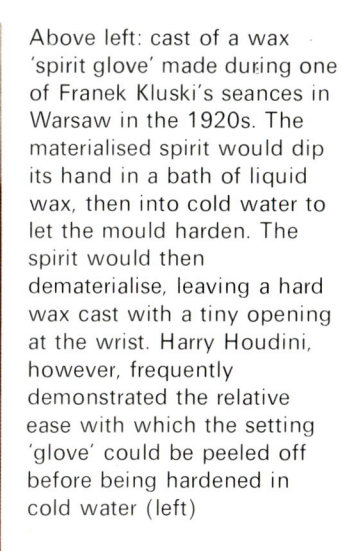

Above left: cast of a wax 'spirit glove' made during one of Franek Kluski's seances in Warsaw in the 1920s. The materialised spirit would dip its hand in a bath of liquid wax, then into cold water to let the mould harden. The spirit would then dematerialise, leaving a hard wax cast with a tiny opening at the wrist. Harry Houdini, however, frequently demonstrated the relative ease with which the setting 'glove' could be peeled off before being hardened in cold water (left)

Physical mediums

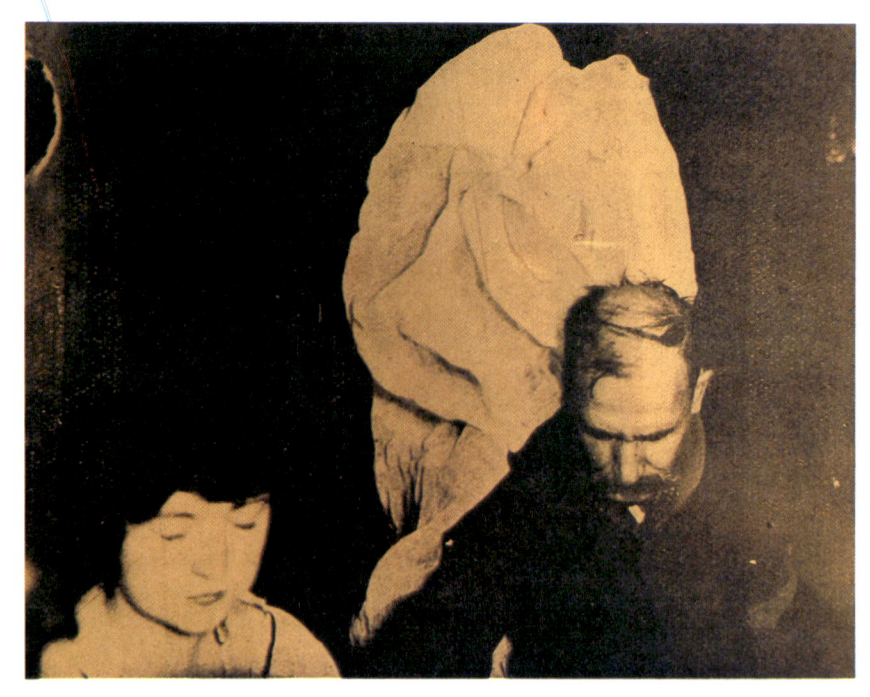

Geley and Dr Charles Richet, who was a professor of physiology in Paris, obtained excellent moulds of materialised hands and limbs with Kluski.

The full-form materialisations that appeared at Kluski's seances (see box) often arrived suddenly, though at other times they were seen to emerge from a faintly luminous cloud above the medium's head.

The materialisations produced by a Cardiff boot and shoe repairer, George Spriggs, seem almost too good to be true, but there is ample testimony from people who witnessed the phenomenon and who were all aware of the precautions that need to be taken against fraud.

Spriggs's paranormal powers developed in a Welsh Spiritualist circle in the late 1870s, beginning with clairvoyance and automatic writing – and culminating in full-form phantoms. He emigrated to Australia in November 1880, taking his psychic powers with him. A prominent Australian named Donovan, a former member of the Legislative Assembly of Victoria, attended Spriggs's seances for 18 months and wrote a book about his experiences, *The evidences of Spiritualism*.

An extraordinary incident occurred at one of the Australian seances when a man materialised and said he wanted to write a letter to a Sydney woman who had visited the seances a couple of times. He was given a pen and paper and wrote a three-page letter, which he placed in an envelope and addressed to the woman. But no one had a stamp. The spirit borrowed sixpence from a sitter and left the seance room to buy one from the shop next door. Word reached the shopkeeper that a phantom was on its way to buy a stamp and he was so flustered that he forgot to give the dead man his change. The spirit realised the error when he got back to the seance room and promptly returned to the shop for the money. The letter was posted and a reply duly received; this was kept until the spirit materialised at another seance, opened it, and read the contents aloud.

Spriggs's ability to produce materialisations faded after six years but he developed the ability to diagnose illness psychically. He returned to Britain in 1900 and between 1903 and 1905 he gave free medical advice in the rooms of the London Spiritualist Alliance.

A demand for healing

Medicine also played an important role in the mediumship of English psychic Isa Northage, and the materialisation seances she gave are perhaps the most astonishing ever recorded. She was a popular medium in the 1940s, visiting churches to demonstrate her psychic powers, which included apport mediumship, direct voice and materialisation. But it was the healing work of her spirit doctor, Dr Reynolds, that was in particular demand and eventually a church was built specifically for this work in the grounds of Newstead Abbey, Northumberland. In time – as the medium's powers grew stronger – Dr Reynolds was able to materialise and carry

Top: a phantom begins to materialise in the gloom of one of Kluski's seances. Spiritualists believe that ectoplasm – the material from which materialisations are formed – is photosensitive; which is why most seances are held in the dark

Above right: the Australian medium George Spriggs. One of his materialisations wrote a letter – and went to the post office to buy a stamp for it

The apeman cometh

Not all of Franek Kluski's materialisations would have been welcome at a party. In July 1919 an apeman made the first of several appearances at a Kluski seance. Dr Gustave Geley reported: 'This being, which we have termed *Pithecanthropus*, has shown itself several times at our seances. One of us... felt its large shaggy head press hard on his shoulder and against his cheek. The head was covered with thick, coarse hair. A smell came from it like that of a deer or wet dog.'

And Colonel Norbert Ocholowicz, who published a book about Kluski's mediumship in Polish, in 1926, wrote: 'This ape was of such great strength that it could easily move a heavy bookcase filled with books through the room, carry a sofa over the heads of the sitters, or lift the heaviest persons with their chairs into the air to the height of a tall person. Though the ape's behaviour sometimes caused fear, and indicated a low level of intelligence, it was never malignant. Indeed, it often expressed goodwill, gentleness and readiness to obey....'

Physical mediums

out 'bloodless' surgery on patients. This account, written by Group Captain G.S.M. Insall, VC, is taken from a book about Isa Northage's mediumship, *A path prepared*, compiled and published by Allan Macdonald:

We prepared the room, donned white overalls and masks, as was the rule with Dr Reynolds. This was not new to me as I had been a student in the most up-to-date French hospital before the First World War changed my career to flying.... The two patients came in. [Both had hernias.] The first, the one with complications, was partially stripped and placed on the operating table. The other was given a chair nearby.

There was a trolley, and I checked over the instruments – tweezers, swabs, kidney basins and bowls; no cutting instruments at all except scissors to cut lint. There was also a small white pencil light. I checked the emergency door and saw that it was locked and bolted on the inside, and draught excluded by a mat placed on the threshold. I was just closing the inner door leading into the church when somebody noticed that the medium had not arrived. I opened it again, and she came in. The light was turned low and somebody opened in prayer. I could see the medium sitting in her usual chair, a curtain hanging on either side.

Immediately the prayer was over a trumpet rose and Dr Reynolds' familiar voice greeted us all. He then re-assured the patients and gave them instructions.... I was assigned a kidney basin to collect swabs and stepped forward to the operating table.

The trumpet went down, and almost immediately the doctor appeared in materialised form on the opposite side of the operating table. He is of small stature. The medium was deep in trance.

He first took the tweezers and swab with a disinfecting cleaner and swabbed the area. The hernia was umbilical. I collected the swab in the kidney basin. Then I saw him place his hands on the patient's flesh, and they just went in deep, nearly out of sight. He stretched out for the tweezers and swabs and I collected eight soiled ones altogether.

The materialised doctor checked that the patient was comfortable – he had felt no pain – and turned the pencil light on his flesh to inspect the area. There was no sign of a wound or a scar. Dr Reynolds then said he wanted to give the medium a rest before the next operation – and he dematerialised.

Above left: Charles Richet, French scientist and psychical researcher who was president of the SPR in 1905. He was impressed with the mediumship of Kluski, finding no natural, or fraudulent, explanation for his phenomena

Above, left and below: three stages of materialisation, based on the experiences of William Eglinton. The mist that seems to grow up from the medium's solar plexus forms a distinct shape – sometimes an object (as in the case of 'apports'), or an animal or human being. But it always disintegrates

Further reading
W.J. Crawford, *The reality of psychic phenomena*, J.M. Watkins 1916
Fred Gettings, *Ghosts in photographs*, Harmony (New York) 1978
Harry Price, *Stella C.*, Longman 1925

The doctor's dilemma

Every unorthodox method of healing has its devoted advocates – and its grateful clients, convinced of its effectiveness. RUTH WEST begins a survey of the treatments that are offered as rivals or as complements to 'scientific' medicine

FRINGE MEDICINE, alternative medicine, natural medicine, complementary medicine – all these are titles that have been applied to a body of therapies practised, in the main, outside the bounds of orthodox medicine by practitioners with no qualifications that a conventional doctor would recognise. The terms include a whole range of practices. Osteopathy is concerned with correcting relationships among the different parts of the body's mechanical structure – the skeleton and musculature – by manipulation and other techniques. Naturopathy rejects the use of drugs and relies on the body's own healing systems, aided by 'natural' agencies – 'healthy' foods, exercise, a moderate regimen. Acupuncture and the associated system of massage, acupressure, are now well-known in the West and have attracted the serious interest of the medical profession (see page 181). Reflexology is a system of healing concerned with the supposed beneficial effects on internal organs of massage applied to the hands and feet. Hypnosis, yoga, meditation, the latest diet – all these, too, can lie on the borderland between conventional and alternative medicine.

There is one thing, however, that these practices have in common. To orthodoxy they are unscientific. They do not fit within the current medical scientific framework explaining the way in which the body works. And they have little or no research behind them to back up their claims to be legitimate, effective treatments. Yet while science awaits satisfactory evidence, the number of satisfied customers of these therapies grows – customers who have often gone as a last resort when all else has failed. Several surveys, some of them commissioned by governments, point to this growth in both the number of practitioners of alternative medicine and the number of their patients, and a concurrent dissatisfaction with orthodox medical care. For example, a survey conducted by the British consumer magazine *Which?* in 1981 found that nine out of ten of the people questioned who had used alternative medicine said that they would use it again. Two thirds of those who had used alternative medicine during the preceding five years said that they had found that orthodox medicine did not help them, or they did not like what it had to offer.

Perhaps the features that attract such warm praise are as much to do with the general attitudes that are common to alternative therapies as with the nature of their specific remedies. The relationships between therapists and their patients are often closer than those between conventional doctors and their patients. Furthermore, fringe therapies generally address themselves to the 'whole person' – to emotions, attitudes and all aspects of daily living: diet, exercise, even relationships with others. Conventional medicine, on the other hand, has achieved its greatest successes in tackling isolated disorders of the body, caused by single, identifiable agents, such as a particular virus or a particular chemical imbalance. The professional worker in conventional medicine prides himself on a 'detached' attitude, and never presumes to guide the patient's general way of life.

That something is fashionable or popular in no way guarantees its truth. So the charge is made that the gullible public, disappointed to find that medicine cannot supply a wonder drug for each disorder that afflicts us, is seeking magical cures elsewhere: and in the course of this irrational and prescientific behaviour people are being duped by charlatans and quacks.

The wisdom of the shaman

Many workers in alternative medicine would claim, on the other hand, that they are extending the range of techniques and drugs in use – adding to the armoury of the medical practitioner. They also claim to be recovering some of the wisdom and some of the healing arts that have been lost with the advent of modern medicine. Certainly the skill of the healer may have been viewed magically in the past: the sick person may have gone to a priest, shaman or medicine man – a person possessing jealously guarded esoteric knowledge – expecting him to be able to manipulate nature on his behalf. Many people, even in advanced societies, may still expect and want that from their doctors. But we are free to learn from the traditional healer while rejecting the magical attitude – to ask just how the shaman or priest contributed to the recovery of the sick.

Healing was a priestly function when Western medicine first developed, in the tradition of the Greek god Asclepius (whom the Romans called Aesculapius). According to René Dubos, a distinguished student of medicine and its history, this tradition had three strands. First there was the cult of Asclepius, which was

under the control of a priesthood which practised faith healing based on

Below: a page from *The book of herbs* of the German botanist Adam Lonitzer. Published in 1557, it was an early example of a new kind of herbal, which described and depicted plants in a scientific spirit. European herbals had hitherto contained mythological and fantastic accounts of plants, with pictures copied from Greek and Roman originals

Alternative healing

Left: 'natural' healing for the rich in 1898. At this luxurious sanatorium near Dresden, in Germany, well-to-do patients could relax, sunbathe, take the air and the local mineral waters, and live on wholesome food

Below: herbal medicine for the poor. Dr Bokanky, the street herbalist, was one of the traders depicted in Henry Mayhew's great work London labour and the London poor, *which appeared in 1851. He described the virtues of his 'Kalibonca root' in these words: 'It'll cure the tooth-ache, head-ache, giddiness in the head, dimness of sight, rheumatics in the head, and is highly recommended for the ague; never known to fail . . . .'*

dreams. Drawn by a widespread and deep belief in the healing power of the god, many patients came to seek cures in sanctuaries dedicated to his worship but not organised for true medical care. . . . Purifying baths, anointments, abstinence, a religious atmosphere, and the interpretation of dreams took the place of medical treatment.

The other two strands of the tradition were purely medical practices, represented by two goddesses: Hygeia (Health) and Panacea (All Heal, or Cure All). They were practised by lay physicians, whose medicine was based on the anatomical and physiological knowledge of their times. Hygeia represented the prevention of disease: live wisely and you will stay healthy. Panacea 'symbolised the belief that ailments can be cured by skilful use of the proper kinds of substances'. Only these last two aspects gave rise, through the great physicians of Greece, Hippocrates, Aristotle and Galen, to modern medicine.

But one further crucial step towards our present-day outlook was made with the rise of modern science: mind was divorced from matter, and health came to be viewed as the quality of performance of the body-machine. Medicine became a matter of making sure, with the use of drugs and surgery, that the parts of the machine were kept in good repair.

Today conventional medicine attacks its unorthodox rivals on two main grounds, as we have seen: that they are reviving magical attitudes towards the practice of medicine, and that they are foisting spurious techniques and ineffective medicines on a gullible public. To examine these questions we shall discuss two important types of alternative therapy (although this is by no means an all-inclusive classification): first, therapies based upon the taking of medicines; secondly, therapies based upon the use of touch or manipulation.

An important branch of the unorthodox therapies based on medicines is herbalism. This, it may be argued, is well on the way to scientific respectability. After all, until the 1930s, medicines came almost wholly from plants and fungi, and many still do. Morphine, digitalis, ephedrine, quinine, senna are a few of these. Nonetheless, our present scientific attitudes stand in the way of a full

1851

Alternative healing

A temple of healing

Medical treatment is administered by Asclepius, god of healing, in a Greek relief of the fourth century BC (above). From being merely a wise, but mortal, physician, mentioned by Homer in the *Iliad*, he rose in stature and came to be regarded as the son of the god Apollo and a nymph, Coronis. He was supposed to have been taught the art of healing by the centaur Chiron. He learned so well that Zeus finally slew him, afraid that his skill would make mankind immortal. His cult extended over the entire Mediterranean world and his temples were places of worship and of healing. The sick would come there, offer up a sacrifice and spend a night in the temple. They would receive advice from priests and then depart. Numerous commemorative tablets survive, relating the names, sicknesses and, invariably, the cures of the patients.

The greatest of the temples devoted to Asclepius was that at Epidaurus, in the Peloponnese. In 293 BC Rome was beset by a plague, and a mission was sent to Epidaurus to bring back the image of Asclepius. It brought instead a snake that was supposed to be inhabited by the god, and a temple to Asclepius was built in Rome.

Contact with a sacred serpent played an important part in the treatment of the sick at the temples of Asclepius. The serpent often appears in representations of the god, and is seen in this statue (left) of Hygeia, one of the daughters of Asclepius. The small figure at her feet is Eros Hypnos, representing sleep, one of the other important factors in Asclepian healing. Today twin serpents of Asclepius, coiled round a staff, are still used as a medical symbol.

---

understanding and acceptance of herbal medicine.

The standard, safe approach to the use of herbal preparations is to spend massive research grants, using very expensive and sophisticated equipment, to analyse each plant for its active compounds. If such a substance has a chemical structure similar to one that is known and understood, then it may be of use. Herbal mixtures in seemingly illogical combinations are to be avoided at all costs and, as one commentator says, they may be 'even more insidiously dangerous when they contain ingredients of non-herbal origin'.

Even if a herbal remedy that seemed to be a likely candidate for medical use were to be prepared according to the criteria of modern pharmacology, it would be required to pass lengthy and expensive tests of its efficacy – on laboratory animals, on small groups of patients and finally in large-scale clinical trials. Scientific critics doubt that the herbal practitioners of the past would have been able to recognise some of the subtle ways in which drugs can be dangerous – in causing cancers or genetic mutations over long periods of use, for example.

This approach dismisses the knowledge of those using herbs as failing to meet modern scientific standards. Yet medical herbalists are often aware of the side effects of particular preparations and will employ other

Alternative healing

ones to counteract them. And it is possible that modern science does not yet know how to analyse fully the action of plants. There are certain enzymes – substances that promote and regulate important chemical reactions in living organisms – that, as one writer says, 'we know little about and cannot isolate, but which seem to do good work'. There is evidence that there can be a difference in action between a whole-plant preparation and that of the isolated substance that is allegedly the active ingredient. It is often better to use the whole plant: trials have shown that the heart drug digitalis, prepared from the whole leaf of the foxglove, is superior to the purified substance extracted from the leaves and often used medically.

A stumbling block to the acceptance of herbal medicine is the sheer variety of ills that each is claimed to help. Medical workers are deeply imbued with the traditional notion that each cure must be tailored to one disorder. But two such 'panaceas' have raised some interest in the scientific community. One is a group of herbs described as 'valuable nutrients': it includes wheat grass and the evening primrose. The other is a group of herbs called adaptogens, which act as tonics: they include ginseng and Russian root.

The oil of the evening primrose is supposed to aid sufferers from high blood pressure, excess weight, eczema, rheumatoid arthritis, multiple sclerosis, alcoholism, pre-menstrual tension – the list is seemingly endless. But it does seem to have a scientific basis for its claims. It is a source of gamma-linolenic acid, which is of vital importance in the chain of body processes leading to the production of prostaglandins, which in turn are of key importance for the smooth working of the body – including, notably, the control of blood pressure. At present, however, the case is undecided: more extensive trials are needed before the biochemical significance of the oil can be properly judged.

A final area of research must be mentioned. From the orthodox viewpoint, talk of the correct times for planting and collecting herbs, according to time of day, season and phase of the Moon, smacks of magic. Yet the evidence is there: some plants can be highly toxic at certain times of year, yet safe at others. The intake of oxygen by plants varies with the phase of the Moon – so why should medical effectiveness not similarly vary? It seems that the folklore regarding the times of planting and collection are not there merely for the purpose of persuading patients that some ritual is being performed to aid their cure.

One of the oldest unorthodox therapies, homoeopathy, is discussed on page 1866

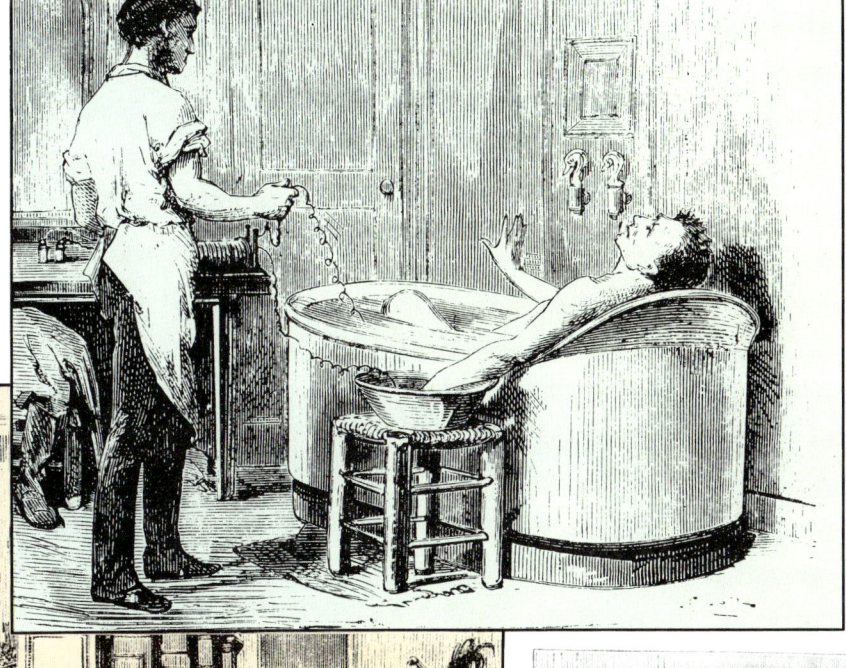

Below: the electric bath of 1874. The patient received electric shocks, intended to be therapeutic, through the bathwater. He could break the circuit when he wished by lifting his hand from the bowl

Left: the vibrating helmet, a treatment for Parkinson's disease invented by the great French neurologist Jean Martin Charcot. In the late 19th century orthodox and alternative medicine could still hardly be distinguished: bizarre treatments such as this typified 'official' medicine

Centre: inhaling ozone at a French clinic in 1895. The amount of gas used would probably have been too small to produce ozone's normal effect: irritation of the nose and throat

Far left: evening primrose, regarded as a remedy for a wide range of ills

Long after the much-publicised disappearance of Franck Fontaine from Cergy-Pontoise, confusion still reigns over whether he was abducted by a UFO. Was it all a put-up job by him and his two friends? Or did it really happen? HILARY EVANS sums up

THE ABDUCTION OF Franck Fontaine by a UFO, though unsubstantiated by scientific evidence, seemed a plausible story on first hearing. Had he and his friends Jean-Pierre Prévost and Salomon N'Diaye been content to tell that story and nothing else, they might have convinced an interested world of its truth. But the two books on the case – one by the well-known science fiction writer Jimmy Guieu and one by Prévost himself – raised questions that cast suspicion on the entire affair. Moreover, there were many interviews and conferences in which widely divergent material was put forward. And Prévost, who had pre-empted Fontaine as the hero of the Cergy-Pontoise UFO affair, even published a short-lived journal in which he kept the public informed of his continuing dialogue with the 'intelligences from beyond' who he claimed had contacted him.

All this increased the doubts of the sceptics. Michel Piccin and his colleagues of the Control organisation had detected inconsistencies and contradictions in the witnesses' statements from the start. And the more they probed, the more discrepancies they found.

It began with trivial, marginal matters, like Prévost's insistence that before the encounter he had no interest in or knowledge of UFOs. The Control investigators found that his brother was a French representative of the American UFO organisation APRO. Even if Prévost did not share his brother's interest in UFOs, he could hardly have been unaware of them. Besides, in his own book, Prévost had said that he saw several spacecraft similar to ones he had 'seen as a child' when the 'intelligences' took him to their UFO base. He also denied seeing a magazine in which a UFO abduction story, very like Fontaine's, was being serialised. Yet Control established that this very magazine was in Prévost's flat at the time of the Cergy-Pontoise abduction.

The events of the night before the abduction became more confused the more they were investigated. Control discovered that there were five people – not three – in

fact, fraud or fantasy?

Cergy-Pontoise affair

Prévost's flat that night. Why had the published accounts almost completely failed to mention the presence of Corinne, Prévost's girlfriend, and Fabrice Joly? One reason suggested itself: knowledge of the presence of the fourth young man, Joly, might throw doubt on one of the facts most favourable to Prévost and N'Diaye. They had claimed that they had gone straight to the police when Fontaine vanished from their car, even though they knew they might get into trouble because they were driving without a licence. But Joly was there because he had a valid licence and had agreed to drive the three friends to the market at Gisors.

Discrepancies abound

Why were Corinne and Joly never questioned about what happened? Did they see and hear nothing? They could certainly have straightened out some of the contradictions, for Fontaine, Prévost and N'Diaye could not even agree on who had been at the flat on the night before the abduction – surely one of the most memorable of their lives. First the three had said they spent the night together. Then Prévost recollected that he had watched a television film with friends elsewhere.

Other discrepancies force us to ask how far we can trust their account. They said that they were dubious about their car's ability to start and pushed it to get the motor running, then left Fontaine in the car to make sure it didn't stop. Why didn't Joly, the only licensed driver, do this so that Fontaine could lend a hand with loading the jeans for the market? Did they really sit outside the block of flats at 4 a.m. with the motor running without any complaint from the neighbours? None of the other residents seem even to have heard the sound. What about N'Diaye's completely opposing statement that they loaded the car first and only then started the motor? Whom should we believe?

The account of the one neighbour who did witness anything only makes matters more confused. Returning home at the time the young men were supposedly loading the car, he said he saw two people get into the Taunus estate car and drive away. Yet the three involved said that Fontaine was alone when he drove up onto the road to get a better view of the UFO they had spotted.

Even though UFOs are notoriously difficult to describe, the three accounts of the one at Cergy-Pontoise are particularly far apart. One saw 'a huge beam', another 'a ball', the third 'a flash'. One said it was moving fairly slowly, taking two minutes to cross the sky; the others said it was moving fast, gone in a matter of seconds. There was further disagreement about the direction in which it was moving.

The circumstances of Fontaine's return a week after his supposed abduction are no less confused as several stories emerged. One of the journalists covering the case was Iris Billon-Duplan, who worked for a local newspaper and lived close by. Apart from the special interest of a case that had occurred almost on her doorstep, the fact that she lived nearby meant she could follow it personally. As a result, she became closely involved with the witnesses. Indeed, she spent the night before Fontaine's return with Prévost, preparing a definitive account of the case.

According to the journalist's published account, N'Diaye went off to bed shortly after midnight, leaving her with Prévost. He told her that he had no food or money because his involvement in the UFO affair was keeping him from working. So she suggested that they go to her flat where she could give him a meal while they continued to work on

Above: Franck Fontaine, whose disappearance for a week – allegedly as an abductee of aliens – stirred worldwide interest. He was never very forthcoming about what had happened to him

Left: the cabbage field in which Fontaine awoke on his return to Cergy-Pontoise

Space briefing

Franck Fontaine remembered things that had happened to him during his week 'out of this world' only slowly and bit by bit, but refused to undergo hypnosis to speed the process. However, strange – and sometimes very disturbing – dreams helped him to recall his experiences, he said.

In one instance that he recalled, he was in a large white room with machines that went all round the walls. They were all the same height and had opaque white glass fronts that lit up and went out almost simultaneously. He was lying on a sort of couch and two small luminous spheres – the extra-terrestrials – were talking to him about problems on Earth and how to solve them.

His abductors, who were always kind, told him that he would be the sole judge of what to reveal of his adventure. He seems to have decided to say as little as possible.

1855

Cergy-Pontoise affair

the article. This explains why Fontaine did not find Prévost in when he returned and went to Prévost's flat. We know that Fontaine then went to N'Diaye's flat and succeeded in rousing him. But according to the journalist's account, N'Diaye then left Fontaine and hurried round to her flat to tell her and Prévost the news.

Should we believe Iris Billon-Duplan or Salomon N'Diaye? For his statement, made to the police, flatly contradicts hers.

His story was that he happened to wake up at about 4.30 a.m., looked out of his window and saw a ball of light on the main road. When he saw a silhouetted figure emerge from it, he recognised his friend Franck Fontaine. He then hurried to a telephone to report the return to Radio Luxembourg, believing he would get a reward for information about Fontaine's whereabouts. (In this he was mistaken; it was Europe Numéro 1 that had offered a reward.)

Radio Luxembourg later confirmed that such a call had been made, but not at 4.30 a.m. because there was nobody on duty at that hour. The implication is that N'Diaye telephoned later than 4.30 a.m. and that he waited to inform the police until he had attempted to claim the reward money – not saying much for his concern about his friend. In the event, it was Radio Luxembourg staff who told the police that Franck Fontaine had returned. According to them, they had received an *anonymous* call from a man who, just as he was going to work, saw Fontaine coming back. Surely N'Diaye would not have made an anonymous call if he wanted to collect the reward.

These contradictions are just a sample from Control's 50-page report. There is confusion, if not outright deception, at every stage of the affair. Some of the discrepancies can be attributed to faulty memory, but such an explanation can hardly be stretched to account for Prévost's extraordinary visit to the tunnel. As a case history, Cergy-Pontoise is so ambiguous that few will be ready to give it serious credence. Yet it caused such a sensation that it is still worth asking what really happened. If the abduction was not genuine, was it a put-up job from the outset? Or did the witnesses gradually distort what was fundamentally a true UFO experience? If so, at what point did deceit and contrivance begin? There are several ways to answer these questions.

An elaborate tale

We may believe that Franck Fontaine was abducted as claimed, that all the witnesses were doing their best to tell the truth and that contradictions crept in because of defective memory. However, the extent of the discrepancies makes it easier to believe that the trio elaborated the story for their own purposes, adding sensational details that they may or may not have believed actually happened.

Alternatively, we may surmise that Franck Fontaine was not in fact abducted, but that he sincerely believed he was. He may have been in, or put into, some altered state of consciousness in which he experienced the illusion of the abduction. That this can happen is an established psychological phenomenon, so we cannot rule it out altogether. But it does raise questions about Fontaine's two friends. If he was deluded,

Top: Jean-Pierre Prévost with Patrick Pottier of the Control group. Control carried out as thorough an investigation as they could without the active co-operation of Prévost and the other two involved

Above: Salomon N'Diaye in front of the Taunus estate car which, he said, he and Prévost saw enveloped by a UFO just before their friend Fontaine disappeared

Cergy-Pontoise affair

Further reading
Jimmy Guieu, with Franck Fontaine, Salomon N'Diaye, Jean-Pierre Prévost, *Contacts OVNI Cergy-Pontoise*, Editions du Rocher (Monaco) 1980
Jean-Pierre Prévost, *OVNI, le grand contact: la verité sur l'affaire de Cergy-Pontoise*, Michel Moutet (Regusse, France) 1980

where do they stand? Were they also in an altered state of consciousness, experiencing or being made to believe in the same illusion? And does this explain the contradictions? If so, who fed them the illusion and made them believe in its reality?

While neither of these explanations can be ruled out entirely, we may consider it most plausible that the whole affair was a fabrication from the start – that there never was any abduction and that the three young men put the story together for fun, for gain or for some undiscovered ideological motive. We know that the trio immediately co-operated with Jimmy Guieu in a commercial enterprise. We learn from Control that Prévost, clearly the dominant one of the three, was noted for practical joking at school. Indeed he told the Control investigators, 'You bet I'm a clown!'

More questions than answers

The reports are consistent with the hypothesis that Prévost persuaded his two companions to stage a hoax, but that Corinne and Fabrice Joly refused to go along. Perhaps none of them expected their story to attract so much attention and they were forced to improvise beyond their prepared narrative. This could explain such muddles as the contradictory accounts of Fontaine's return.

Another question then arises: was Guieu a party to the deception? Did he suspect the story from the start but, as a professional writer, recognise its money-making potential? Did he start by believing them, as he claimed to do, then discover the hoax but decide to go along with it – perhaps because he was already committed? Or did he believe that the affair was genuine? The last supposition seems unlikely in the light of Guieu's long involvement with ufology, unless he was unusually gullible. On the other hand, it is hard to believe that he would risk his reputation by endorsing a case that he knew to be a fake. We are probably left with the surmise that he discovered a hoax but decided not to reveal it for reasons of his own.

If the Cergy-Pontoise contact was indeed all a hoax, it would explain why the trio committed themselves to the uncritical Guieu and his *Institut Mondial des Sciences Avancés* (World Institute of Advanced Sciences). IMSA has little following or reputation, but Guieu offered the backing of a big name, sympathetic support and the chance to make a substantial profit from a book bearing his name. And other UFO organisations might have uncovered the deceit in a short time, if deceit it was.

In the absence of any definite proof, all this is merely speculative. Will the truth ever be established? There are hopes that it may be. During their researches, Control came across a tantalising clue that they were unable to follow up. It seems that during Fontaine's disappearance, a school in Cergy-Pontoise was working on a project about it with the local newspaper – the one that was later to carry Iris Billon-Duplan's version of Fontaine's return. Some of the children learned that one of the school workers was an aunt of Fontaine and interviewed her as part of their project in the presence of one of the teachers and one of Iris Billon-Duplan's colleagues from the paper. During the interview, Fontaine's aunt said angrily that she knew perfectly well where her nephew was. He was, she said, staying with a friend.

Was she stating a fact or simply saying what she thought to be true? Who was the friend and where did he or she live? The answers to these questions could settle the Cergy-Pontoise mystery. But until we learn if someone knew where Fontaine was all the time, the case must remain open.

Right: a UFO base in a disused railway tunnel, as described by Jean-Pierre Prévost in his book on the Cergy-Pontoise affair. The tunnel also contained an abandoned Nazi train carriage left over from the Second World War. Prévost, always the dominant member of the trio of witnesses, quickly became the 'star of the show' and the other two receded into the background – for, said Prévost, the aliens had simply used Fontaine to establish contact with himself

Riddle of Racetrack Playa

The stones move – and no one sees them do it. Yet thousands have seen their tracks in the dry lake beds that dot the Sierra Nevada mountains in the western United States. BOB RICKARD **tells how the moving stones make their mysterious journeys**

HIGH IN THE Sierra Nevada mountains, in the remote region of California's border with Nevada, there are places where stones move at night. Once, a band of pioneers was trapped in these rough, deeply channelled hills and unexpected dried-up lake beds, on their way to prospect or to settle in more hospitable places. Now it is part of the vast Death Valley National Park, of which the moving stones are a great attraction.

Perhaps the most famous of these dry lake beds, or playas, is Racetrack Playa, about 1¼ miles (2 kilometres) wide by 3 miles (5 kilometres) long and nearly 4000 feet (1200 metres) above sea level. The visitor's eye is immediately drawn to the scattered boulders and stones that litter this plain of hard, cracked mud. The quality of light at this altitude adds to the surreal effect, so that the rocks, with their snaking furrows behind them, give the impression of being both stationary and stirring. No one has ever seen the stones move – but move they do.

Over the years it was noticed that the rocks that moved had not rolled along but were pushed, leaving a groove the same size as their width behind them. Then in 1955 a geologist called George M. Stanley wrote in the *Bulletin* of the Geological Society of America (GSA) that he believed wind and ice were involved. Stanley was intrigued by the fact that groups of rocks often moved together. He suggested that sheets of ice formed around a group of rocks and that the wind raised the whole sheet slightly and propelled it along. This sounds plausible and was accepted for many years, especially after ice sheets embedded with rocks had been seen moving on other Californian playas. However, the ice layers on the Death Valley playas are extremely thin, and while they may be capable of moving smaller stones, even Stanley did not suggest they could shift the 300- to 600-pound (135- to 270-kilogram) boulders that had made tracks.

The mystery of Racetrack Playa became world-famous in the 1960s, and in 1969 it attracted the attention of Dr Robert P. Sharp, of the California Institute of Technology's geology department, who began a study of the moving stones that lasted seven years. He selected 25 stones of a variety of shapes and weights, up to about 1000 pounds (455 kilograms), named them, and used a metal stake to mark their position. Later he included five more rocks. When he was able to make the arduous journey to the playa over more than 30 miles (50 kilometres)

Death Valley

Opposite: the trail of a moving stone is marked by clear tracks behind it in the arid landscape of Racetrack Playa – one of the dried-up lakes of the Sierra Nevada mountains. The moving stones are a tourist attraction of the Death Valley National Park

These two sets of tracks show how far some of the moving stones travel (right) and how they can change direction (below)

of rough dirt road, he looked for any tagged rocks that had moved, staked their new position and measured the distance travelled.

During the seven-year study period, 28 of the 30 rocks moved. The longest track measured 860 feet (262 metres) but, as in all cases, this distance was reached by a number of smaller moves rather than all at once. The longest single movement was 659 feet (201 metres) by a 9-ounce (250-gram) cobble called Nancy. The direction of these movements was north-north-easterly, with a few deviations to the east and south-east, which matched the direction of the prevailing winds in the playa.

Sharp soon noticed that there was a ridge on the edges of the furrow and that a small heap of debris was pushed up at the front of the rock by its movement. This indicated that the rocks must have moved when the playa surface was soft, not during its hard-baked or frozen state. Sharp found that most of the recorded movements occurred in three periods: the particularly wet or stormy winters of 1968 to 1969, 1972 to 1973 and 1973 to 1974. Although only some of the stones moved during all three periods, Sharp could infer that rain was as important a factor as wind. The playas get very little rain – about 0 to 3 inches (0 to 8 centimetres) annually – but they are surrounded by about 70 square miles (180 square kilometres) of hills, which make a fine catchment area. Even a light rain in the area could result in a thin layer of water over most of the playa.

Because the surface of the playa is made of fine clay, the action of the rain creates a sheet of water with clay particles in suspension. If the water soaks the surface deeply enough or for long enough, the rocks get bogged down in soft, sticky clay. But when about a quarter of an inch (0.6 centimetres) of water collects, the surface is firm enough to support the rocks. 'The secret,' Sharp wrote in the GSA *Bulletin* in 1976, 'is to catch the play of wind and water at precisely the right moment.' He thinks that movement probably occurs within one to three days of wet or stormy weather when the surface is 'as slick as a whistle'. A powerful gust of wind is all that is needed to make the rock slide, and a slighter wind afterwards will keep it going. Sharp maintains that the surrounding hills scoop

Death Valley

One of the 'walled lakes' in the state of Iowa, USA. According to Professor Charles A. White in a *Scientific American* article (1884), these walls were formed by deposits of compacted gravel, earth and boulders through the action of ice expansion in the shallow lakes. An early theory about the moving stones of the playas maintained that ice formation had caused their movement

and channel the winds into the playa at sufficient speeds to start the rocks moving – and the smoother the bottom of a stone, the farther it will skid. He has also calculated the maximum velocity of a moving stone as about 3 feet (1 metre) per second.

The phenomenon of moving rocks is not unique to Racetrack Playa. Tracks have been observed on at least 10 other playas in California and Nevada, and from time to time, in the literature of geology, similar anomalies have been reported. In an article written in 1879 for the periodical *Nineteenth Century*, Lord Dunraven told of a strange sight on the shore of a lake in Nova Scotia the previous year:

One day my Indian told me that in a lake close by all the rocks were moving out of the water, a circumstance I thought not a little strange. However, I went to look at the unheard of spectacle and, sure enough, there were the rocks apparently all moving out of the water on to dry land. The lake is of considerable extent, but shallow and full of great masses of rock. Many of these masses appear to have travelled right out of the lake and are now high and dry some 15 yards [14 metres] above the margin of the water. You may see them of all sizes, from blocks of, say, 6 or 8 feet [1.8 or 2.4 metres] in diameter, down to stones which a man could lift. Moreover, you find them in various stages of progress, some 100 yards [90 metres] or more from the shore and apparently just beginning to move; others halfway to their destination; and others again. . . high and dry above the water. In all cases there is a distinct groove or furrow, which the rock has clearly plowed for itself.

Lord Dunraven noticed one enormous specimen some distance from the water's edge; earth and stones were heaped up in front of it to over 3 feet (1 metre) in height. A furrow the exact width of the rock extended down the shore and into the water until it was lost from sight in the depths.

This weird scene, remarkably similar to that on the playas, was explained in a letter to the *Scientific American* later in 1879. The writer, who signed the letter 'J.W.A.', claimed to have seen identical effects in other Canadian lakes. The effect is most prominent in shallow lakes that are partly bounded by steep banks or cliffs, according to the explanation. As ice forms it expands and pushes outwards in all directions. The cliffs form an immovable obstacle on one shore, however, doubling the thrust on the opposite, open shore. In shallow water the ice extends to the lake bottom and embeds the rocks there. As the ice expands, it takes the rocks and any other debris with it, depositing them farther along when expansion stops and a thaw sets in. As the lake ice expands and melts each winter, cumulative movements would be enough to drive the rocks onto the land. A similar explanation was proposed by Professor Charles A. White (*Scientific American* 1884) to account for the mystery of the so-called 'walled lakes' of Iowa, which were originally thought to be 'the work of an extinct race'. He said that successive expansions of ice in shallow prairie lakes gradually deposited substantial ridges of compacted earth, gravel and boulders around the perimeter of the lakes.

So we may know how the rocks move. But the surrealistic scene of playas, rocks and their snaking track marks can still awaken a keen appreciation of the wonder and mystery of the natural world.

Further reading
Jim Brandon, *Weird America*, E.P. Dutton (New York) 1978
John Michell and Robert J. M.Rickard, *Phenomena, a book of wonders*, Thames and Hudson 1977

The Old Testament is full of 'signs and wonders', miraculous events that seem frankly impossible to the sceptic. But, as DAVID CHRISTIE-MURRAY shows, they bear a similarity to many paranormal events down the ages

THE BIBLE CONSISTS OF 66 books (80 including the Apocrypha) written over about a millennium, although some of its material is derived from far older oral tradition. Like most ancient writings it recounts paranormal incidents, though a student of psychical research will be surprised by their comparative absence and the general soberness of the history. Psychical researchers have, however, investigated the Bible comparatively little, partly because of a distrust of records so ancient by writers with such different outlooks from their own, partly because they hold that it is psychical research that throws light upon the Bible, not the Bible that contributes to psychical research.

Many people also feel that Holy Writ is sacrosanct, the Word of God, to be accepted, not studied – except as a guide to devotion and righteous living – and never to be criticised. Others see in it no more value than is contained in any collection of ancient writings. But it is possible to take a middle way: one can apply the principles of scholarly criticism to the Bible as to any other book, though without preconceptions, recognising that further discoveries are continually modifying present knowledge, and respecting the views of others. Whatever the findings of modern critics, the book has a unique value, recording the evolution of the conception of God from primitive animism to the most ethical monotheism, influencing three major religions, Islam, Judaism and Christianity.

Certain types of paranormal activity are

For it is written...

Above: Jacob's momentous dream of the ladder that reached down from heaven, upon which angels climb. The Lord spoke to him, bestowing on him the land on which he slept, adding: 'For I will not leave thee . . .'. Could this dream have been a subconscious safety mechanism to reassure the exiled Jacob and to give him a sense of purpose? Whatever its cause, it drastically altered not only his own life, but that of the entire Israelite nation

Right: Saul consults the 'witch' of Endor, who was probably a medium. Such consultations were strictly forbidden by Judaic law

Bible mysteries

missing in the Old Testament because its editors were followers of Yahweh (Jehovah), whose worship included prohibitions such as, 'Thou shalt not suffer a witch to live.' Their 'good' kings annihilated those with familiar spirits (mediums). Only one account of spiritist activity in Israel is extant, that of Saul's visit to the medium – 'the witch' – at Endor, to enquire his fate of the dead prophet, Samuel (1 Samuel 28). That visit is recorded as his final sin against God.

Other paranormal phenomena in the Old Testament include divination, possibly dowsing, precognitive dreams, mystical experiences, healing and precognition.

Divination had to be carried out under the auspices of Yahweh. Old Testament 'prophets' were regarded not as diviners but as religious and political commentators, and therefore were judged to be 'true' or 'false' not so much by the accuracy of their forecasts as by the gods they followed. The prophets of Baal were 'false' because their god was Yahweh's rival, whereas Jeremiah was 'true', even though his oracles were sometimes mistaken, because he served Jehovah. So Yahweh's high priest was provided with means of divination, 'the Urim and the Thummim' ('Lights and Truths'), apparently semi-precious stones set in his breastplate, which he may have used for a kind of crystal-gazing (Exodus 28). But on the whole, individuals devised their own methods of divination or of reading meaning into symbolical 'signs'. Thus Gideon knew that God would grant him victory because one night dew fell on a fleece while the ground around was dry and the next night the process was reversed (Judges 6).

Moses, finding water in the desert by the use of his rod (Exodus 17 and Numbers 20), may have used dowsing techniques. But though a visionary, he was no dreamer, and revelatory dreams are possibly the commonest paranormal phenomena in the Old Testament. Jacob's ladder dream (Genesis 28) repeated the promise made to his grandfather, Abraham, that his descendants should possess the very land on which the vision was dreamed. Joseph dreamed of his future lordship over his family (Genesis 37) and foresaw from the dreams of Pharaoh's imprisoned butler and baker that the former would be restored and the latter executed. His successful interpretation of Pharaoh's dreams foretelling seven years of plenty followed by seven of famine – of seven healthy kine (cattle) being eaten by seven feeble kine – resulted in his own promotion to high office (Genesis 40).

Right: Elijah is taken up by God in a 'chariot of fire' and disappears from the sight of men. Some modern writers believe that this is a primitive description of a UFO abduction, while many consider the language visionary, as in Blake's *Jerusalem*: 'Bring me my bow of burning gold, bring me my chariot of fire . . . .' But whatever really happened, the Bible records several sudden disappearances, mainly of the chosen prophets of the Lord

Far right: Moses hears the Lord speaking to him from the burning bush. Was this an hallucination – or genuine paranormal combustion?

Above: Joseph finds favour with Pharaoh by interpreting his dreams. The dream of seven healthy cattle being eaten by seven lean cattle Joseph interpreted as a prediction of seven years of prosperity being followed by seven years of famine. This happened, but because of the dream's warning Pharaoh had been able to build up stocks of food for the time of famine. Modern psychologists have confirmed that we often dream in symbols – such as cattle – and precognitive dreams may be widespread, but unfortunately such dreams are often ignored

Dreams of yesterday

In the light of modern dream research, from experiments carried out by such agencies as the Maimonides Dream Laboratory, we could conclude that these dreams happened as recorded. Jacob, leaving territory in which he had spent his youth, with thoughts that it might be for ever, could have been comforted by his dreams reminding him of God's promise to Abraham, which in turn made his own return probable. Joseph, knowing the reasons for the butler's and baker's imprisonment, needed no remarkable insight to interpret correctly the symbolism of their hope and fear.

The mystical experiences of different individuals vary in type and intensity. At a crisis of his life, Jacob wrestles with a mysterious but beneficial supernatural being (Genesis 32). An angel (that is, a messenger – not necessarily supernatural, though often so) appears to Samson's parents, foretelling their hero son's birth, and leaves them by ascending in an altar flame (Judges 13). The child Samuel, first of the great biblical prophets, has his first experience as a sensitive when he clairaudiently hears the voice of

Bible mysteries

God (1 Samuel 3). Every prophet seems to have had similar experiences, from Isaiah's vision in the Temple of 'the Lord . . . high and lifted up', attended by seraphim (Isaiah 6), to Ezekiel's sight of four great rings, full of eyes, their motion accompanied by a rushing sound (Ezekiel 1).

Other questions arise when one considers the wonder-stories surrounding the biblical folk heroes. Around individuals such as King Arthur and Robin Hood, who have a kernel of historicity, tales gather that are self-evidently legendary accretions. While fundamentalists deny that the Bible contains anything of the kind, most scholars would say that many stories, such as those of Samson's carrying away the city gates of Gaza (Judges 16) and Elisha making iron float (2 Kings 6), are of this kind, and that every account must be examined according to the principles of normal historical and literary criticism. A balance must be held.

Modern knowledge shows that some incidents that would have been considered pure legend at the beginning of the 20th century are at least possible, especially in the realm of healing. Although healing comes into its own in the New Testament, there are a few examples of paranormal healing in the Old Testament. Miriam, punished with leprosy for a revolt against Moses, is restored by his prayer (Numbers 12). Gazing upon the brazen image of a serpent heals Israelites bitten by snakes in the wilderness (Numbers 21). The image survived until its superstitious veneration caused it to be destroyed by Hezekiah, King of Judah, himself cured of an otherwise fatal abscess by a fig poultice. This event was signalled by a marked retreat of the shadow on the sundial (2 Kings 20), an event for which fundamentalist apologists claim there is astronomical evidence. Naaman, the Syrian general, was cured of leprosy by distant healing when Elisha, without seeing him, sent a message instructing him to bathe in the river Jordan seven times (2 Kings 5). Elijah restored a dead boy to life by stretching himself three times upon him (1 Kings 17). Elisha apparently used a 'kiss-of-life' technique on another, placing 'his mouth upon his mouth, and his eyes upon his eyes, and his hands upon his hands; and he stretched himself upon the child: and the flesh of the child waxed warm' (2 Kings 4). Since there are, in the literature of psychotherapy and psychical research, well-attested instances of chronic skin diseases being cured by hypnosis, and others of cures being effected by mental action at a distance, it would be unwise to reject dogmatically the possible truth of these stories.

And there are several other parallels with unexplained phenomena today. Mysterious disappearances occurred then as now (see page 281). Genesis 5:24 states dramatically that 'Enoch walked with God: and he was not: for God took him.' Moses was cryptically recorded as being 'buried by God' (Deuteronomy 34) – where is not known – but Josephus, the Jewish historian, records a tradition that 'a cloud stood over him [Moses] of a sudden and he disappeared in a certain valley.' And Elisha tells of Elijah's departure alive in 'the fiery chariot' (2 Kings 2).

Paranormal fire occurs frequently in the Old Testament, not unparalleled today if the stories of spontaneous human combustion (see page 24) are true. Such could have been the poetic justice of the rebels Nadab and Abihu, devoured by fire for offering 'strange fire' before the Lord in rivalry to Aaron, the appointed high priest (Numbers 3). The spontaneous combustion of 250 other rebels (Numbers 16) is more difficult to accept, though one can imagine the possible occurrence and exaggerated report of a number of deaths occurring simultaneously from

Right: God shows his power by igniting his prophet Elijah's sacrifice – while that of the Baal worshippers remains unlit, despite their frantic pleas. Spontaneous combustion is common in the Bible – and, according to Charles Fort and other collectors of tales of anomalous phenomena, not unknown in the lives of ordinary people even today

Below: the 'pillar of cloud' that assured the Israelites of God's presence during the daytime

Bible mysteries

The literal truth?

A river that turns to blood, plagues of frogs, and the mysterious deaths of the firstborn – these are among the plagues of Egypt as recorded in the Old Testament. Even many theologians maintain that these afflictions cannot possibly have happened as described, although similar events are recorded today.

Red rain fell in Newfoundland in 1890; frogs cascaded onto a bewildered Athens in 1980, and the large hailstones that fell near Clermond-Ferrand, France, in 1873 did no harm for they fell *slowly*. And on 14 June 1880 red, blue and grey hailstones fell in rapid succession in one small area of Russia.

Grievous afflictions such as the deaths of the Egyptian firstborn could well have been the effects of a curse for, as reports suggest, curses can work (see page 1761). The plagues, and other paranormal manifestations such as the parting of the Red Sea (left), may have been brought about by Moses himself, using psychic means. American parapsychologist Rex G. Stanford's theory of psi-mediated instrumental response – PMIR – (see page 1570) allows that quite ordinary people can psychically cause things to go their way, but only when in extreme need. But Moses was no ordinary man and his people were being threatened with extinction – a combination that may well have unleashed formidable powers.

lightning. Cloud and fire were symbols of the divine presence, cherubim and seraphim being originally cloud and lightning spirits. The Israelites were led through the wilderness by a 'pillar of cloud' by day and a 'pillar of fire' by night (Exodus 13), though for those who like rational explanations, the smoke and fire may have come from a brazier carried at the head of the wanderers – for them, however, it may have been none the less symbolic of God's guidance.

On many occasions God 'answers by fire' in mysterious ways, though the origins of the stories may often lie in priestly legerdemain. Heaven-sent fire ignites altars for Moses and Aaron (Leviticus 9), Gideon (Judges 6), David (1 Chronicles 21) and Solomon (2 Chronicles 7). Elijah calls down divine fire to consume bands of men sent to apprehend him (2 Kings 1). The supreme example of God's fire is in the dramatic scene on Mount Carmel, when Elijah's sacrifice, drenched with water, bursts into flame after Baal's prophets had failed to win fire from their god to ignite their offering (1 Kings 18). Perhaps, say the rationalists, lightning, preceding the storm that ended three years of drought, ignited Elijah's sacrifice. Or does the answer lie in conjuring tricks, or the fictional accretions of folk legend? Are all such 'paranormal' events explicable by natural law? After so many centuries, nothing can be proved or disproved.

Other instances of apparent paranormalities in the Bible could well have had natural causes. The 'burning bush' from which God's voice called Moses to lead Israel from Egypt (Exodus 3) could have been a wisp of gas escaping from the oil-rich desert and ignited by the Sun's rays, concentrated by the burning glass of a crystalline stone. Flickering in the wind, it could have looked like a bush blowing from side to side. The plagues of Egypt (Exodus 7) could have occurred because excessive deposits of red clay turned the water to stagnant 'blood', which bred an excess of frogs whose piled-up, decaying bodies bred 'lice', the larvae of swarms of flies that caused the horrifying disease in cattle and the 'plague of boils' in humans. The crossing of the 'Red' – or 'Reed' – Sea can be explained in different

Joshua and his men, having marched repeatedly around the walls of Jericho, sound their trumpets – and the walls crumble. Some modern commentators suggest that the vibrations set up by the marching were reinforced by the bugle blast, having a disastrous effect on walls that were perhaps already in a state of bad repair

Bible mysteries

ways according to the various locations where the crossing may have occurred. It has been suggested that the similar miracle, which occurred years later, of the dry-shod crossing of the river Jordan (Joshua 4) was caused by the temporary blocking of the river by an earth tremor. The same tremor could so have weakened Jericho's walls (shown archaeologically to have been shoddily built) that the rhythmic tramping round them of the Israelite army and the resonance of the blast of the rams' horns were enough to 'bring them tumbling down' (Joshua 6).

Bread of heaven?

Crossing the desert the Israelites were fed with 'manna' from heaven. This is widely believed to have been the exudation of tamarisk shrubs, which is still used as food by Bedouin. It is, however, produced only in small quantities, and the paranormality of the biblical account lies in the quantity produced – enough to feed an entire nation – and the fact that twice as much was produced every Friday so that the work of gathering manna should not profane the Saturday Sabbath. And Elijah was fed morning and evening by 'ravens', which brought him meat and bread. But the Hebrew word for ravens is the same as that for 'merchants' or 'Arabs'.

Nearly a quarter of the Old Testament is occupied by writings of the political commentators known as the 'prophets'. Precognition – 'prophesying' – is therefore the paranormal phenomenon most associated with it, for in popular thought prophets foretell the future. There are indeed many stories of prophecies that were fulfilled, most of which can be paralleled in other cultures. One example is Elisha's forecast that within a day the starving city of Samaria, besieged by the Syrians, would have a wealth of provisions, and that a certain lord, who had scorned his prophecy, should see the food but not eat it. Against all expectations the food arrived; the lord, supervising its distribution at the city gates, was trampled to death in the rush for it (2 Kings 7).

When the prophets spoke of the future they nearly always did so conditionally – if you do not walk in God's way, this [disaster] will happen; if you do, it will not. Other prophecies are not what they seem. 'Behold a virgin shall conceive and bear a son' (Isaiah 7:14) is not, as widely believed, a prophecy of the virgin birth of Christ. The word that was translated as 'virgin' means, in fact, a young married woman. The text continues: 'For before the child shall know to refuse the evil, and choose the good, the land that thou abhorrest shall be forsaken of both her kings.' It seems that Isaiah in effect pointed at a pregnant young woman – possibly his own wife – and indicated that King Ahaz's two enemies would be destroyed before the child could grow up. This is one case where a parochial interpretation of the text makes most sense.

The prophets aimed not so much at foretelling the future as at describing what they saw as the will of God in the circumstances of their time. But in doing this, their prophecies *were* fulfilled, often in ways more profound and long-lasting than they ever imagined. Isaiah's 'virgin' statement is one example of this. These multi-meaning prophecies that reverberated down the ages culminated, Christian scholars claim, in the miraculous life of Jesus Christ in the New Testament.

The miracles of Jesus are examined in the light of psychical research on page 1886

The Israelites gather manna in the desert. Rationalists say that the sticky, sweetish substance must have been the exudation of the tamarisk shrub. However, the manna appeared in precisely the right amount, even according to individual appetite, and twice as much appeared on Fridays to avoid breaking the law by collecting it on the Saturday Sabbath. It seems possible that some paranormal mechanism was involved, but whether induced by some outside intelligence – 'the Lord' – or through the psychokinetic powers of Moses we shall never know

Jonah emerges from his ordeal in the stomach of a whale. As with the Old Testament book of Daniel, there is no point in assuming a literal interpretation, for both books were written as fictional moral tracts

Enormously diluted solutions of natural remedies are the medicines used in homoeopathy, which has flourished for nearly two centuries. RUTH WEST describes evidence suggesting that homoeopathy may have a sound – if highly obscure – basis

THE STATUS OF THE UNORTHODOX medicines is problematic. Do they have a direct physico-chemical effect on the body that can be measured and understood? Or are they placebos, depending on the faith of the patient in their efficacy – a faith that may be enhanced by a good therapeutic relationship between practitioner and patient?

The problem is acute in the case of homoeopathy. Homoeopathic medicine claims to deal with more than the physical condition of the sick person. The selection of the correct remedy takes into account the psychological make-up of the patient and his current emotional state, as well as the physical complaint.

Furthermore, the homoeopathic physician does not send his patient off for numerous tests. Rather he builds up a picture of the symptoms, derived from what he can observe together with what the patient reports of himself: how he feels at certain times of day, what aggravates or relieves his symptoms, what his habits are and so on. The doctor believes that all the details of each patient together constitute a meaningful pattern that can suggest the correct remedy. As James Tyler Kent, one of the 'fathers' of homoeopathy, has said:

> The homoeopathic physician has no remedy for the name of a disease. Homoeopathy is an exact science. It is based upon a natural law, and the true physician must prescribe in accordance with this law of nature. Homoeopathy has no specific for any disease by name, but it has a true specific for each individual case of disease.

Homoeopathic treatment is based upon the successful application of the 'law of similars': treat like with like. Homoeopathy was founded by Samuel Hahnemann, a German physician, in the late 18th century. He came to believe that the appropriate medicine for a sick person was one that, when given in small doses to a healthy person, produced precisely the same set of symptoms presented by the sick person. He regarded the symptoms as the person's own healing reaction to whatever disease was assailing him. The idea had been presented before, notably in the writings of Hippocrates and in the *Medical observations* of the English physician Thomas Sydenham, written in 1676.

As Harris Coulter has pointed out, there are a number of drugs used in orthodox medicine that produce the same symptoms, when administered to a healthy person, that

A potent remedy?

Above: old tincture bottles line the shelves of A. Nelson and Co., the British makers of homoeopathic medicines, at their London premises. The pharmacy was begun by Ernest Louis Ambrecht, a fellow countryman and contemporary of Samuel Hahnemann (inset), the founder of homoeopathy. Hahnemann taught three fundamental principles: that a disease can be cured by very small doses of a medicine that in large doses causes the symptoms of the disease; that extreme dilution enhances the medicine's curative properties and removes its harmful side effects; and that a medicine must be prescribed only after study of the whole person, including his temperament characterise the disorders for which they are prescribed.

There are also superficial resemblances between homoeopathic practice and vaccination. A vaccine stimulates the body's defensive system so that it will be able to deal with future attacks by particular disease-causing organisms. The person vaccinated often develops mild symptoms of the disease. But the differences between the two procedures are significant. Homoeopathy does not seek to immunise but to heal. Vaccines are administered in doses that are identical in composition and quantity. The homoeopath searches for the particular remedy that will produce just those symptoms displayed by the patient and so will trigger the healing response.

The feature that truly separates homoeopathy from present-day 'scientific' medicine, however, is that its medicines are administered in doses that are minute – in fact, infinitesimal. They are so enormously diluted that probably not a single molecule of the original therapeutic substance remains.

There is scientific backing for the value of a certain degree of dilution. According to the

Alternative healing

Arndt-Schulz 'law': 'every drug has a stimulating effect in small doses, while larger doses inhibit, and much larger doses kill.' Although this dual action of drugs is well-established, orthodox medicine nonetheless balks at the extreme dilutions used in homoeopathy. A 'small' dose in ordinary medicine is massive by homoeopathic standards. It is felt by conventional doctors that drugs are meant to kill off diseases, rather than to help bodies to heal themselves.

The preparation of the medicines adds to the mystique surrounding homoeopathy. The therapeutic substance is converted into the medicine by vigorous shaking alternating with successive dilutions. This must be done in just the right way to 'potentise' the medicine: mere dilution is held to be less effective.

Homoeopaths are concerned with producing scientific evidence and explanations for their treatments, and they are open to scientific scrutiny. A great deal of research has been undertaken, mainly in France, Germany, Switzerland, India, Britain and the United States. It has been conducted on plants, animals and micro-organisms.

But a study of the results is not likely to reassure doubters or convert sceptics. An informal report made by Dr Jean Kollerstrom for the British-based Scientific and Medical Network was forced to conclude that very little published work in this field stands up to rigorous statistical analysis, or meets the necessary standards of repeatability.

For example, between 1941 and 1954 Dr William Boyd of Glasgow University carried out research that had striking results. He measured the rate of chemical reactions involved in processes of growth, and the effect of mercuric chloride on the rate. Normally mercuric chloride acts to inhibit growth. But his results showed that minute doses stimulated growth. His work was analysed independently by four teams of statisticians, and they confirmed Boyd's conclusion. Unfortunately this impressive result has never been repeated, and a fundamental demand of scientific research – that a claim cannot be regarded as substantiated until the same effect has been obtained by more than one researcher – remains unsatisfied.

In 1980 the Scientific and Medical Network attempted to replicate the work of two Dutch scientists, Amons and Manavelt, carried out a few years previously. They had measured the effect of highly diluted mercuric chloride on the growth of cells called lymphoblasts, produced by a mouse tissue culture in the laboratory. The Dutch workers found, again, that the mercuric chloride affected the growth of the cells.

However, the Network team found no such effect in two series of their own experiments. In fact there was neither stimulation nor inhibition of the growth of the lymphoblasts. Dr Kollerstrom commented:

Our results afford another example (of which there are several in the literature) of non-repeatability in this type of experiment. For the benefit of sceptical readers who would like to discard this tiresomely inexplicable phenomenon by assuming that it is due to sloppy experimentation or to inadequate experimental details having been given in the literature, I would like to state that in my opinion this is not often the case . . . . The point I am making, hesitatingly and with reluctance, is that one may be forced to admit that non-repeatability, when one is working on the fringe of what one hopes may be considered scientific, may have to be accepted as a 'fact' not due to human carelessness or to wishful thinking (in the first place), and presumably not due

Above right: beautiful structures formed by crystallisation from a solution of chromium and nickel salts, to which a small amount of a homoeopathic 'mother tincture' has been added. The patterns that appear depend on the chemical nature of this tincture, which is a relatively concentrated homoeopathic solution from which the highly diluted medicines are prepared

Alternative healing

to bloody-mindedness on the part of the cell or organism. Thus we seem to be left only with the choice of 'experimenter effect' or 'other factors beyond our knowledge'.

The writer Fritjof Capra, formerly a physicist, has said that homoeopathy lacks any scientific explanation. He asks whether homoeopathy should not be understood in terms of a 'resonance' or 'tuning' between the patient and the medicine. The metaphor suggests a strong response being called forth from the patient's healing systems by a relatively weak, but finely adjusted stimulus, the medicine – just as a loud note is given out by a piano string if it is precisely in harmony with some note played on another instrument. But Capra goes on to state that 'one is tempted to wonder whether the crucial resonance . . . is not the one between the patient and the homoeopath, with the remedy merely a crutch.'

It may be tempting to see homoeopathic approaches to medicine more in terms of psychotherapy or faith healing than as a form of drug treatment, but this is to ignore other aspects of the research literature and the more informal evidence from clinical case studies.

A clinical trial was conducted in 1980 in Glasgow, Scotland, on the effect of homoeopathic therapy in rheumatoid arthritis. The results showed that patients receiving orthodox drug treatment together with individually prescribed homoeopathic drugs improved more than patients receiving orthodox treatment together with a placebo – some inert substance that they were led to believe was a medicine. This difference was due to the drugs and not to the doctors involved. By 1982 only one such trial had been conducted.

One major breakthrough in replicating homoeopathic research was, however, achieved in 1981. Raynor Jones and Michael Jenkins, working at the Royal London Homoeopathic Hospital, successfully repeated experiments first carried out by Pelican and Ungar. They had found that substances in extremely high dilutions affected the growth of wheat seedlings. The original work had been described by Dr Kollerstrom as 'the most exhaustive and meticulous study yet carried out on seedlings'. With its corroboration we may now have a body of scientific evidence validating the claim of homoeopaths that their remedies – even when diluted so much that not a single molecule is left – have an effect on living things.

Another impressive piece of evidence that has to be taken into account before homoeopathy is dismissed is the record of successful homoeopathic treatment given during the great cholera epidemic that swept Europe in the 1830s. And the Royal London Homoeopathic Hospital has well-documented evidence stretching over many years,

Above: a medicine cabinet used by Samuel Hahnemann. Since homoeopathic tinctures are used in extreme dilution, only a small quantity of each is required. Hahnemann's own handwriting appears on the stoppers of the phials

Below: in a homoeopathic laboratory the potency, or power, of a medicine is, paradoxically, increased by a sequence of dilutions, each followed by 'succussion', a vigorous shaking. A commonly used potency is '30c' – the result of 30 successive hundredfold dilutions. No physical trace of the tincture then remains

Alternative healing

Left: monkshood, a poisonous plant. The homoeopathic medicine made from it is used at the onset of certain acute conditions, such as fevers and colds, and also for treating chronic anxiety

Right: the Christmas rose, used to make homoeopathic remedies for certain severe disturbances, involving unconsciousness, muscular weakness, grinding of the teeth, and so on. An advantage of homoeopathic remedies in such cases is that only a little needs to be slipped into the mouth, where it can be absorbed even if it is not swallowed

Below: the Royal London Homoeopathic Hospital was granted royal patronage in 1948, immeasurably raising the status of homoeopathy

which seems to show the superiority of homoeopathy over orthodox medicine.

There is also a mass of anecdotal testimony that is hard to dismiss. Just try telling a mother who has been desperately worried over a child with a high fever that its temperature fell minutes after taking a homoeopathic drug because the child got on well with the doctor!

Homoeopathy just does not fit in with current ways of scientific thinking. Neither does another group of unorthodox treatments: the flower remedies. To the conventional mind their use as anything other than placebos is sheer lunacy. A flower head, from a wild plant, tree or bush, is placed in water in sunlight for a number of hours. The water then constitutes the remedy. Any matter that may have found its way into the water from the plant can only be minute in quantity. Certain commentators speculate on some kind of 'energy' from the Sun causing remarkable structural changes in the water, changes that happen to have beneficial effects upon sick people.

But we have no real understanding of how these 'medicines', or those of the homoeopaths, could be valuable additions to the physician's armoury of drugs. If they do not work by a straightforward chemical action, the alternatives are to say that their beneficial effects must be imaginary; or that they are real, but work through the patient's confidence in the treatment; or that they are real and psychically caused – that they are paranormal phenomena.

Healing by touch, massage and manipulation is surveyed on page 1914

Does the Sun control terrestrial life in ways that are little understood? GUY LYON PLAYFAIR **suggests that the incessant turmoil on the Sun's surface is linked to chemical, biological and social activity on Earth**

A touch

THE DARK BLOTCHES on the face of the Sun have been observed and recorded for 2000 years. But they have been studied in detail only since the telescope was first used in astronomy, in the early 17th century. We now know that these 'sunspots' come and go in cycles of just over 11 years and that they are closely associated with solar flares, intense outbursts of radiation on the Sun's surface. But why sunspots appear when and where they do, how they are formed, and what effects they have upon life on Earth are matters still far from understood.

Sunspots first become visible as 'holes' in the swirling, granular surface of the Sun. Some of them cluster together to form groups. These can reach enormous dimensions: an average group is several times the diameter of the Earth. Groups can merge into larger groups, with areas of up to 7000 million square miles (18,000 million square kilometres).

The number and extent of sunspots are estimated by a somewhat arbitrary procedure, and the result is expressed as a number, called the Wolf number after the German astronomer who devised the method. It can vary from 0 to 300, and it can increase very rapidly. From 8 to 18 February 1956, for example, it shot up from 26 to 270 and then in the next 10 days fell back to 125. This fluctuation formed a small peak within the overall cycle.

The main sunspot cycle averages 11.1 years in length, although individual cycles have ranged from 7 to 17 years. There is also a longer cycle of 179 years, apparently related to the movement of the Sun around the centre of mass of the solar system. And there is also a 25-month sunspot cycle, apparently linked to changes in the rate of emission of particles called neutrinos from the Sun's deep interior (see page 1898).

Disturbing the Earth

Orthodox scientists recognise that sunspots influence the Earth in certain fairly well-understood ways. Flares are associated with them, and the electrically charged particles that issue from flares cause auroral displays in the Earth's atmosphere. They can also cause sharp fluctuations in the Earth's magnetic field. A major solar flare can even cause minute changes in the Earth's rotation by its effect on the terrestrial magnetic field.

Mankind's most costly attempt to study the Sun was brought to a premature end by sunspot activity. The 80-tonne Skylab space satellite, empty after having been occupied by a number of crews on scientific missions, was circling the Earth in 1979. Solar activity affected the Earth's atmosphere, causing it to

Right: the vast globe of the Sun, capable of swallowing up a million Earths, is blotched by huge sunspot groups. Each group is like a great magnet: the two poles of the magnet are represented in different colours in this computerised picture. Magnetic fluctuations on the Sun influence the Earth's magnetic field – and this in turn may affect us and other living things

Below: the pulse of the Sun. The number and extent of sunspots vary in a cyclic way, reaching a peak roughly every 11 years. Superimposed on this are longer cycles. Flares and other outbursts of activity on the Sun keep rough step with the sunspot number

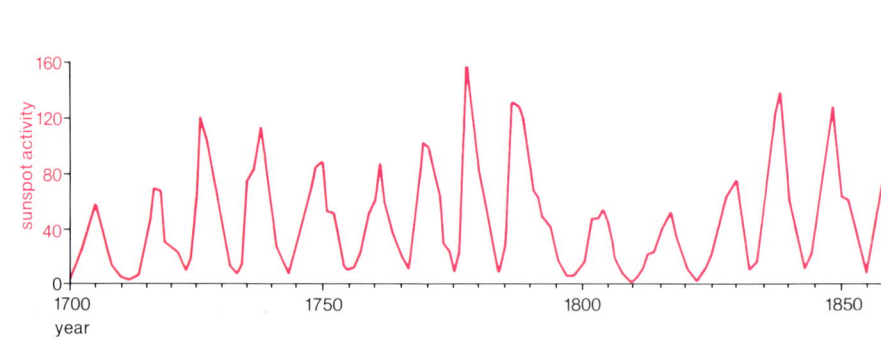

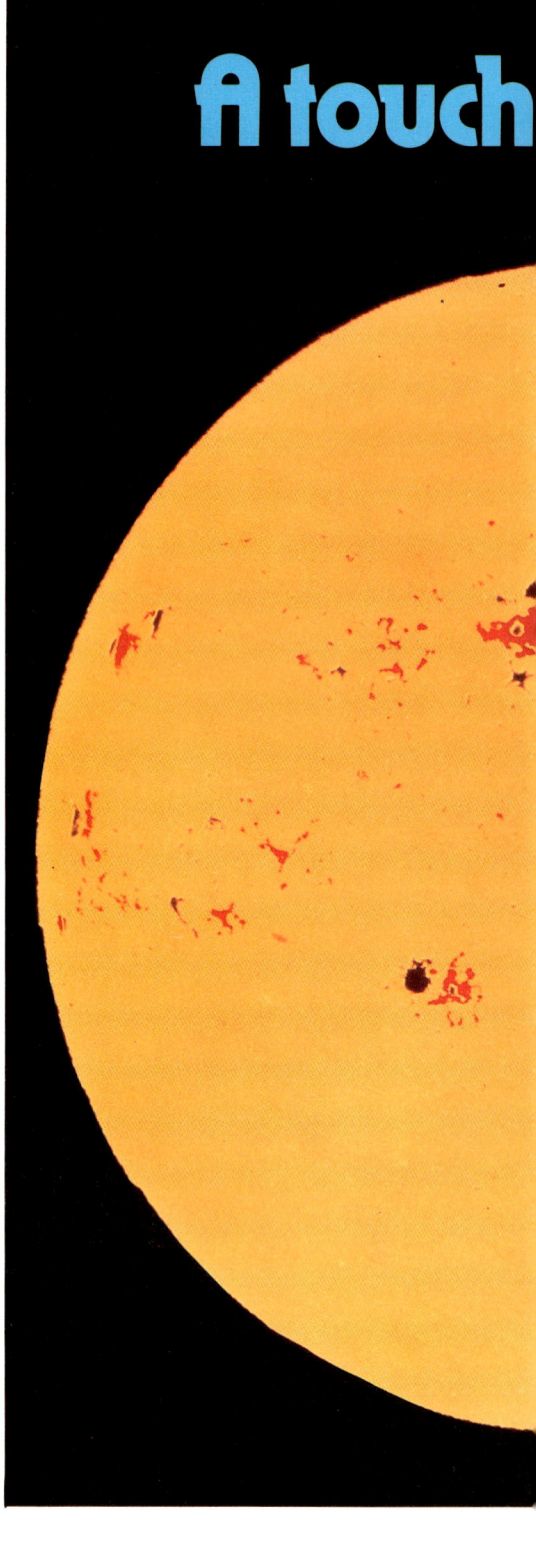

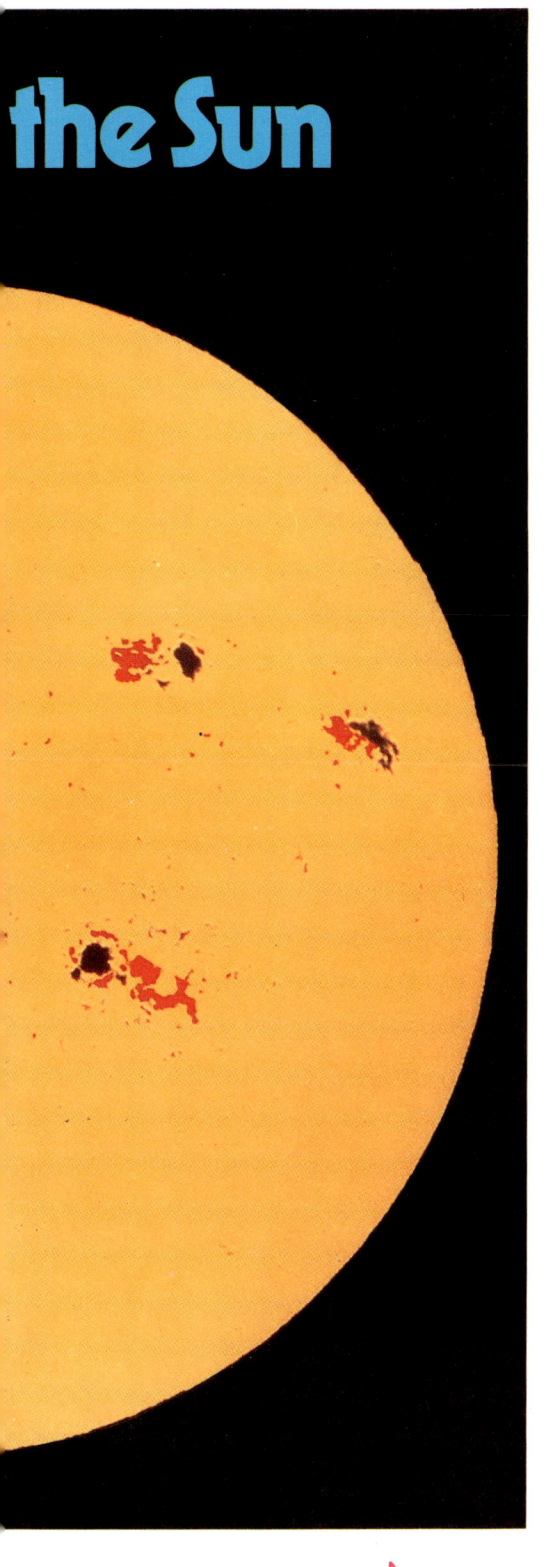

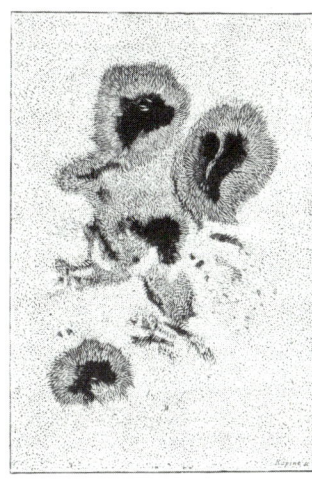

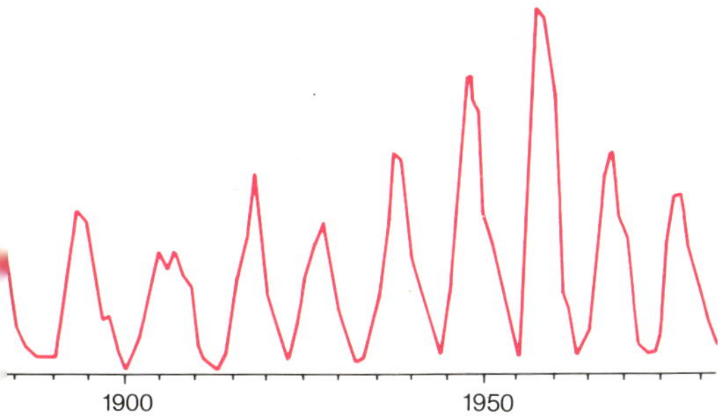

The Sun

expand and increase the drag experienced by Skylab. The craft fell to Earth in July 1979, long before it could be moved into a higher orbit by the space shuttle, which had not then made its maiden flight.

What else, we might ask, is the Sun doing to us, apart from knocking our satellites out of orbit and putting an occasional brake on the Earth's rotation?

The close correlation that has now been established between the solar cycle and variations in the Earth's magnetic field may imply a corresponding influence on life on the Earth. There is now good evidence that the Earth's magnetic field influences a wide variety of processes in living things from micro-organisms to human beings. Electromagnetic ecology is now a scientific discipline in its own right, in the opinion of Dr A. P. Dubrov, a pioneer in this challenging new field.

According to Dubrov, nervous activity, the skin's electrical resistance, blood count, blood clotting rate, heart and eye function, onset and duration of the menstrual period, and even the incidence of neurosis, epilepsy and schizophrenia can be influenced by variations in the Earth's magnetic field. The mechanisms by which fluctuations in the field, which are known as magnetic storms, affect us are still largely speculative, although much has been discovered since the 1960s about the magnetic fields of the body, associated with the heart and brain.

A living sundial

In experiments that lasted more than 20 years, Dr Maki Takata of Japan showed that blood clotting rates responded precisely and immediately to both short- and long-term cycles in solar activity. 'Man is a living sundial,' he concluded. His findings supported those of Professor Giorgio Piccardi of Florence, in Italy, concerning ordinary water. Piccardi claimed, after conducting a series of thousands of tests throughout an entire solar cycle, that the rate of chemical processes in water exactly matched day-to-day sunspot counts, the occurrence of magnetic storms and the occurrence of solar flares. The process in question was the precipitation from water of a dissolved compound – that is, the substance involved, bismuth oxychloride, came out of solution and formed a solid deposit. Piccardi turned his attention to blood, and found that its coagulation time could be increased, by up to 50 per cent, by shielding it from the Earth's magnetic field. 'All living beings,' he concluded, 'are bound more intimately to the external world than one would think.'

The claims of Takata and Piccardi have been supported by numerous reports from the Soviet Union, where heliobiology – the study of the Sun's influence on life – is an accepted discipline. Scientists there are particularly interested in the Kursk anomaly. In the region around the Russian city of Kursk

Soviet scientists have emphasised Sun-Earth links in books such as *The geomagnetic field and life* (top) by A.P. Dubrov and *Complete harmony in nature* (centre) by L.V. Golovanov. They think the Sun's influence is due to the magnetic fields that burst through the surface at sunspot sites (above)

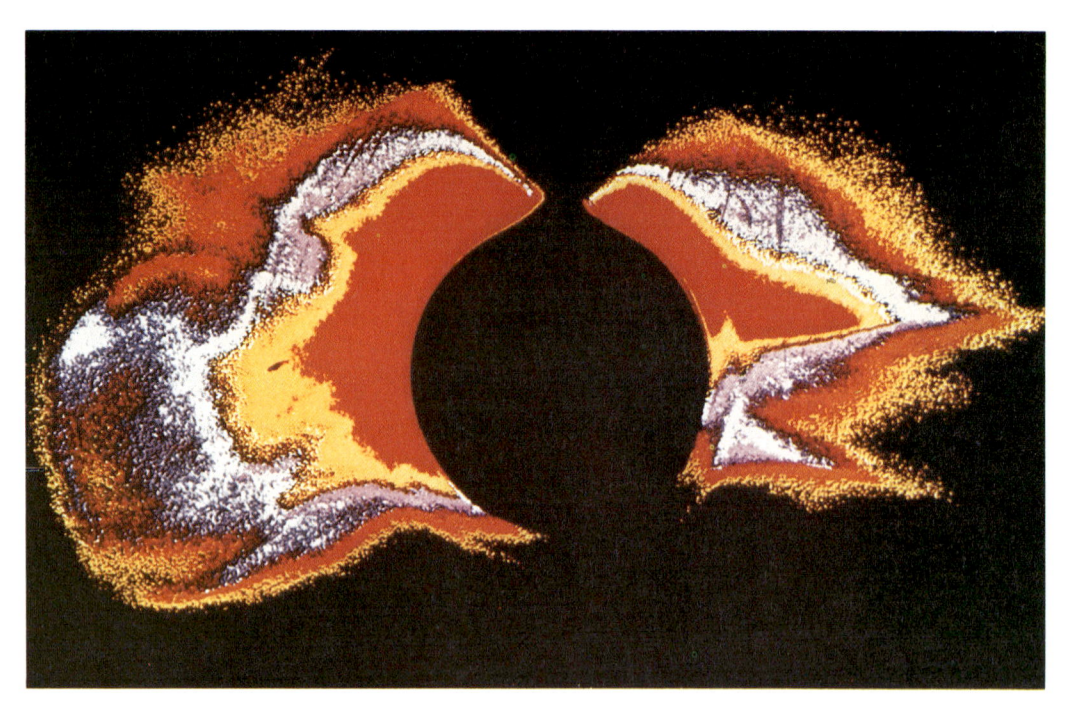

The Sun

the Earth's magnetic field reaches three times its average strength. The incidence of some diseases is 160 per cent higher than the average, and yields of a wide range of crops are consistently lower.

There have been all too few attempts in the West to follow up Soviet research in heliobiology. However, there have been some surprises: in 1979 a report published in the prestigious scientific journal *Nature* described a significant correlation between fluctuations in the terrestrial magnetic field and emergency cardiac admissions to two Indian hospitals over a six-year period. This lends some support to Dubrov's claim, based on at least 14 Soviet studies, that magnetic storms are 'one of the direct causes of cardio-vascular accidents [heart attacks]'.

The boldest claims of all in this field were made by the versatile Russian scientist A. L. Chizhevsky, who died in 1964. He studied sunspots for 10 years and correlated their appearance with his own state of health. In 1926 he declared:

We must assume that there exists a powerful factor outside our globe which governs the development of events in human societies, and synchronises them with the Sun's activity . . . we must assume that the electrical

Above left: the huge extent of the solar corona, the Sun's 'atmosphere', is revealed in this Skylab computerised picture. The corona is shaped by the Sun's magnetic field

Above: John H. Nelson projects an image of the Sun onto a circular screen at the RCA observatory in New York. Nelson predicted radio 'weather' from sunspots and planetary positions

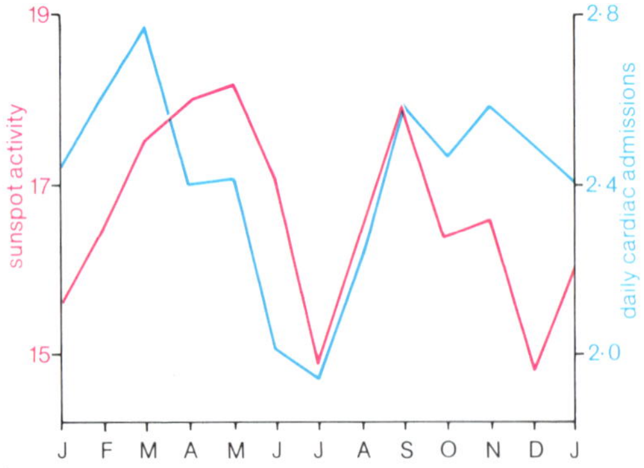

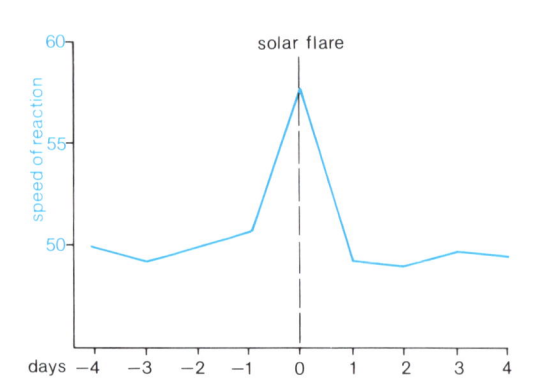

Some of the countless suggested influences of solar activity. Admissions of heart cases (blue) at an Indian hospital keep step through the year with disturbances in the Earth's magnetic field (left). A chemical reaction performed in the open went faster on the day of a solar eruption (below left). The number of warm days in the year (blue), measured at a Scottish site, kept in step with sunspot numbers over a 50-year period (above right). Even Soviet government purchases of white hares (blue), valuable for their fur, seem to depend on sunspot numbers, though there is an interval of five years between a sunspot peak and a peak in hare purchases (right)

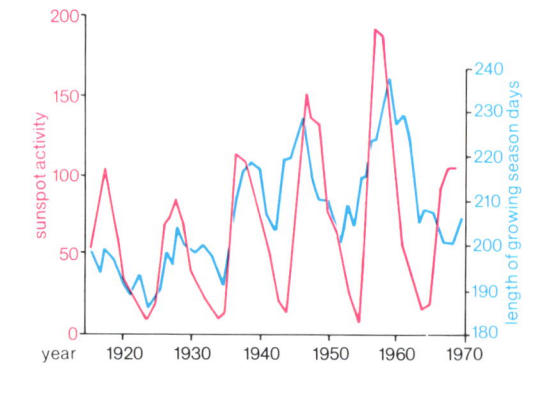

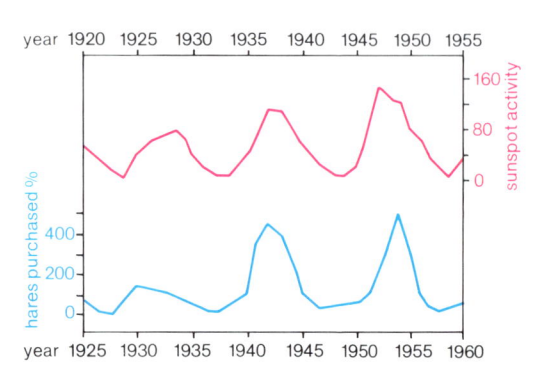

energy of the Sun is the superterrestrial factor which influences historical processes.

He supported this startling claim with a mass of evidence covering 2400 years. It revealed, he said, the existence of a 'universal cycle of historical events' locked to that of the Sun. Each cycle came in four phases of roughly equal duration. In the first, people were peaceful but apathetic; in the second, new ideas and leaders emerged; in the third (coinciding with a maximum of solar activity) nations reached 'maximum excitability', realising their greatest achievements, good or bad; while in the fourth, everybody became exhausted and slipped into the first phase of the next cycle.

Chizhevsky believed he had found cycles everywhere: in the emigrations of Jews, the outbreaks of diphtheria and influenza epidemics, strikes, terrorism, all major wars and even the voting patterns in Britain. Absurd as some of these claimed correlations may seem, Chizhevsky might not have been surprised by the coincidence of maximum solar sunspot activity and, for instance, the Soviet invasions of Hungary, Czechoslovakia and Afghanistan, the agitation by Polish workers in 1980 and the still officially unexplained influenza pandemics of 1957 and 1968.

Maverick sunspots

One man who put the study of sunspots to practical use was J. H. Nelson, chief analyst of shortwave radio propagation for RCA Communications in New York. He studied them carefully for more than 20 years, until his retirement in 1968. Before the days of satellite communication, radio companies were at the mercy of the Sun, for the state of the ionosphere influenced the range and quality of shortwave radio communication. After careful study of individual sunspots and solar flares, Nelson made an important discovery: some sunspots heralded radio blackouts, while others did not.

Looking more closely at the disruptive 'maverick' sunspots, as he called them, Nelson made an even more important discovery: they were invariably associated with certain positions of the planets. Nelson was not a professional astronomer, and certainly not an astrologer, but a technician with a practical job to do. By 1951 he was able to announce that there was a direct relationship between bad radio 'weather', severe magnetic storms, and planetary angles. Moreover, the 'maverick' angles of 0°, 90° and 180° coincided with the traditionally unfavourable angles of astrology, while the 'favourable' angles of 60° and 120° were also favourable in astrology.

By taking into account the positions of all the planets, even distant Pluto, Nelson eventually achieved, he believed, an accuracy of 85 per cent in his forecasts of radio 'weather'. His former chief acknowledged his work to have been of enormous importance to his company, the world's largest in this field.

Nelson never discovered the nature of the influence that could cause this relationship. The planets raise 'tides' on the surface of the Sun by their gravitational attractions, but these are minute. Furthermore, the gravitational fields of the planets differ considerably from each other: that of Jupiter is over 30 times stronger than that of Mercury, which is much closer to the Sun, but much less massive than Jupiter. Yet Nelson found that his forecasting system worked only when all the planets were taken into account. Gravity could not give them all an equal 'vote' in this manner. Nelson was led to conclude, somewhat lamely, that 'unknown forces' were involved in the process.

Whether or not the radiation from solar flares reaches us according to a timetable drawn up by the planets, it certainly has a direct effect on our magnetic environment and this in turn is known to affect many biological processes. Such radiation is certainly not the only influence on worldwide events, but it is a cyclic influence, and may determine the timing of a wide variety of events: heart attacks, influenza epidemics, the very moment of birth (see page 634) – or even the rise of political and religious movements. Today, after three centuries of research and speculation, we still cannot give a definite answer to the question asked by Chizhevsky: 'Are we all slaves of the Sun?'

On page 1898: has the Sun gone out without our knowing about it?

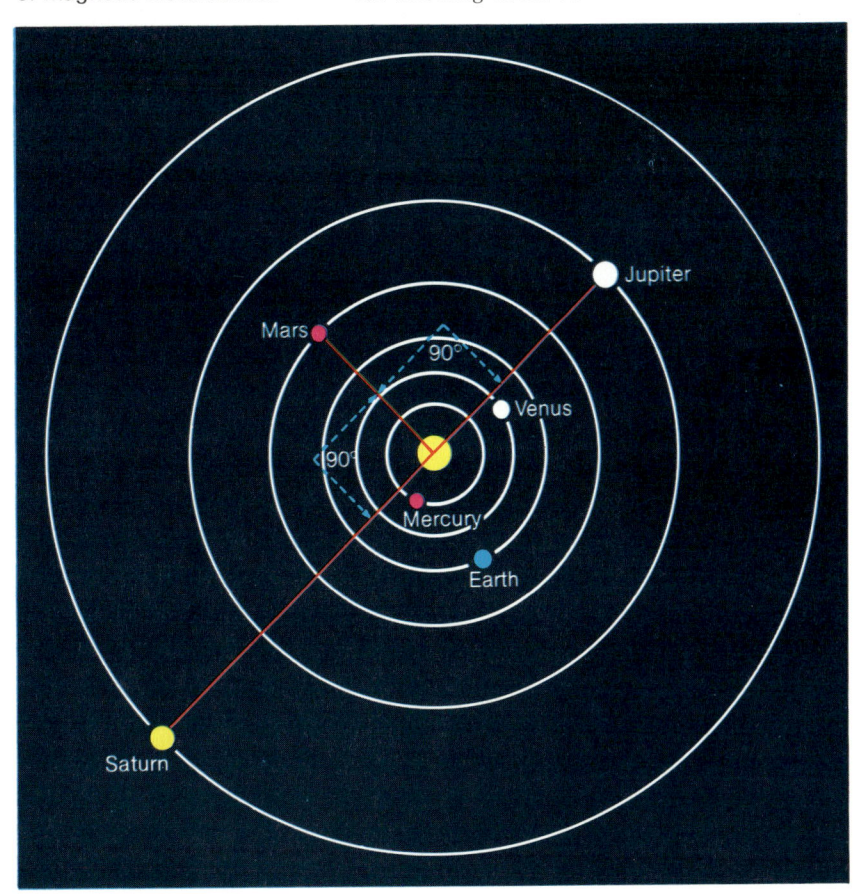

The influence of the planets on the Earth's broadcasting conditions, according to the radio engineer J.H. Nelson. When Sun–planet directions make angles of 90° or 180° with each other, as here, sunspots that happen to occur at the same time will cause magnetic 'storms' on Earth. Any planets can be involved, including the three outer planets, not shown here. Angles of 60° and 120°, on the other hand, are associated with an absence of magnetic disturbances

The king and the covens

Many primitive societies practised ritual sacrifices of their kings to ensure the continued well-being of the tribe. Could it be, asks STAN GOOCH, that this practice continued, even in Western Europe, well into historic time?

THE STORY OF THE FOUNDING of the Most Noble Order of the Garter is as follows. Edward III of England (1312-1377) was dancing – either with the Fair Maid of Kent or the Countess of Salisbury according to which tradition one follows – when his partner dropped her garter. The king immediately seized the garter and pinned it to his own leg, saying '*Honi soit qui mal y pense*' – shame to him who thinks evil of this incident. Going still further, in fulfilment of a vow to restore the Round Table of Arthur, the king then founded two groups of Garter knights, 12 for himself and 12 for the Prince of Wales, adopting as their motto *Honi soit qui mal y pense*. These two groups, plus the respective leaders, form two bands of 13. The rise of this number appears to have been deliberate: it is significant that the king's mantle as Chief of the Order is powdered over with 168 garters. These, together with the one worn on the leg, make a total of 169; that is 13 times 13.

The garter or cord as the mark of a sorcerer is known from oldest antiquity, and can be seen in prehistoric cave paintings of sorcerers. In the medieval witch trials in France, also, it was frequently stated that the leaders of each coven wore a garter as a sign of rank.

Some 40 years before the founding of the Order of the Garter, there had been among the charges levelled at the Knights Templar by the Inquisition that, when worshipping the severed heads or skulls at their secret rituals, 'they surrounded or touched each head of the aforesaid idols with small cords, which they wore around themselves next to the shirt or the flesh.'

There is even a legend linking King Arthur with the sorcerer's garter. According to local folklore, King Arthur and Guinevere sleep in a cave under the castle of Sewingshields in Northumberland. A farmer allegedly once found his way into this cave, and near the entrance saw a stone sword, a garter and a horn. He took up the sword and cut the garter, but his nerve failed when he saw the sleepers awakening. As he ran out of the cave he heard King Arthur say:

O woe befall the evil day
that ever the witless wight was born
who took the sword, the garter cut
but never blew the bugle horn.

The most obvious explanation of Edward III's behaviour in the incident that led to the founding of the Order of the Garter is that he was covering up some kind of sexual liaison with the lady concerned. There is another interpretation, however: the time was marked by a number of witch trials involving members of the aristocracy in which the noble leaders went unpunished while their followers were imprisoned or executed. Edward III could have been putting under his personal protection a woman who was at risk from these infamous witch trials. He could also have been announcing publicly to a secret band of his pagan followers that he himself was the grand master of the witches they revered.

Above: the knights of the Most Noble Order of the Garter in procession to St George's chapel, Windsor. Legend says that the order was founded after King Edward III (1312–1377) picked up a garter that his dancing partner had inadvertently dropped (right). Exclaiming '*Honi soit qui mal y pense*', or 'Shame be on him who thinks evil of this incident', he picked up the garter – and went on to found the Order of the Garter, adopting his remark as its motto. The garter is an ancient sorcerers' symbol: could Edward have been announcing his sovereignty over British witches?

Holy blood, Holy Grail

There is an intriguing connection between Edward III and the Knights Templar. In *The holy blood and the Holy Grail*, Michael Baigent, Richard Leigh and Henry Lincoln report a very curious incident, known as 'the cutting of the elm'. It took place in 1188, and marked the formal break between the Order of Sion and the Order of Templars, which had hitherto been synonymous. Adjacent to the Templar fortress of Gisors was a field, a place sacred since pre-Christian times, and which had often served as a meeting place for the kings of England and the kings of France. In the centre of this field was an ancient, gigantic elm. On this particular occasion a quarrel, whose details we do not know, arose between Philippe II of France and Henry II of England. A fight ensued, in which blood was shed, and one of Henry's sons, Richard Lionheart, attempted to defend the tree – but the French succeeded in cutting it down. At this point, it seems, the Order of Sion split from the Templars, changed its name to the Priory of Sion, and adopted as a sub-name 'Ormus'. *Orme* is the French for elm.

What all this signifies is impossible to say, but it seems that there is a covert connection between Henry II and the founding of the Priory of Sion. And, some 60 years later in 1252, Henry III, the grandson of Henry II, was publicly threatened by the Templars: 'So long as thou dost exercise justice, thou wilt reign. But if thou infringe it, thou wilt cease to be king.' This statement amounts to an extraordinary threat; the implication is both that the king has somehow offended the Templars, and is also somehow beholden to them. Finally, a further hundred years later, we find Henry III's great-grandson, Edward III, founding the Order of the Garter.

Top: a fragment of a limestone tablet from Ur, in ancient Babylonia. The king is pouring libations to the Moon god Nannar. The religions of many ancient societies involved worship of the Moon in the form of the Horned God or Goddess – as in Celtic mythology, where Cernunnos, 'the Horned One' (above, flanked by a wolf and a stag), rules over the entire animal kingdom. The Horned God or Goddess was essentially a fertility deity, neither good nor evil. It is likely that the personification of the Satan of the Christian Church as a horned creature is the result of a deliberate attempt to stigmatise the Horned God

There are many more hints of connections between Templars, the Priory of Sion, witches and the nobility of England and France. Let us now dispense with hints and bring a whole section of the central mystery into the open.

In the 1920s Margaret Murray, a distinguished Egyptologist, enraged a previously admiring academic world with the publication of her two books *The witch cult in western Europe* and *The god of the witches*. In her view, the study of the religion of pre-Christian times had been completely neglected – this was slightly unfair to J. G. Frazer's *The golden bough* (1922) – and she proceeded to redress the balance. The standard religion of Europe and the Middle East, she claimed, had been close to what is today called witchcraft. It involved the worship of the Horned God or Goddess, who ruled over both good and evil, and was the creator of both. In essence the original paganism-witchcraft was a fertility religion, pre-dating the discovery of agriculture and farming methods, and concerned with producing abundance in game animals and wild plants.

In the centuries following Christ, the kings and rulers of Europe were gradually persuaded to declare their public support for Christianity, but Murray suggests that even in post-medieval times the mass of people and many of the nobility continued to worship the old gods in the old ways. Murray comments that 'even in the highest offices of the Church the priests often served the heathen deities as well as the Christian God and practised pagan rites.' Such a view is supported by the mystery labyrinths inlaid on the floors of French cathedrals, by the discovery in the 1940s of a stone penis carved inside the altar of an English church, and a complete Celtic altar bearing the names and portraits of the Celtic gods (including Cernunnos, the horned stag god, flanked by a bear) built into the choir of Notre Dame

1875

Holy blood, Holy Grail

church in Paris; or even by Robert Graves's evidence, presented in *The white goddess*, that the old 13-month year was still commonly observed in medieval rural Britain.

It is against the formidable background of the wide-scale continuance of pagan tradition that we must seek to understand the Templars, the Priory of Sion, *qabalists*, Cathars, alchemists, the witches themselves and many allied manifestations.

The king of the world

Baigent, Leigh and Lincoln have demonstrated some of the many interconnections between Cathars, gnostics, Templars, *qabalists* and others. Nicolas Flamel, Grand Master of the Priory from 1398 to 1418, was also a famous alchemist. The documents found at Rennes-le-Château (see page 161) prominently feature the phrase *rex mundi* ('king of the world'). This concept is a notion central to all forms of gnosticism, of which the sect of the Cathars in France represents one variant. These sects held that God, being pure spirit and goodness, could not have produced the world, which is both material and at least partly evil. The world, Christ and mankind were held to be the product of another entity, capable of immersion in matter. This usurper god, or *rex mundi*, has much in common with Satan, Lucifer and ultimately with the Horned God of paganism.

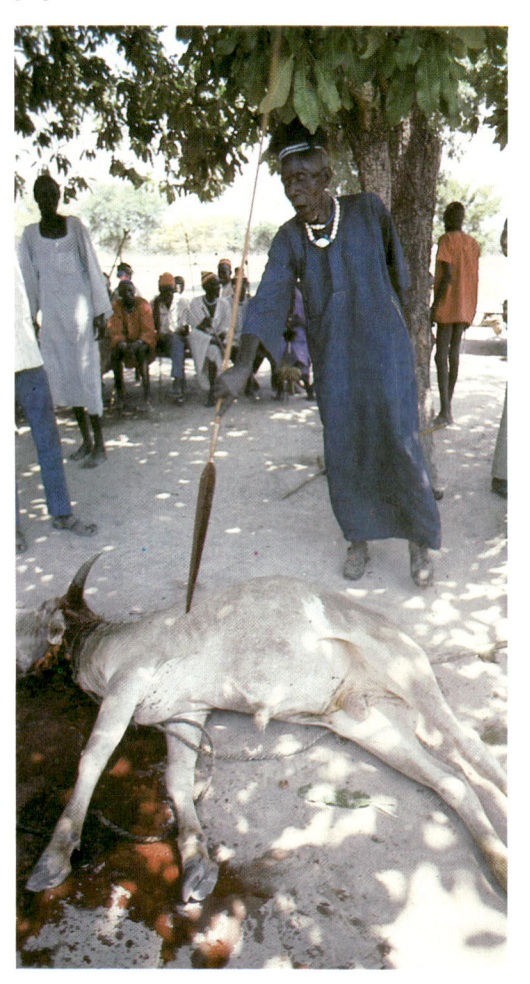

Below: a ritual sacrifice of a goat, made by the Dinka tribe of the Sudan, north-east Africa, to ensure the recovery of a sick man. Most primitive tribes practise animal, and sometimes human, sacrifice. The ancient Druids of Britain were one such society; this highly romanticised engraving (below right) shows a mother's grief as her son is sacrificed during a Druid ritual

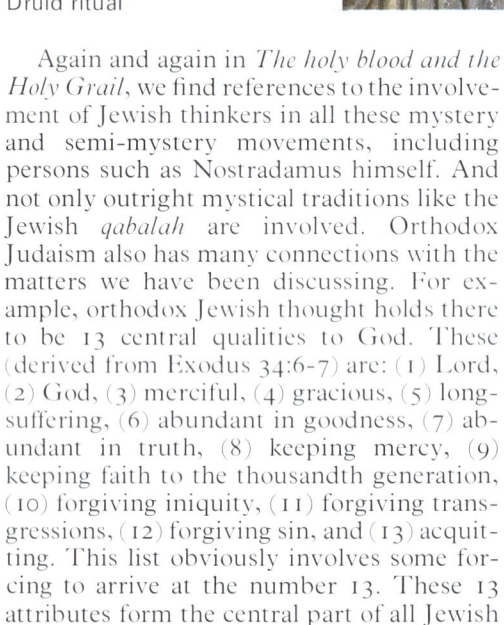

Again and again in *The holy blood and the Holy Grail*, we find references to the involvement of Jewish thinkers in all these mystery and semi-mystery movements, including persons such as Nostradamus himself. And not only outright mystical traditions like the Jewish *qabalah* are involved. Orthodox Judaism also has many connections with the matters we have been discussing. For example, orthodox Jewish thought holds there to be 13 central qualities to God. These (derived from Exodus 34:6-7) are: (1) Lord, (2) God, (3) merciful, (4) gracious, (5) long-suffering, (6) abundant in goodness, (7) abundant in truth, (8) keeping mercy, (9) keeping faith to the thousandth generation, (10) forgiving iniquity, (11) forgiving transgressions, (12) forgiving sin, and (13) acquitting. This list obviously involves some forcing to arrive at the number 13. These 13 attributes form the central part of all Jewish penitential prayers.

The power of the number seven in both Judaism and Christianity is manifest (see page 1327); the sacred Jewish seven-branched candlestick, the Menorah, which is described as 'the seven eyes of God which range through the whole earth' and 'the seven stars', appears to have some connection with the seven stars of the Plough – part of the Great Bear constellation.

Unlike the number seven, however, the number 13 seems to have undergone considerable purging from the text of the Bible.

Holy blood, Holy Grail

Left: detail of a carving showing the murder of Thomas à Becket in 1170. The anthropologist Margaret Murray has suggested that the ancient practice of ritually sacrificing important figures in order to ensure continued fertility of crops and livestock continued into historic times – and that among its victims were Becket and (right) William Rufus (1087–1100), who died in suspicious circumstances while hunting. There is a further intriguing possibility: that the ritual murderers are guardians of the old religion, descendants of the last king of the Merovingian dynasty, Dagobert II – whose trepanned skull (below right) is now lodged in a convent at Mons, Belgium – himself a descendant of Christ

Nevertheless, it is clear, for instance, that Israel is regarded as yet another group of 13 – Jacob and his 12 sons. As one religion succeeds another, those elements of the old religion that can be assimilated become part of the new religion; the remaining elements are strongly suppressed. It seems reasonable to suppose that the purging of the number 13 from the Bible indicates that it was of significance in the religion that Judaism, and later Christianity, replaced – perhaps the old pagan religion of Moon worship, in which the number 13, the number of full or new moons in the 13-month year, was held in great reverence.

Blood sacrifice

Another piece of evidence for the nature of the old religion, not cited by Baigent, Leigh and Lincoln, is the persistent medieval story that Jews used the blood of a Christian child to make their Passover bread. Of course, they did nothing of the kind. The fact of the matter is that Jews are forbidden to consume blood in any form, so that all meat must be bled dry by ritual slaughter, and an egg with a speck of blood in it must be thrown away. But this very strong prohibition of blood in the Jewish religion suggests that back in pagan times blood was at the very centre of their religious practice. Margaret Murray, indeed, assures us of the importance of allowing the blood of a human sacrifice to strike the earth in pagan ritual.

Much to the point here is also that the words 'blood', 'bless' and 'blossom' all come from the same root: again the fertility element is quite clear.

Could this be a key to the puzzle? Perhaps. The many strands of the central mystery at last begin to form a coherent and recognisable pattern.

New ships were originally sanctified by sacrifice; and we still bless a new ship by breaking a bottle of champagne over the bows. The victim was doubtless once a human being – for human sacrifice was undoubtedly at the heart of the old religion. The most important sacrifice of all was that of the king. The chosen king had to die – originally every year, subsequently every seventh or ninth year – in order to ensure the continuing fertility of the tribe itself, of the game and the wild plants. Probably Murray's most outrageous claim is that many kings and notables of historical times were ritually killed by the witch cult. She cites, in Britain, King Edmund (AD 946), Edmund Ironside (1016), William Rufus (1100) and Thomas à Beckett (1170); and in France Joan of Arc (1431) and Gilles de Rais (1440). Could it be that such ritual killings did indeed continue in the heart of Western society far into historic time?

On page 1906: could Christ's death have been a ritual sacrifice?

A UFO comes to town

PHOTOGRAPHS OUGHT TO BE good evidence of a UFO sighting, but they are not always so. Sometimes, for example, a UFO can appear on a picture when the photographer did not actually see one. Sometimes, too, the object appears different on the photograph from the way that the observer remembers seeing it.

Sightings of UFOs over large cities are rare, but Anthony Russell's photographs show that he saw one in the London suburb of Streatham.
CHARLES BOWEN reports

So the evidence from even genuine pictures is often ambiguous.

In this case, the photographer remembered the UFO as different from the picture. And, after all, if the UFO was in such a highly populated area as south London, why was there only one witness?

'Strange shadow effects'

Close encounter of the first kind: Streatham, London, 15 December 1966

Sightings of true UFOs over London are a rarity. Many reports are made, but these often prove to be misidentifications of lights in the sky. This is hardly surprising considering the great volume of aircraft flying over the city on the way in or out of Heathrow airport. There are also many other aircraft flying over at great height and, at night, satellites that reflect the rays of a Sun already well below the western horizon. Few who report sightings in fact fulfil the condition of having seen a UFO at close range – near enough to be classified as a close encounter of the first kind.

One sighting towards the end of 1966, however, may have fulfilled this condition – and the report was reinforced by photographs. These photographs seem to show remarkable changes in the shape of the images, and the changes cannot be due entirely to changes of aspect of the photographed object.

The day of the sighting was Thursday, 15 December 1966. It was one of the shortest days of the year: the Sun set at 3.53 p.m. The weather was unpleasant – misty, dull and damp, with drizzle, rain and low cloud – and maximum visibility was 2 miles (3 kilometres).

At approximately 2.30 that afternoon, Anthony Russell was standing by the open window of his flat in Lewin Road, Streatham, south-west London. Lewin Road is at the southern end of Streatham High Road and just west of Streatham Common. The window by which Russell stood faces approximately north-north-west. A keen photographer, he was testing for resolution two new 2× converters for his Zenith 3N single lens reflex camera (focal length 135 millimetres increased to 270 millimetres by one converter). During the testing, Russell was aiming the camera at the gable of a house on the far side of Lewin Road, about 28 yards (26 metres) from the lens. The camera was loaded with 35-millimetre Gratispool colour film.

Suddenly Russell became aware of an

This is the first photograph taken by Anthony Russell of a UFO that he sighted from his flat window. There is a hint of an efflux from the base of the object on the right. The bar seen on the gable of the house across the road supports a chimney that is off camera

UFO CASEBOOK

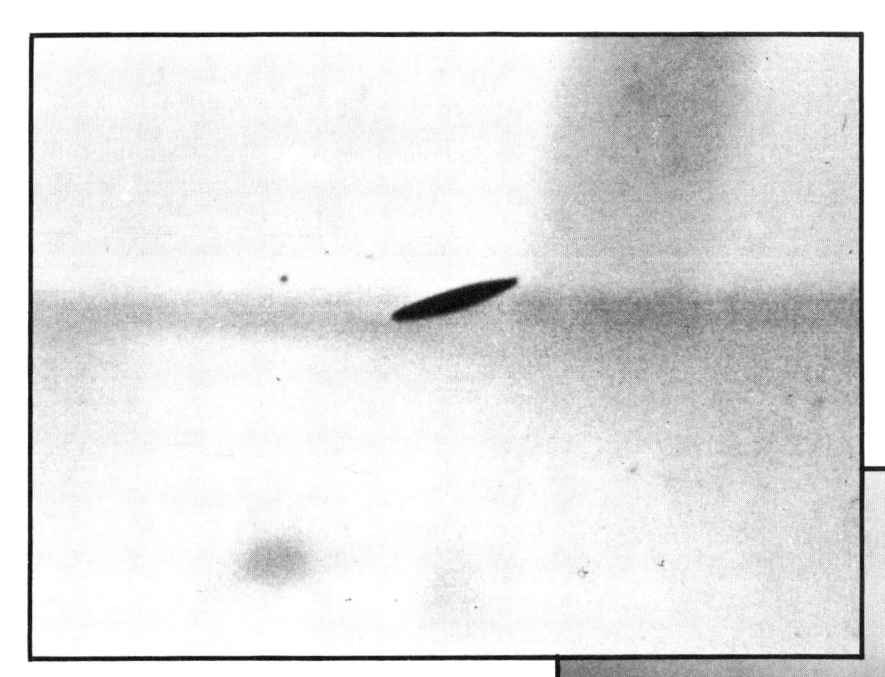

well. A fourth – the last to be taken – revealed a dim shape that had little definition. Russell was puzzled by the object's apparent changes of shape because he did not recall seeing such changes. He recalled seeing only changes of aspect of the UFO.

It is reasonable to assume that the eight blank frames were due to the speedy rolling on of the film between shots in the witness's excitement, occasioned by an incident that lasted two minutes at most. Here is a reconstruction of those two minutes:

After the initial swift descent and abrupt halt of the UFO, Russell took his first two shots. He used the single converter that he

object in the sky falling suddenly, stopping dead, and then drifting slowly earthwards with a pendulum-like motion. Amazed at first, but rapidly collecting his wits about him, he 'slapped the camera to infinity' and began snapping. He thought he got 12 photographs. The last two shots were taken as the object moved away, at first slowly and then at much greater speed.

The witness had had limited contact with UFO literature before in as much as his father had designed a cover for the book *Flying saucers have landed* (1953) by George Adamski and Desmond Leslie. Russell did not think much of the book and, after meeting Adamski, thought even less of the subject. But his scepticism received a jolt as he stood photographing the strange object in the sky.

Russell left the rest of the film in the camera so that he could take photographs at Christmas and sent it away for processing after the holiday period. In the meantime he told a few friends what had happened. They were inclined to laugh off the incident, but he felt it was worth investigating. He did not wish for the publicity a newspaper might have brought him, but he was not sure who would be genuinely interested. Fearing he would get short shrift from established bodies such as the Royal Astronomical Society or the Royal Aeronautical Society, he looked through the telephone directory under the word 'flying' and so happened on *Flying Saucer Review*. He wrote to the magazine, explaining what he expected to be found on his pictures when the film was returned, and the magazine arranged for R.H.B. Winder, an engineer, and Gordon Creighton to help in an investigation once the pictures were available for study.

From the start of the investigation there was a measure of disappointment for the witness, for only 3 of the 12 frames came out

Top: the second photograph shows the UFO edge-on, which emphasises its disc shape. The expert who examined the photographs for fraud could not explain the strange shadow effects on this shot

Above: the third photograph caught the UFO in a slanted position, perhaps in the ascent since it was taken just before the object sped away. When enlarged, the picture revealed a marked efflux to the left

had been testing, set at 1/125 second (f/5.6). He then hurried away from the window and fitted the second (Panagar) converter. With a focal length now of 540 millimetres, he set the exposure at 1/25 second (f/11). Returning to the window, he saw the object 'stand on end' and present its full circular shape to him before turning through 90° about a vertical axis until it was edge on. The UFO then started to move to his right. During all that period, Russell shot only two successful snaps, though he could not have known this at the time. It was during the moment of movement to the right that the third good picture was captured. Then the fourth followed as the UFO accelerated away. By the time Russell reset the camera for the next shot, the object had gone.

After investigation, the researchers handed the transparencies to *Flying Saucer Review*'s photographic consultant, Percy Hennell. After examining them he made plate negatives from the first three. He stated that they were 'genuine photographs of an object in the air, and, in the case of the first, some distance beyond the house opposite the position where the photographer stood'. He could detect no signs of the transparencies

1879

UFO CASEBOOK

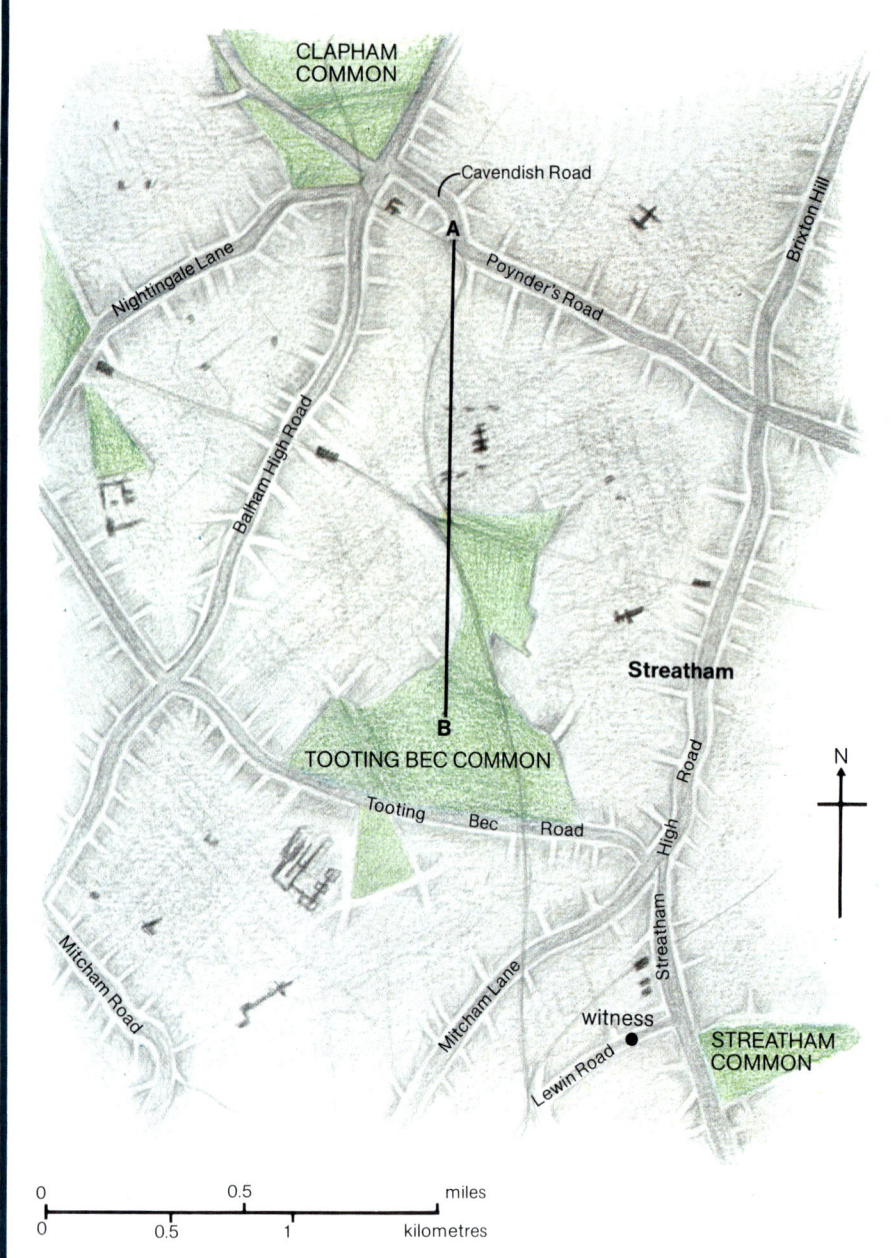

seen when the image had been enlarged and viewed on a projector.

Winder pointed out that the silhouetted image of the UFO on the first photograph bore a remarkable similarity to the shape drawn by Police Constable Colin Perks after his sighting of a UFO at Wilmslow, Cheshire, on 7 January 1966, at 4.10 a.m. Constable Perks was checking the back door of a shop when he heard a high-pitched whine. He turned and looked over the car park behind the shops, which was east. There he saw a solid-looking object – stationary – some 35 feet (10 metres) above the grass of the meadow beyond the car park. It was about 100 yards (90 metres) from him. Perks said the UFO's upper surfaces glowed steadily with a greenish-grey colour, a glow that did not hide the definite shape of the object. He said the lines in his sketch 'represented rounded, but fairly sharp changes in the profile, matched by shading in the glow'. Nowhere could he see openings like portholes or doors. His estimate of a diameter of 30 feet (9 metres) for the base was based on a mental comparison with a 30-foot (9-metre) long bus. After about five seconds the object moved off east-south-east with no change of sound. Then it disappeared.

Russell's other photographs brought no further comparisons to mind. In the second picture there are strange shadow effects, particularly one that slants away in the '7 o'clock' position. Hennell could offer no explanation for this.

The third photograph seems to have been blurred either by the motion of the object – it was beginning to move away – or by camera shake. An efflux effect is also noticeable to the left of the object. This in fact was quite pronounced when the picture was enlarged.

Judging from Russell's position and the 2-mile (3-kilometre) visibility limit, the object appears to have been somewhere on a line from the sighting point via Tooting Bec

having been tampered with. Later the transparencies were projected onto a 12-foot (3.5-metre) square screen. Close inspection revealed nothing untoward.

The investigators ascertained that the object was not luminous, and that it was virtually impossible for the witness to distinguish any colour owing to the fact that it was being viewed as a dark object against a light background. Russell merely suggested it might have been maroon.

The first photograph shows the gable of the house opposite Russell's flat with a near-horizontal bar to the right that acts as a support for a chimney that is off camera. Winder estimated that the bar would have been at an angle of elevation of 10° from the lens of the camera. Russell thought the object might have been anything up to a mile (1.6 kilometres) away. In the photograph there is a hint of an efflux streaming to the right from the base of the UFO – a feature more clearly

Top: map of the area in which Russell spotted the UFO over Streatham. The object appears to have been somewhere along line A–B

Above: a drawing made by PC Colin Perks of the UFO he saw in Cheshire about a year before Russell's sighting. The two reports were strikingly similar

Common to Cavendish Road.

A contact at Heathrow airport told the investigators that the object was not observed on the radar screens, but it is possible that it missed the radar sweep by virtue of its plummeting fall in between sweeps.

The Ministry of Defence (Air) was asked about weather balloons on 15 December 1966. The answer was that four were released in south and south-west England earlier than the sighting, but that they would not have migrated to the London area.

A spectral figure has often turned up on a photograph when nothing of the kind was visible at the time it was taken. How do these 'extras' appear? Are they genuine? FREDERICK GOODMAN focuses on spirit photography

THE EASE WITH WHICH 'EXTRAS' may be imposed upon photographs has led most people to believe that all spirit photographs are in some way fraudulent. However, the evidence suggests otherwise. While the greater number of so-called psychic pictures are indeed intended to amuse or defraud, a few spirit photographs have been made in circumstances that place them on a level beyond ordinary understanding. What makes the discussion of spirit photography so difficult is that no one knows how genuine images come to be on plates and film. And no one knows exactly what these spirit images are.

The most extraordinary spirit photographs have been made in seances, often under rigid test conditions, but a few interesting ones have been made unexpectedly by amateurs. People take a snapshot of a friend, or of an interior, or of a pet, and afterwards find, to their astonishment, the image of a face or figure – sometimes recognisably that of a deceased relative or friend – on the print. This happens rarely, but it does happen; and many examples, with written accounts, have been preserved by archivists and librarians interested in psychic phenomena. The earliest preserved examples of spirit photographs were of this order: they were taken by amateur photographers who had no specialist interest in psychic effects, and who indeed were disappointed that their portraits and landscapes were 'spoiled' by extra images.

It is generally accepted that spirit photography as such began in Boston, Massachusetts, USA, on 5 October 1861, when William Mumler accidentally produced his first spirit picture. But this date may not be entirely accurate. For, according to an early pioneer of Spiritualism in Boston, Dr Gardner, a few portraits exhibiting a second figure that could not be accounted for had been made before that at nearby Roxbury. The Roxbury photographer was an 'orthodox Christian' who, after hearing about Mumler's pictures, refused to print any negatives containing 'spirits' on the grounds that 'if it had anything to do with Spiritualism, it was the work of the Devil.'

The fact is that, well over a century later, we still do not know how spirit photography

An embracing couple not seen by either the photographer or the subject (far left) appeared on this picture taken in a churchyard in 1928 by a Mrs Wickstead. The 'spirits' could not be identified – and the Society for Psychical Research, who investigated the matter, could not explain them

Unexpected developments

Spirit photography

actually works. The majority of psychical researchers involved with spirit photography claim it occurs by the direct intervention of the spirits themselves. By such reasoning, of course, the result is not so much 'spirit photography' as 'photography by spirits'. The famous journalist W. T. Stead was an early champion of spirit photography, and many portraits of him show images of recognised extras alongside. After he died in the *Titanic* disaster in April 1912, he continued to converse in spirit with his daughter Estelle, as she reported. And then the matter went further, for his image began to appear as an extra alongside her in pictures. When Estelle asked him to say something about the actual production of such psychic photographs, Stead insisted that the spirits were themselves involved with producing the images – mainly in order to convince people of the reality of life after death.

The spirit photographs made by professionals and participants in seances are fascinating enough. But it is the innocence and the element of the unexpected that permeate the accidental spirit photographs of amateurs that intrigue the historian of the genre more.

Perhaps the most famous of the early

Above: a spirit portrait of William T. Stead, who had died in the *Titanic* disaster, with his living daughter Estelle. According to her, she asked him how psychic photography actually came about; he replied that the spirits themselves were involved in producing the unexpected images

Above right: the ghostly heads of two drowned sailors photographed by a passenger on the boat, *Watertown*. The spectres were seen in the waves for several days after the drowning and the photographer deliberately took the picture to record this psychic phenomenon

Negative findings

The faking of spirit photographs seems to have begun almost as soon as the genuine product appeared in the 19th century. One of the common faking techniques was the double exposure – marginally easier with the large plates then in use. A more cunning method involved the painting of a background screen with a special chemical invisible to ordinary sight, but which showed up on photographic film. This screen was pre-painted and placed behind the sitter. Still other techniques were devised by ingenious and unscrupulous photographers.

The case called the 'Moss photographic fiasco' is among the most interesting of the proven frauds. In the early 1920s, G.H. Moss was employed as a chauffeur by a man who was interested in the paranormal. Moss was an amateur photographer, and one day he brought a print with a ghostly 'extra' to his employer. The employer showed interest and, after some experiments on his own, introduced Moss into the British College of Psychic Science. About 1924, Moss was given a year's 'contract' to work under test conditions at the college, on a fixed salary. His work there was impressive and well-received – until he was exposed as a fraud.

Moss produced a number of spirit images that were recognised as the likenesses of dead relatives and friends by sitters. In one of these (below) the sitter was a trance medium. She recognised the extra as her dead sister. A cut-out photograph of that sister was mounted alongside the extra to illustrate the resemblance. In another (right), the image was recognised by a person observing the photographic session, though it was not clear whether the recognised spirit was dead or alive.

A third example of Moss's work (far right) was made in a seance with the well-known medium Mrs Osborne Leonard on 5 January 1925. The sitter was informed by 'a voice from beyond' that he would be sitting for a photograph in 8 days. The invisible speaker promised that she would reveal herself then.

Spirit photography

examples of amateur spirit photography is the 'Lord Combermere's ghost' picture (see page 574). The circumstances surrounding the taking of this photograph have been well-recorded and documented. The picture was a study of the splendid library in Combermere Abbey, Cheshire, taken by Miss Sybell Corbet in 1891 as a souvenir of her visit. She was surprised, if not disappointed, to discover on the plate the transparent image of an old man sitting in a chair at the left of the room.

Only the head, the body and arms of the figure are relatively clear – the legs are missing. Subsequent research by psychical investigators revealed that at the precise time that the plate was being exposed, the body of Lord Combermere was being buried in the local churchyard at Wrenbury, a few miles away from the abbey. Lord Combermere had died in London a few days previously as a result of a road accident. In this accident his legs had been so badly damaged that, had he lived, he would never have walked again.

The touch of drama that characterises this photograph came to light well after it was taken. Indeed only rarely do amateur photographers take pictures in the knowledge that they are recording psychic phenomena. One of the few exceptions is the case of the *Watertown* pictures, which contain images of drowned seamen. These were deliberately taken by one of the passengers on board a boat, the *Watertown*, from which two seamen had been swept overboard and drowned during the course of the journey. For several days afterwards, passengers and crew insisted that the seamen's spectral heads could be seen in the waves and spray.

Much more typical is the account of the curious extras on a snapshot taken by Mrs Wickstead in 1928. The snapshot – now quite faded, but never of first-rate quality – was one of two taken at the church in the village of Hollybush, not far from Hereford. Mrs Wickstead was on a car tour with friends and had stopped to see the church. She decided to take a photograph of her friend Mrs Laurie, who, in the event, can barely be seen in the photograph. After the picture had been taken, Mrs Laurie drew Mrs Wickstead's attention to the grave of a soldier who had died in service. Alongside this grave was one of a girl who had died shortly afterwards.

'I wonder if they were lovers?' Mrs Laurie had asked.

In a letter to Sir Oliver Lodge, later

That sitting, which had already been arranged without Mrs Leonard's knowledge, did indeed produce an extra – and some of the sitter's friends insisted that the image bore a strong likeness to his recently deceased wife. A portrait of her was pasted alongside so that a comparison could be made.

Moss was unmasked by the astute F. Barlow, at that time the Honorary Secretary for the now defunct Society for the Study of Supernormal Pictures. While Barlow was examining a group of Moss's negatives containing extras, he noticed a roughness on the edges of certain plates. Closer examination showed that each negative bearing a spirit image had one edge filed. Detailed examination of the plate wrappings revealed that they had been skilfully opened by steaming and resealed.

Moss vehemently denied fraud and even signed a statement declaring his innocence. However, when faced with the filed plates, he made a confession. He had secretly opened certain plates and superimposed an image on them, marking them for later use by filing the edges.

Spirit photography

Emile le Roux in 1909, and is one of the very few stereoscopic spirit photographs.

The instructions came from a spirit who claimed to be the uncle of le Roux's wife. The spirit made contact through her when she was practising automatic writing in le Roux's presence. Through the automatic script, the 'uncle' said that he could be photographed at a later point in the day and gave instructions as to the time and the exposure. Le Roux, a keen amateur photographer, considered the exposure to be far too long; but he followed instructions and took the picture with his stereoscopic camera at the time indicated. The image of the deceased uncle not only appeared but was quite recognisable. In its day, the plate became very famous – but time after time le Roux had to defend himself against the usual charges of fraud. His own simple words reveal the recurrent story of the amateur caught up in a process that he or she cannot explain:

> In reality, this photograph was made under the most simple circumstances, and I would say that except for the strangeness of the spirit head, there were so few difficulties both before and after its execution that, in spite of the

president of the Society for Psychical Research (SPR), Mrs Wickstead wrote that Mrs Laurie had seemed impressed by the two graves and had made a point of showing them to her husband. 'We thought no more about it until about six weeks later when the film was developed and came out as you see with these two figures on the path in the shadow of the yew tree,' Mrs Wickstead wrote. The two figures were in an embrace. The picture was investigated by the SPR, but the mystery of the extras was never solved.

Invisible spirits

There have been rare cases of sensitives seeing and photographing spirits that have remained invisible to others present. One famous example of this is known as the 'Weston' photograph.

The Reverend Charles Tweedale and his family lived in Weston vicarage, a much haunted house in the town of Otley in West Yorkshire. While having lunch on 20 December 1915, Mrs Margaret Tweedale saw the apparition of a bearded man to the left of her son. The others around the table could see nothing. However, her husband immediately fetched the camera and took a picture of the area indicated by his wife. When the negative was developed, a portrait of the apparition appeared on the print.

One extraordinary picture session that took place in Belgium seems to support the belief that the spirits intervene directly in psychic photography. In this instance, a spirit actually instructed an amateur photographer in the most precise manner how and when to take a picture in which the spirit would manifest. The picture was taken by

Above left: the spirit of a dead child appears with her father on a portrait taken by Dr Hooper, a clairvoyant. Hooper claimed that he saw the girl when he took the picture, though she was invisible to others present

Above: an 'extra' of Madame le Roux's uncle appeared on this picture of her, taken by her husband during an automatic writing session. Through the script, the spirit gave instructions on taking the photograph

Left: an unidentified extra in Gloucester Cathedral taken about 1910

Above right: a picture of a bottle allegedly made by the direct transfer of a thought onto a photographic plate in 1896 – called a 'thought-photograph' before the word 'thoughtography' came into use. It was made in France by a Commandant Darget

Right: the ghost of a woman, dead a week, is seen in the back seat in a picture taken by her daughter. Experts said the photograph had not been tampered with

Spirit photography

scepticism which arose within me, and which has not yet quite vanished, I am forced to admit that in order to explain this negative it is necessary to look in another direction than 'fraud' or the double exposure of the plate.

This tantalising image of the deceased uncle is stereoscopically adjusted for depth – an indication that, photographically at least, the psychic entity is subject to the same optical laws as a living being.

The subject of spirit photography greatly excited psychical investigators in the 1870s and 1880s, but no organised and sustained study seems to have been made. There are many references to the phenomenon in the *British Journal of Photography* and a number of articles in the *Journal* of the SPR. But the issue was clouded by the controversy over Spiritualism and no undistorted and full treatment of psychic photography itself has come down to us.

In any event, psychic photography did not end with the unexplained appearance of spirit forms on prints. One new form that has emerged in recent times is the manifestation of UFOs. And, since the main question is whether images on film can be produced without optical processes, thoughtography is of relevance too.

The term 'thoughtography' came into use in Japan in 1910 following a series of tests by Tomokichi Fukurai of a clairvoyant who accidentally imprinted a calligraphic character on a photographic plate by psychic means. Later the sensitive was able to do this by concentrated effort. Fukurai's work was published in English 20 years later and some experiments similar to his were then undertaken in Europe and the United States. But it was not until 1962 that interest in thoughtography was activated by Pauline Oehler, of the Illinois Society for Psychic Research, through her work with the American psychic Ted Serios

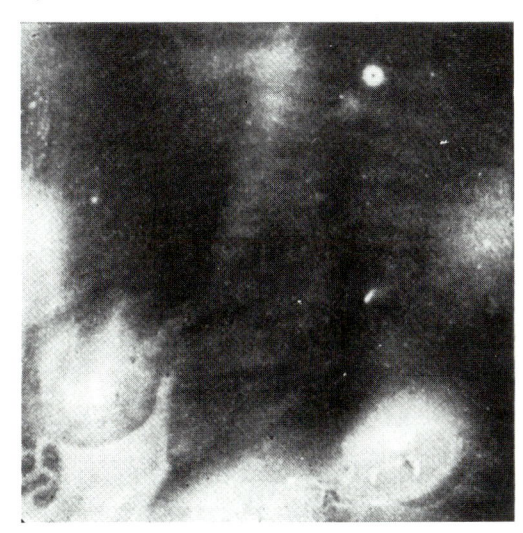

Serios was much investigated under strictly controlled conditions, particularly by Dr Jule Eisenbud (see page 710), a psychical researcher working mainly in Denver, Colorado, USA. In many experiments planned by Eisenbud over a period of two years, Serios could at will produce pictures of what he was thinking about – an old hotel, cars, a corner of a room, and many other mental images. He could also produce an image of a target set by himself or others. For example, one day he glanced casually at a travel magazine in Eisenbud's waiting room. The next day he decided to produce a picture of Westminster Abbey, which he had noticed in the publication. And he did so.

Thoughtography has since become an integral part of modern psychical research. And although Serios's ability to transfer his thoughts onto film has never been explained, neither has it ever been proved fraudulent.

Among the professional spirit photographers of the late 19th century, however, there were undoubtedly frauds – and a number of them were exposed. But does that negate the important fact that many photographic images have been produced by paranormal means?

Not all professional spirit photographers were frauds. We give the evidence on page 1930

His wonders to perform

Levitation, psychokinesis, ESP and paranormal healing are all, apparently, described in the New Testament. But did the conventions of the gospel writers obscure the facts? Were they as miraculous as reported? DAVID CHRISTIE-MURRAY investigates

IF JESUS WAS GOD incarnate, as Christianity teaches, his life could scarcely be expected to be anything but miraculous. Beginning with a virgin birth (a claim not made for him until after his death), an event surrounded with portents – as was the birth of his cousin, John the Baptist – the Bible implies that he lived an uneventful life until he was about 30. Then he burst on his world like a meteor. For some three to four years he taught and worked miracles in Palestine and, if the records can be believed, whatever else he was, he was the greatest and most beneficent healer who has ever lived. By his followers he came to be recognised as the all-conquering Messiah whose coming had been foretold by the prophets. They could not, however, accept his teaching that his kingdom was spiritual, not political, and they were appalled when he went unresisting to execution. To the members of the Jewish religious establishment whose authority he challenged he was a dangerous upstart who might cause trouble with their political masters, the Romans. According to the gospels, the climax came at the Passover festival, when the chief priests allied with an unwilling Roman governor to bring Jesus to crucifixion.

That should have been the end of it. But, at the next great feast, Pentecost, his followers proclaimed that Jesus had risen – in his physical body – from the dead. They then went out into the world and preached with such conviction that within a decade the new religion of Christianity had permeated almost the entire Roman Empire.

In assessing miraculous events as reported in the New Testament, three elements need to be considered – the records, the truth or falsehood of the facts chronicled and their interpretation.

First, the records. Apart from a few fragments, the oldest New Testament manuscripts date back to about the fourth century AD and are copies of copies. Part of the work of textual scholars is to reconstruct the original texts by comparing and collating surviving manuscripts and eliminating the inaccuracies, additions and annotations of copyists. Mark's gospel was written about AD 65, approximately 30 years after the events recorded, Luke's probably about AD 70, Matthew's late in the first century and John's about AD 100. They were based on earlier written material, in turn collected from oral tradition and statements of eyewitnesses, contemporaries of Jesus. Mark probably

Right: a conventional Nativity scene, complete with adoring magi and heavenly choir, typical of the Midrash, or embroidered scriptural commentary. Angels appearing to shepherds, and the star of Bethlehem are, say biblical scholars, attempts by the gospel writers to create an atmosphere appropriate for the birth of the Son of God. Yet, if that were the true identity of Jesus of Nazareth, why should 'signs and wonders' not have accompanied his birth?

Far right: Jesus walks on the water, while Peter begins to sink the moment he takes his eyes off Jesus's face. Is this another example of the Midrash style – or did Jesus hypnotise Peter, releasing paranormal powers?

Right: the gospel writers. Mark's gospel was written about 30 years after the events it recorded, Luke's shortly after that; Matthew and John's gospels were probably written around the end of the first century. Were their memories hopelessly muddled after such a long time – or were the events they recorded too amazing to forget?

Below right: Peter raises the dead Tabitha; early Christian propaganda or literal truth?

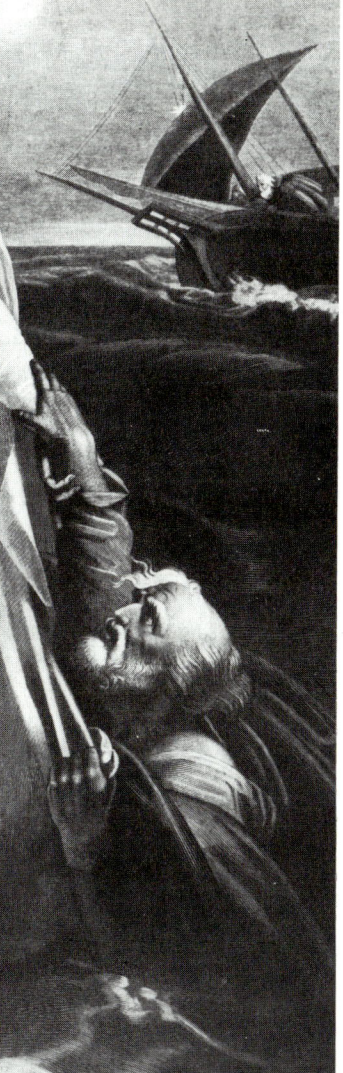

Bible mysteries

obtained information from Peter, leader of the Apostles, and Luke from Mary, Jesus's mother. Sceptics may therefore claim that the fallibility of memory and the unconscious exaggeration of each other's recollections by enthusiastic believers can explain away everything, and that records written so long after the events are worthless. Believers can argue that the records were based on the recollections of contemporaries of Christ, that events so astounding would imprint themselves upon the memory, that mere illusion could not have transfigured lives and made the impact on history that Jesus's career did, and that the most scholarly investigation by hostile critics has not succeeded in destroying the main fabric of the New Testament story, including its paranormal elements.

Star of wonder

In judging the records the writing conventions of the time must be considered. Ancient narratives were not as obsessed as 20th-century journalists with the literal accuracy of words and the reporting of events – the interpretation was more important than the happening, and their readers understood this. Thus Matthew, a Jewish Christian writing for Jews, used the technique of the Midrash, or embroidered commentary. This technique poetically and symbolically enhanced events that were, perhaps, wonderful in themselves, creating a suitable atmosphere to convey the wonder to the reader. So, the birth of Jesus was accompanied by the appearance of angels to shepherds, the star over Bethlehem and the visit of the wise men from the East. An earthquake, the rending of the Temple veil, darkness and the appearance of spirits in the streets of Jerusalem signalled the death of Jesus. None of these events may have actually happened, but for all believers, what matters is not the physical events men experience but the spiritual experiences they symbolise.

Matthew also emphasises the fulfilment of prophecy, a favourite phrase being, 'that it might be fulfilled which was spoken by the prophets'. However, for 'fulfilled' read 'paralleled', for a rabbinical tradition was to quote Scripture as commentary; as when a rabbi, given a basin of oil in which to wash his feet, commented, 'that it might be fulfilled what is written in Deuteronomy, "let him dip his feet in oil".' Matthew never intended – any more than the rabbi – to state that the prophets foresaw the actual events.

Intervention of angels

Another Jewish convention is the device of ascribing the apparent intervention of God in the affairs of men to the action of 'an angel of the Lord'.

Prediction and precognition have a place in the New Testament but only, research reveals, as a matter of faith. Jesus predicted his death at Jerusalem at least three times. He prophesied the obliteration of the Temple, which occurred in AD 70. He foresaw Peter's denial of him. Agabus, a Christian prophet, warned Paul that the Jews of Jerusalem would deliver him to the Romans (Acts 21:9). But the records of these predictions were all written *after* their apparent fulfilment and are therefore useless as evidence for the power of prediction.

Mystical experiences, dreams and visions

Bible mysteries

abound. If the dreams of Joseph, Mary's husband (Matthew 1:20; 2:13; 2:19; 2:22), are not Mishradic, they can be accepted as dramatisations of solutions to problems of which he was aware when awake. Jesus, at his baptism, saw the heavens open, the Holy Spirit descending upon him like a dove and heard a voice saying, 'Thou art my beloved Son,' all of which was, apparently, personal to him. No bystander is reported as having seen or heard anything. Paul's conversion occurred when a light from heaven (lightning?) temporarily blinded him on a journey to Damascus and a voice addressed him. Acts 9:7 claims the voice was heard by Paul's companions while Acts 22:9 denies this. The discrepancy cannot be denied – but neither can the fact that the arch-persecutor of the Christians became, as a result of his experience, their principal advocate. There is also a possible psychological explanation. Watching the heroic death of the first Christian martyr, Stephen (Acts 7), Saul – later Paul – was subconsciously convinced of the truth of Christianity. The conviction violently conflicted with his upbringing as a rigorous Pharisee, and the conflict had to be resolved by a cataclysmic personal experience.

More than psychology, however, is needed to explain the experience of Peter and Cornelius. Cornelius, a Roman centurion, given Peter's very name and address in a vision, sends for him. Peter, forbidden by Jewish law to enter a gentile's house, has a vision of creatures 'clean' and 'unclean'. Told to 'kill and eat', he replies that he has never eaten anything unclean. The reply comes, 'Do not call unclean what God has cleansed.' The vision coincides with the arrival of Cornelius's emissaries, and Peter, his scruples removed, visits Cornelius who is converted to Christianity – and the new faith is for the first time communicated to the gentile world (Acts 10).

Below: an angel announces to Mary that she will bear the 'Son of the Highest'. The Holy Ghost is shown here as a dove – a symbol of God's especial favour – which is also mentioned in the New Testament description of Jesus's baptism (bottom)

Below right: Peter is freed from his chains by an angel. Is this an example of the Apostle's own PK ability activated by his dire need?

The go-between

The psychical researcher can see in this story an unusual case of extra-sensory perception, the Roman's thoughts reaching out to the Jew and inspiring the reflection expressed in a vision that the whole of humanity was acceptable to God. But there is an extra dimension in that the communications are inspired by something or someone beyond the two men, an 'angel' who instructs Cornelius and a 'voice' that addresses Peter. Some parapsychologists, however, believe that this sort of disembodied voice may be an exteriorisation of one's own inner conviction – in effect, one literally hears not merely what one wants to hear but what one *needs* to hear. Thus the Apostles heard 'divine' voices at critical moments in their lives. Rex G. Stanford's theory of 'psi-mediated instrumental response' (PMIR) embraces the idea that prayers are answered, not by any outside agency, but by the person who prays, through the unconscious activation of a form of psychokinesis, but only when the need is greatest (see page 1620).

The delivery of Peter from prison, when he was sleeping chained between two guards, is frankly miraculous (Acts 12); but the story has a ring of truth about it and is paralleled in the similar release of a modern Christian, Sadhu Sunder Singh in the early 20th century. This is only one of a number of biblical miracles that although superficially incredible, can be matched by personal experiences today.

During Jesus's mission – a time of great spiritual outpouring – his followers may well have experienced the blossoming of psychic powers. If there is any truth at all in the strange experiences reported by saints and mystics down the ages, these continue to manifest in holy people. Many of the experiences, such as 'speaking with tongues', are explicable psychologically (see page 444), others, such as some of the well-attested healing miracles at Lourdes, are inexplicable.

At the same time a truly balanced view often actively cries out for a healthy and reasonable scepticism. Some of the miracles in the New Testament are ethically suspect – is the striking dead or blind of deceivers and opponents, as Peter did to Ananias and Sapphira (Acts 5) and Paul to Elymas the sorcerer (Acts 13), albeit temporarily – reconcilable with Christ's teaching of 'Love thine enemies'? Was it ethical of the Lord of creation to send evil spirits into a herd of swine (Matthew 8) so that they were all drowned? (Although there is some evidence that this incident was misreported.)

Christians prefer to assess each miracle individually, according to its consonance with the true spirit of Christianity as they see it. Thus, Jesus's calming of the tempest at sea (Matthew 8:24) can be believed of a man so in tune with nature that he could read its signs, and his walking on the sea (Matthew 14:24) as an example of levitation – which has been reputed in different cultures and at different ages to be a property of holy men.

One outstanding characteristic of Jesus's life was his healing ability. The literature of the paranormal is crammed with stories of healing, many of them as well-authenticated as such events can be; and there is no reason why Jesus's reputation as an exceptional healer should not be accepted at face value. His raising from the dead of Jairus's daughter (Matthew 9:18) – of whom he said, 'The maid is not dead, but sleepeth' – and of the widow of Nain's son (Luke 7:11-17) could both have been recoveries from comas. The raising of Lazarus (John 11) is a different matter. Not only is there here a man raised to life four days after his burial, but this astounding miracle – which finally decided the authorities to destroy Jesus – is ignored by the first three gospels. Yet the modern Hindu leader, Sai Baba, is also credited with raising from the dead a man whose body had actually begun to decompose (see page 237).

But for Christians, there remains a miracle of raising that, if it happened, must be the most remarkable and significant event of all time: the physical resurrection of Jesus himself, three days after he died on the cross.

Did Jesus really – as the gospels claim – rise from the dead? See page 1934

Bottom: Lazarus is raised from the dead. Some commentators suggest that Lazarus was in fact in a cataleptic trance, or a coma, and that Jesus, realising this, released him from the appalling fate of being buried – or entombed – alive. Yet in the 1970s, the Hindu leader Sai Baba is said to have 'raised' a man who had been dead for days and who had actually begun to decompose; perhaps Lazarus truly was dead when Jesus raised him

Half human and half fish, mermaids and mermen have appeared many times over the centuries. But, asks PAUL BEGG, are the merfolk merely colourful figments of our imagination – or do they really exist?

ACCORDING TO THE South African *Pretoria News* of 20 December 1977, a mermaid had been found in a storm sewer in the Limbala Stage III township, Lusaka. The reports are garbled and it is difficult to tell who saw what – and what exactly it was they saw – but it seems that the 'mermaid' was first seen by some children and, as the news spread, so a crowd gathered. One reporter was told that the creature appeared to be a 'European woman from the waist up, whilst the rest of her body was shaped like the back end of a fish, and covered with scales.'

Legends about mermaids and mermen stretch back into antiquity and can be found in the folklore of almost every nation in the world. Merfolk have been seen and vouched for down the ages by witnesses of attested integrity – and they continue to be seen today.

The earliest merman in recorded history is the fish-tailed god Ea, more familiarly known as Oannes, one of the three great gods of the Babylonians. He had dominion over

A fishy tale

the sea and was also the god of light and wisdom, and the bringer of civilisation to his people. Originally Oannes was the god of the Akkadians, a Semitic people of the northern part of Babylonia from whom the Babylonians derived their culture, and was worshipped in Akkad as early as 5000 BC.

Almost all we know about the cult of Oannes is derived from the surviving fragments of a three-volume history of Babylonia written by Berossus, a Chaldean priest of Bel in Babylon, in the third century BC. In the 19th century, Paul Emil Botta, the French vice-consul in Mosul, Iraq, and an enthusiastic archaeologist – albeit one whose primary concern was loot – discovered a remarkable sculpture of Oannes dating from the eighth century BC, in the palace of the Assyrian king Sargon II at Khorabad, near Mosul. The sculpture, along with a rich collection of carved slabs and cuneiform inscriptions, is now held in the Louvre in Paris.

Another early fish-tailed god was Dagon of the Philistines who is mentioned in the Bible: 1 Samuel 5:1–4. The Ark of the Covenant was placed next to a statue of Dagon in a temple dedicated to Dagon in Ashod, one of the five great Philistine city states. The following day the statue was found to have 'fallen upon his face to the earth before the ark of the Lord'. Amid much consternation and, no doubt, great fear, the people of Ashod set the statue of Dagon in its place again, but the following day it was again found fallen before the Ark of the Covenant, this time the head and the hands having broken off.

It is also probable that the wife and daughters of Oannes were fish-tailed, but the surviving representations of them are vague and it is impossible to be sure. However, no doubts surround Atargatis, sometimes known as Derceto, a Semitic Moon goddess. In his *De dea Syria* the Greek writer Lucian (c. AD 120–c. 180) described her: 'Of this Derceto likewise I saw in Phoenicia a drawing in which she is represented in a curious form; for in the upper half she is a woman, but from the waist to the lower extremities runs in the tail of a fish.'

Fish-tailed deities can be found in almost every culture of the ancient world but by medieval times they had become humanoid sea-dwellers. One of the most important scientific influences on the Middle Ages was Pliny the Elder (AD 23–79), a Roman administrator and encyclopedic writer who died in the eruption of Vesuvius that destroyed Pompeii (and whose 15th-century statue outside Como Cathedral looks disconcertingly like Harpo Marx). As far as medieval scholars were concerned, if Pliny said that something was so then it was

Top left: the 'Fejee mermaid' that was the star attraction of Phineas T. Barnum's touring show in 1842. Barnum, a cynical American showman who coined the phrase 'every crowd has a silver lining', advertised the creature with posters depicting voluptuous mermaids, similar to the painting by Waterhouse (top). The 'mermaid' was perhaps a freak fish

1890

Merfolk

undeniably so. Of mermaids, Pliny wrote:

> I am able to bring forth for mine authors divers knights of Rome ... who testifie that in the coast of the Spanish Ocean neere unto Gades, they have seen a Mere-man, in every respect resembling a man as perfectly in all parts of the bodie as might bee....

Why, if the man so perfectly resembled a human, the 'divers knights of Rome' thought they had seen a *mer*man is not clear, but Pliny was convinced that merfolk were real and that they were seen regularly.

Tales of merfolk proliferated and were, oddly, encouraged by the Church, which found it politic to adapt ancient heathen legends to its own purpose. Mermaids were included in bestiaries, and carvings of them were featured in many churches and cathedrals. A fine example of a mermaid carving can be seen in the church at Zennor, Cornwall, on a bench end. It is thought to be about 600 years old and is associated with the legend of Mathy Trewhella, the son of the churchwarden, who one day inexplicably disappeared. Years later a sea captain arrived at St Ives and told how he had anchored off Pendower Cave and seen a mermaid who had said to him: 'Your anchor is blocking our cave and Mathy and our children are trapped inside.' For the people of Zennor the mystery of Mathy's disappearance was explained.

On the whole, mermaids were not a sight to be relished. Their beautiful song, it was said, had captivated many a ship's crew and, like the fabled sirens, lured vessels to grief on dangerous rocks.

Above: the mermaid who is said to have abducted one Mathy Trewhella, carved for posterity on a pew in the church at Zennor, Cornwall. The carving is about 600 years old, but the legend may be considerably older

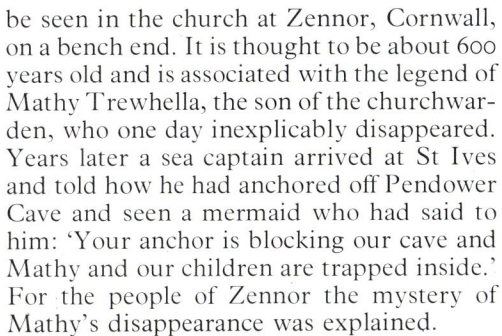

Left: mermaids, mermen and mer-children disport themselves in the turbulent sea

Below: the mermaid as erotic fantasy figure. She was widely believed to prey on drowning sailors, making them her sexual slaves

When mermaids surface

In the late Elizabethan, early Jacobean age belief in the mermaid waxed and waned. Men such as Frances Bacon and John Donne gave rational explanations for many natural phenomena, including the mermaid – yet it was also a time of blossoming maritime travel and some of the great seamen of the age told of personal encounters with merfolk. In 1608 Henry Hudson, the navigator and explorer (after whom the Hudson Bay territories are named), made the following matter-of-fact entry in his log:

> This morning, one of our companie looking over boord saw a Mermaid, and calling up some of the companie to see her, one more came up, and by that time she was come close to the ship's side, looking earnestly on the men: a little after, a Sea came and overturned her: From the Navill upward, her back and breasts were like a womans (as they say that saw her) her body as big as one of us; her skin very white; and long haire hanging down behinde, of colour blacke; in her going downe they saw her tayle, which was like the tayle of a Porposse, and speckled like a Macrell. Their names that saw her were Thomas Hilles and Robert Raynar.

Hudson was a very experienced seaman who surely knew the calibre of his men and presumably would not have bothered to record a blatant hoax. Also, the report itself shows that his men were familiar with the creatures of the sea and were of the opinion that this creature was exceptional – which, if their description is accurate, indeed it was.

But the great age for mermaids was the 19th century. More mermaids were faked and displayed to awed crowds at fairs and exhibitions than at any other time. It was also the period in which several remarkable sightings were reported, including two of the best authenticated on record.

On 8 September 1809 *The Times* published the following letter from one William Munro:

> About twelve years ago when I was Parochial Schoolmaster at Reay

1891

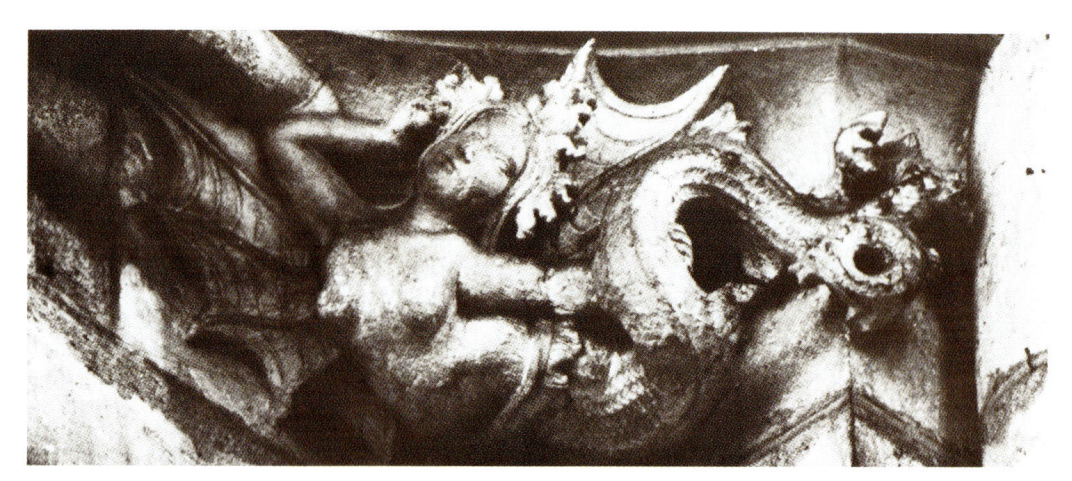

Merfolk

Left: a mermaid cornice decoration in Sens Cathedral, France

Below: the sirens attempt to lure Ulysses and his crew to their doom with their irresistible singing. Seen here as mermaids, they are more often thought of as half woman, half bird (below right)

Bottom: a predatory mermaid seizes a sailor and carries him off to her lair

[Scotland], in the course of my walking on the shore at Sandside Bay, being a fine warm day in summer, I was induced to extend my walk towards Sandside Head, when my attention was arrested by the appearance of a figure resembling an unclothed human female, sitting on a rock extending into the sea, and apparently in the action of combing its hair, which flowed around its shoulders, and of a light brown colour. The resemblance which the figure bore to its prototype in all its visible parts was so striking, that had not the rock on which it was sitting been dangerous for bathing, I would have been constrained to have regarded it as really a human form, and to an eye unaccustomed to the situation, it most undoubtedly appeared as such. The head was covered with hair of the colour above mentioned and shaded on the crown, the forehead round, the face plump, the cheeks ruddy, the eyes blue, the mouth and lips of natural form, resembling those of a man; the teeth I could not discover, as the mouth was shut; the breasts and abdomen, the arms and fingers of the size of a full-grown body of the human species, the fingers, from the action in which the hands were employed, did not appear to be webbed, but to this I am not positive. It remained on the rock three or four minutes after I observed it, and was exercised during that period in combing its hair, which was long and thick, and of which it appeared proud, and then dropped into the sea. . . .

Whatever it was that William Munro saw and described in such detail, he was not alone, for he adds that several people 'whose veracity I never heard disputed' had claimed to have seen the mermaid, but until he had seen it himself he 'was not disposed to credit their testimony'. But, as they say, seeing is believing.

In about 1830 inhabitants of Benbecula, in the Hebrides, saw a young mermaid playing happily in the sea. A few men tried to swim out and capture her, but she easily outswam them. Then a little boy threw stones at her, one of which struck the mermaid and she swam away. A few days later, about 2 miles (3 kilometres) from where she was first seen, the corpse of the little mermaid was washed ashore. The tiny, forlorn body brought crowds to the beach and after the corpse had been subjected to a detailed examination it was said that:

> the upper part of the creature was about the size of a well-fed child of three or four years of age; with an abnormally developed breast. The hair was long, dark and glossy; while the skin was white, soft and tender. The lower part of the body was like a salmon, but without scales.

Among the many people who viewed the tiny corpse was Duncan Shaw, factor (land agent) for Clanranald, baron-bailie and sheriff of the district. He ordered that a coffin and shroud be made for the mermaid and that she be peaceably laid to rest.

Of the many faked merfolk of this period, only one or two need be mentioned to

Merfolk

Below right: the Reverend Robert S. Hawker, who, in his youth, impersonated a mermaid off the shore of Bude, Cornwall. For several nights he draped himself over the rocks, with plaited seaweed for hair and oilskins wrapped round his legs, and sang off-key. The citizens of Bude flocked to see the 'mermaid' but, tiring of his joke, Hawker launched into *God save the King* and dived into the sea – his mermaid days over

illustrate the ingenuity of the fakes and the fakers. A famous example is recounted in *The vicar of Morwenstow* by Sabine Baring-Gould. The vicar in question was the eccentric Robert S. Hawker who, for reasons best known to himself, in July 1825 or 1826 impersonated a mermaid off the shore of Bude in Cornwall. When the Moon was full he swam or rowed to a rock not far from the shore and there donned a wig made from plaited seaweed, wrapped oilskins around his legs and, naked from the waist upwards, sang – far from melodiously – until observed from the shore. When the news of the mermaid spread throughout Bude people flocked to see it, and Hawker repeated his performance.

After several appearances Hawker, having tired of his joke – and his voice a little hoarse – gave an unmistakable rendition of *God save the King* and plunged into the sea – never to appear (as a mermaid) again.

Phineas T. Barnum (1810–1891), the great American showman to whom are attributed two telling statements – 'There's one [a sucker] born every minute' and 'Every crowd has a silver lining' – bought a mermaid that he had seen being shown at a shilling a time in Watson's Coffee House in London. It was a dreadful, shrivelled-up thing – probably a freak fish – but Barnum added it to the curiosities he had gathered for his 'Greatest Show on Earth'. His trick, however, was to hang up outside his 'mermaid' sideshow an eye-catching picture of three beautiful women frolicking in an underwater cavern; under this he had a notice that read: 'A Mermaid is added to the museum – no extra charge.' Drawn by the picture and the implication of what would be seen within, many thousands of people paid their admission fee and went to see this spectacle. As Barnum said, if the shrivelled-up 'mermaid' did not meet with their expectations, the rest of the exhibits were worth the money.

Mermaids have continued to be seen in more recent years. One was seen in 1947 by a fisherman on the Hebridean island of Muck. She was sitting on a floating herring box (used to preserve live lobsters) combing her hair. As soon as she realised she was being observed she plunged into the sea. Until his death in the late 1950s the fisherman could not be persuaded to believe that he had not seen a mermaid.

In 1978, a Filipino fisherman, 41-year-old Jacinto Fatalvero, not only saw a mermaid one moonlit night but was helped by her to secure a bountiful catch. Little more is known, however, because having told his story, Fatalvero became the butt of jokes, the object of derision – and, inevitably, hounded by the media. Understandably he refused to say another word.

It is widely accepted that the mermaid legend sprang from the misidentification of two aquatic mammals, the manatee and dugong, and possibly seals. Obviously many reports can be thus explained, but does this explanation satisfactorily account for what was seen by Henry Hudson's sailors in 1608 or for the mermaid seen by the schoolmaster William Munro? Were these and other similar sightings sea-mammals or mermaids?

One suggestion, perhaps slightly tongue in cheek, is that the merfolk are real, the descendants of our distant ancestors who came ashore from the sea. The merfolk, of course, are descended from those ancestors who either stayed in the sea or chose to return to it. Human embryos have gills that usually disappear before birth, but some babies are born with them and they have to be removed surgically.

But, whatever she is, the mermaid has a long history of sightings and continues to be seen. For this we should be thankful; the romance and folklore of the sea would be all the poorer without her.

Large, dark and ugly, Borley Rectory seemed to invite haunting. And with the arrival of ghost hunter Harry Price, it became a hive of paranormal activity. Was someone helping things along? FRANK SMYTH continues his examination of the Borley case

ALTHOUGH IT SERVED as rectory to the 12th-century Borley church, which stood amid ancient gravestones on the opposite side of the Sudbury road, the 'most haunted house in England' was only 76 years old when it burned to the ground in the winter of 1939. Borley Rectory was an ugly two-storey building of red brick, its grounds dotted with tall trees that cast gloom on many of its 23 rooms. It was built in 1863 by the Reverend Henry D. E. Bull, who was both a local landowner and rector of Borley church, to house his wife and 14 children.

Immediately behind and to one side of the house lay a farmyard bounded by a cottage, stabling and farm buildings. When an extra wing was added to the house in 1875, a small central courtyard resulted. The dining-room fireplace was carved with figures of monks, a decoration suggesting that the Rev. Bull may have believed a local legend that a 13th-century monastery had once occupied the spot. One of the monks from this monastery gave rise to the first ghost story about the site. He was said to have eloped with a nun from a convent at Bures, some 8 miles (13 kilometres) away. But the couple were caught and executed, he being beheaded and she walled up in the convent. And their ghosts haunted the area. The roots of this picturesque tale were cut away in 1938 by a letter from the Essex Archaeological Society to Sidney Glanville, one of the most diligent and

Above: the Reverend Henry (Harry) Bull and the choir of Borley church. Like his father before him, Harry Bull perpetuated the story of the haunting of the rectory by a nun

Below: the gloomy 23-room rectory as seen from the tower of the church

Borley: the tension mounts

honest volunteer investigators for the ghost hunter and author Harry Price. It stated that neither the monastery nor the nunnery had ever existed.

However, there is evidence that both the Rev. Henry Bull and his son and successor as rector, the Rev. Harry Bull, enjoyed telling the story. It gained currency particularly among Sunday school children, many of whom presumably grew up believing it – in view of its source – to be 'gospel'.

Before this first 'nun's tale' was replaced by a later version, reports grew that various members of the Bull family – notably two of the sisters, Millie and Ethel – had seen a shadowy figure in the long rectory garden moving across what then became known as the 'nun's walk'. This route followed the path of an underground stream, along which clouds of gnats were inclined to drift on warm summer evenings. The two sisters told Price that they had seen the nun in July 1900, adding only that it was 'evening' and 'sunlit' – so no one can be sure it was not a formation of gnats. A later rector, the Rev. G. Eric Smith, told of being startled by a 'white figure' that turned out to be the smoke from a bonfire, while V. C. Wall, a *Daily Mirror* reporter, saw a similar apparition that proved to be the maid.

The Bull family lived at Borley Rectory in basic discomfort – without gas, electricity or mains water – for almost 65 years. When his father died in 1892, Harry took over as rector and continued to live in the house with his numerous siblings. At least three of the family remained in occupation until Harry's death in June 1927. He himself moved across the road to Borley Place when he married in 1911, but returned to the rectory in 1920, presumably after his wife's death.

Above: the summerhouse in which Harry Bull dozed away his last years. He claimed that he saw the ghostly nun and other apparitions while he rested here

Below: the place where the ghost of the nun disappears after her walk in the rectory garden. Up to this point – and where she walks – the stream is underground

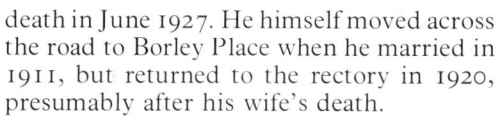

Despite the architectural gloom of their surroundings, the younger Bulls seem to have been a lively crowd, according to the testimony of friends and acquaintances who contacted researchers in the late 1940s and early 1950s. The house had curious acoustics that lent themselves to practical jokes. According to Major the Hon. Henry Douglas-Home of the Society for Psychical Research, footsteps in the courtyard at the rear of the house and voices in the adjoining cottage could clearly be heard in the rectory, along with the noise made by the hand pump in the stable yard. These provided plenty of thumps and groans, he said. Another source told researchers that the young Bull sisters took a delight in telling maids that the house was 'haunted', and one old servant mentioned that after being primed in this way by Edith Bull, she had heard 'shuffling' noises outside her room.

As he grew older, Harry Bull added his own contributions to the village gossip. He appears to have had narcolepsy, a condition in which the sufferer is always drowsy, and took to sleeping for most of the day in a summerhouse. After his snoozes, he claimed he had seen the nun, heard the phantom coach in which she had eloped with the monk, and spoken to an old family retainer named Amos, who had been dead for years. By 1927, when Bull died and the family finally left the rectory, it had become a 'haunted house' in local imagination. This reputation was probably enhanced as the house lay empty and dilapidated for over a year.

On 2 October 1928, the new rector of Borley arrived with his wife. The Rev. G. Eric Smith had spent his early married life in India, but following his wife's serious illness there, he decided to return home, take holy orders, and seek a living. Desperation may

Borley Rectory

have been setting in when he accepted Borley, for he took it on trust and both he and his wife were dismayed when they discovered the condition of the rectory.

To add to their troubles during the first winter, the Smiths soon heard that the house was 'haunted'. The 'ghosts' themselves did not trouble them, however. As Mrs Smith was to write in a letter to the *Church Times* in 1945, neither of them thought the house haunted by anything but 'rats and local superstition'.

Smith's main worry was that the more nervous of his parishioners were unwilling to come to the rectory for evening meetings. When he failed to talk them out of their fears, he took what was perhaps the fatal step of writing to the editor of the *Daily Mirror* to ask for the address of a psychical research society. He hoped that trained investigators could solve the mystery in a rational way and allay the fears of the locals.

Instead, the editor sent a reporter, V. C. Wall, and on Monday, 10 June 1929, he filed the first sensational newspaper account about Borley Rectory. His story talked of 'Ghostly figures of headless coachmen and a nun, an old-time coach, drawn by two bay horses, which appears and vanishes mysteriously, and dragging footsteps in empty rooms....'

The *Mirror* editor also telephoned Price, who made his first visit two days later. With Price's arrival, 'objective phenomena' began for the first time. Almost as soon as he set foot on the premises, a flying stone smashed a window, an ornament shattered in the hallway, showers of apports – pebbles, coins, a medal and a slate – rattled down the main stairs. The servants' bells jangled of their own accord and keys flew out of their locks. During a seance held in the Blue Room – a bedroom overlooking the garden with its 'nun's walk' – rappings on a wall mirror supposedly made by the late Harry Bull were heard by Price and his secretary, Wall, the Smiths, and two of the Bull sisters who were visiting the house.

Price made several trips to the house during the weeks that followed, each visit being accompanied by strange phenomena that were duly reported in the *Daily Mirror* by Wall.

The results were predictable: far from quelling his parishioners' fears, the Rev. Smith had not only unwittingly increased them but added another dimension to his catalogue of woes. The district was invaded by sightseers night and day. Coach parties were organised by commercial companies and the Smiths found themselves virtually under siege. On 14 July, distressed by the ramshackle house and its unwelcome visitors, they moved to Long Melford. Smith ran the parish from there before taking another living in Norfolk in April 1930.

Price must have been made uneasy on at least two occasions at Borley. One of these was when some coins and a Roman Catholic medallion featuring St Ignatius Loyola 'materialised' and fell to the ground at about the same time as some sugar lumps flew through

Below: the spectral nun and the phantom coach haunting the site of Borley Rectory (seen on the left). In some versions of the story, the drivers of the coach were beheaded – which accounts for the headless figures in this picture. The nun was eloping with a monk, who was hanged when the two were caught. She was bricked up into a wall, we are told

Bottom: pointing out the place where the apparitional coach vanishes

Borley Rectory

the air. When they were picked up, they were, recalled Mrs Smith, strangely warm to the touch, as if from a human hand. Her maid Mary Pearson, a known prankster, gave her the solution: 'That man threw that coin,' she explained, 'so I threw some sugar.' An even more farcical incident marked the second near-miss for Price during a further seance in the Blue Room. Heavy footsteps were heard outside, accompanied by the slow rumble of shutters being drawn back. In the doubtless stunned hush that followed, Price asked aloud if it were the spirit of the Rev. Harry Bull. A guttural voice, clearly recognisable as that of a local handyman, replied: 'He's dead, and you're daft.'

Rats, Mrs Smith later averred, lay behind the bell ringing – the bell wires ran along rafters under the roof. As for a mysterious light that 'appeared' in an upstairs window, it was well-known locally as a trick reflection of light from the railway carriages that passed along the valley.

For six months after the Smiths left Borley parish, the rectory was unoccupied once more. Then on 16 October 1930 the Rev. Harry Bull's cousin, Lionel A. Foyster, moved in as the new rector. The Rev. Foyster, a man in his early fifties, had moved back home from his previous post as rector of Sackville, Nova Scotia, which he had held between 1928 and 1930. He suffered from rheumatism but, despite his painful illness, he was a kindly and well-liked man. He was deeply devoted to his attractive wife Marianne, who was 31, and their adopted daughter Adelaide, a child of about two and a half.

During the five years that the Foysters lived at Borley, an estimated 2000 separate 'incidents' occurred, most of them within a period of about 14 months. These included voices, footsteps, objects being thrown, apparitions and messages scribbled in pencil on walls. It is probably true to say that with one possible exception, none of these could be attributable to Harry Price, who visited the rectory only once while the Foysters were there. The day after his visit, on 15 October 1931, he wrote one of the few straightforward statements he was ever to make on the Borley mystery in a letter to a colleague: '... although psychologically, the case is of great value, psychically speaking there is nothing in it.'

Six months had elapsed since the Smiths' departure and the Foysters' arrival, and in that time Borley Rectory had become more dilapidated than ever. According to her husband's cousins, the Bulls, Mrs Foyster hated the place from the moment she saw it. She made no friends locally, and her only companion, apart from Lionel, was a family friend, François D'Arles, a French-Canadian much nearer her own age. He rented the cottage at the rear of the house, and SPR investigators got the impression that he dominated the household. By 1932 Marianne Foyster and D'Arles had opened a flower shop together in London and returned to Borley only at weekends, the implication being that they had become lovers. Mrs Foyster often behaved oddly, if not hysterically, fainting when frustrated. Once she flung herself on her knees before assembled investigators to pray to St Anthony for 'vindication' when no manifestations were forthcoming – as though she expected to be able to produce them.

When the 'hauntings' of Borley Rectory began again shortly after the Foysters' arrival, the villagers accused Marianne Foyster – to her face – of being behind them.

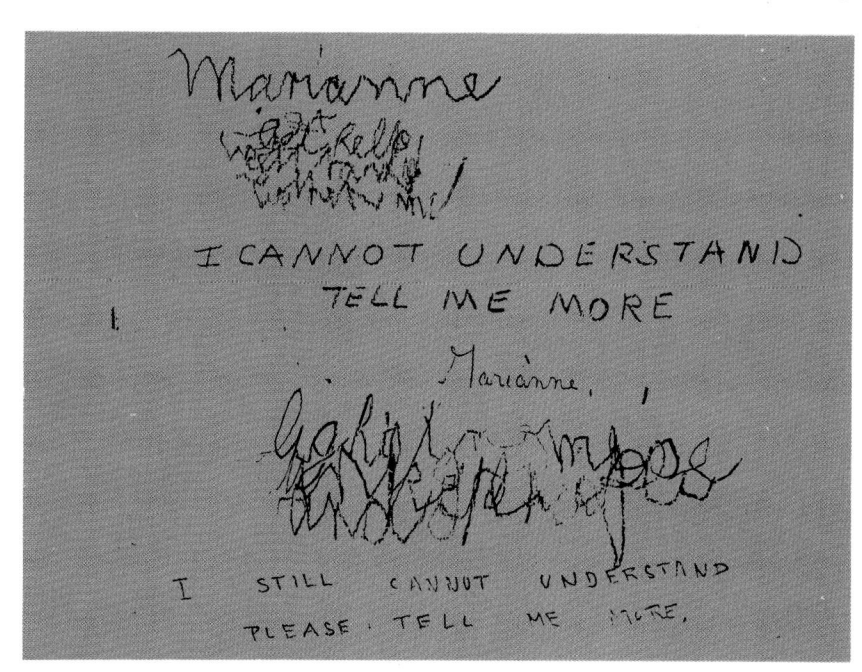

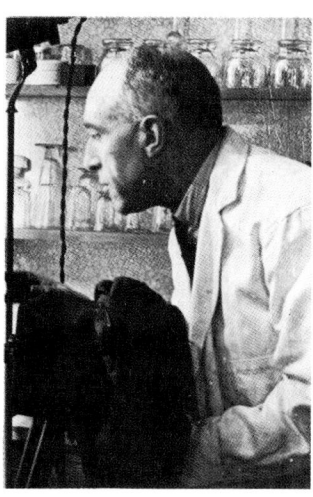

Top: an example of the 'spirit' writing on the wall of the rectory, addressed to Marianne Foyster. Paranormal phenomena increased when the Foysters came to live at Borley

Above: Harry Price at work in his own laboratory. His investigation of the Borley haunting is one of the most controversial of his career

Left: the foot of the main stairs of the rectory, scene of a rain of apports – coins, pebbles and other materialised objects. This happened almost immediately after Price arrived

Was Borley Rectory ever haunted? Or was it a glorified publicity stunt? See page 1918

1897

Did the Sun catch a chill a few million years ago? Has it been 'off colour' throughout mankind's existence – and will it threaten human life by warming up again? JOHN GRIBBIN discusses new evidence about the processes at the heart of the Sun

DURING THE 1930s, nuclear physics and astrophysics came into head-on collision in a debate that made headlines, even in the popular press. Physicists knew that the only processes that could keep the Sun hot were nuclear reactions. Since hydrogen is the most abundant element in the Sun, and helium the second most abundant, it was clear that hydrogen nuclei must be fusing together to make helium nuclei – a reaction that would release energy.

But according to astronomers, the centre of the Sun must be at a temperature of about 27 million degrees Fahrenheit (15 million degrees centigrade). And the nuclear physicists said that, according to their most reliable theories, this temperature was too low to permit the hydrogen fusion reaction to sustain itself.

Confident that, whatever the nuclear physicists might say, the Sun continues to shine steadily as it has done for millions of years, the pioneering astrophysicist Arthur

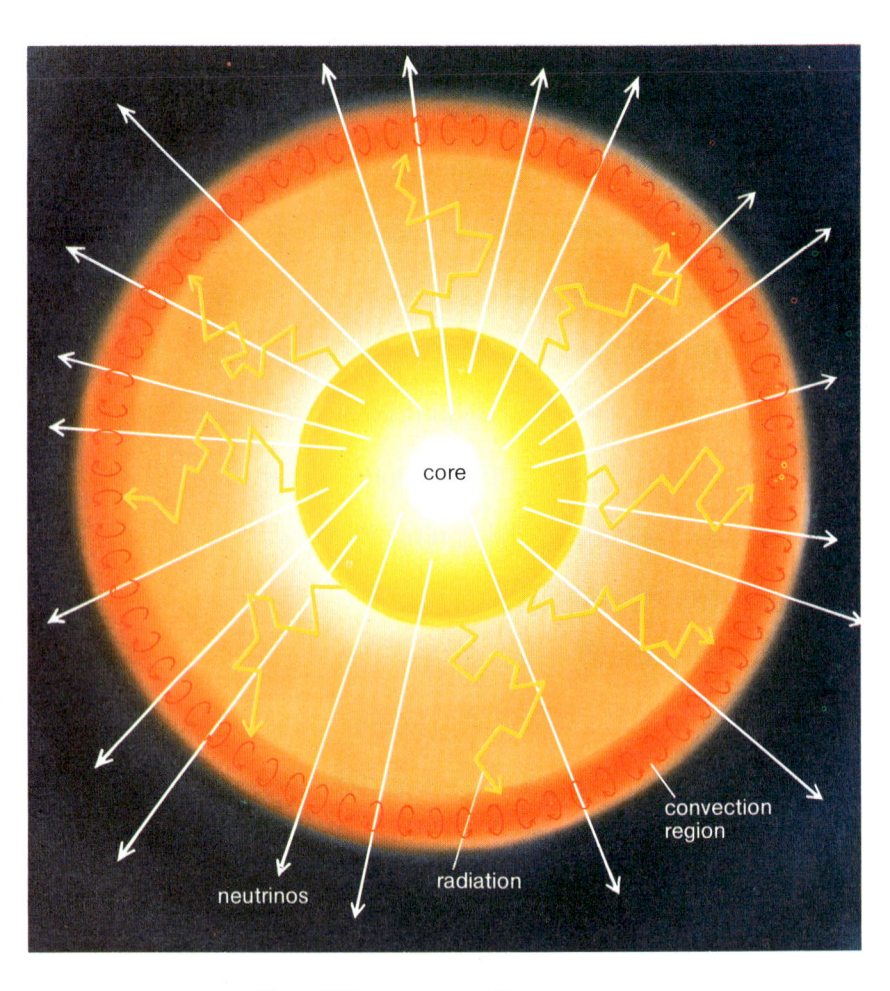

The heart of the Sun

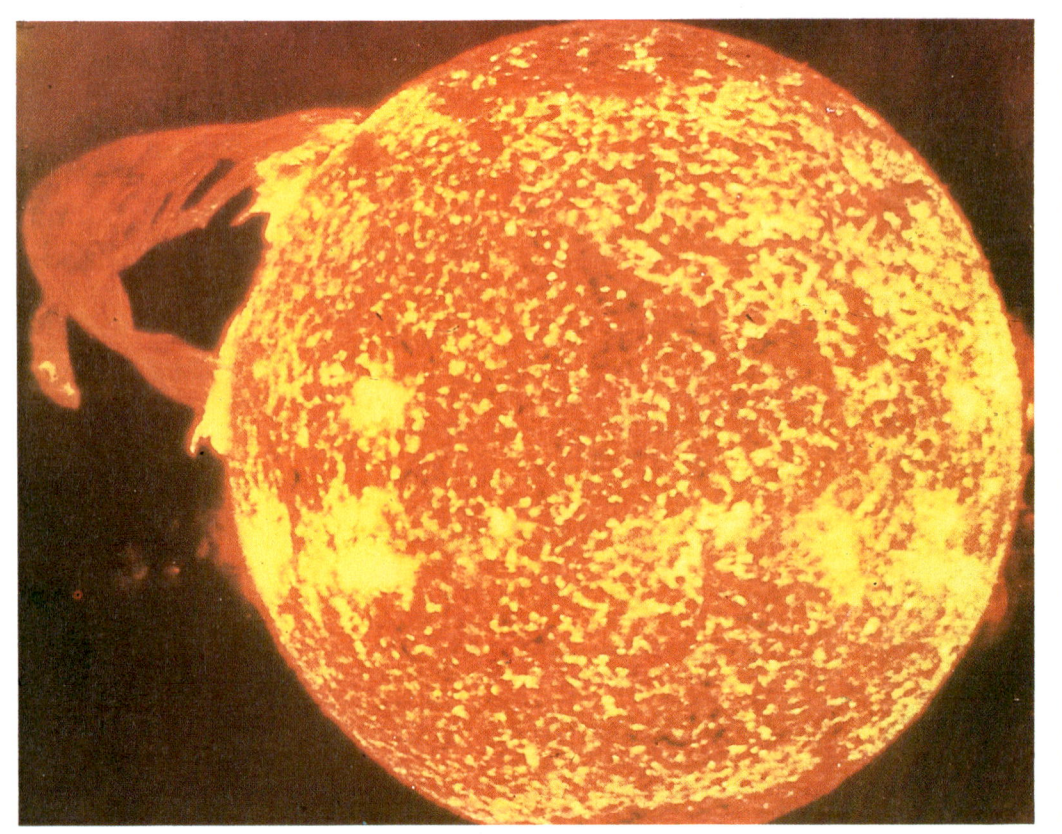

Above: the solar powerhouse is a relatively small region at the centre of the Sun. Four million tonnes of matter are annihilated and converted into energy every second in nuclear reactions. Some of this energy appears in the form of neutrinōs, which flood outwards at the speed of light, unimpeded by the Sun's matter. Heat, light and other radiation take a million years to struggle out through the Sun's middle layers. In the outer layers heat is transferred by convection: hot gas moves outwards, radiates heat and light into space, cools and moves inwards again

Left: hotter and cooler areas on the Sun appear as brighter and darker patches when viewed through an ultraviolet light filter

Eddington is reported to have told his colleagues to 'go and find a hotter place' – a polite way of telling them to go to hell!

In due course the nuclear physicists found that their theories were incomplete; improved theories showed how the fusion reactions could indeed go on inside the Sun, with no need for a 'hotter place'. Those improved theories led eventually to the hydrogen bomb and now point the way towards taming the power of the Sun in fusion reactors on Earth.

Today a new mystery surrounds the nuclear physics that describes conditions inside the Sun and the reactions that go on there. Those same equations that successfully explain how the Sun's heat is maintained predict that a flood of particles called neutrinos should be streaming out of the Sun and across space towards the Earth and beyond: but the neutrinos, or most of them, are missing. Once again there is a head-on clash between observation and theory.

The Sun began its life as a large, cool cloud of gas. It was made chiefly of hydrogen and helium, which have the simplest of all atoms. But it contained a smattering of elements with heavier atoms, debris from earlier generations of stars. The cloud collapsed and as it did so its centre warmed up. It was warmed first by the release of gravitational energy (just as water at the foot of Niagara Falls is warmed by its fall) and then by the nuclear 'burning' of hydrogen.

Originally the Sun was approximately 25 per cent helium and 75 per cent hydrogen. These figures are not exact, and a small proportion of heavier elements was also present. The Sun has been converting hydrogen into helium for nearly 5000 million years since then. Today in the centre of the Sun the proportions are nearly reversed: 65 per cent helium and 35 per cent hydrogen.

How can we be so sure? The basis for these statements is the success of our 'models', or theories, of stellar evolution. From a given original mass of a star, the proportions of the original hydrogen-helium mix, and the laws of physics, the model predicts how the star will 'evolve' as it burns its fuel. The calculations require powerful computers: they are regarded as successful because they successfully 'predict' the sizes and temperatures that stars – and especially the Sun – are observed to have.

The picture of the Sun's interior that is provided by our present knowledge is a dramatic one. Half of the total mass lies close to the centre – inside a sphere with a quarter of the Sun's radius, or just 1.5 per cent of the total volume. In this tiny volume 99 per cent of the Sun's energy is released, and conditions are extreme indeed: the temperature

Below left: how the Sun 'burns'. At the high temperatures and pressures in the Sun, atoms are stripped of their outer electrons. The atoms' nuclei, made of positively charged protons and uncharged neutrons, collide continually. Hydrogen nuclei (single protons) are built up in a series of steps to form more complex nuclei. This can happen in a variety of ways. In the sequence shown here, deuterium ('heavy hydrogen') is formed, while a positron (a positively charged electron) and a neutrino are emitted. Then helium 3 ('light' helium) is formed, and a photon – a 'packet' of electromagnetic energy – is given out. Nuclei of helium 3 collide to form ordinary helium 4, releasing two protons

Below: the Helix Nebula, an enormous globe of gas, shows us the fate of the Sun in the far future, as its nuclear fires die. First the Sun will become a 'red giant'. Then its outer layers will swell, engulfing the Earth, and ultimately the entire solar system

The Sun

is close to 27 million degrees Fahrenheit (15 million degrees centigrade), as we have seen, and the density is 12 times that of lead – yet the material of the Sun's centre is still a fluid, not a solid.

The temperature and pressure prevailing here support the vast weight of the overlying matter. The Sun's mass is one third of a million times that of the Earth. Occupying a volume that could comfortably accommodate 1,300,000 Earths, however, this gives rise to an average density only 1.4 times that of water.

It is surprising that any particle can escape from the depths of the Sun. Yet the neutrino is such an elusive particle that it does just that. The neutrino has no electrical charge; it is not known whether it has zero mass, as long believed, or a very small mass. The chance of a neutrino interacting with any other particle it meets is incredibly small: the result is that it behaves like a ghost, able to slip through immense quantities of matter without any effect whatever. Neutrinos created by nuclear reactions at the Sun's core fly outwards at the speed of light – scarcely noticing the surrounding matter, which has a maximum density of 4.5 tonnes per cubic foot (160 tonnes per cubic metre) – and some of them reach the Earth just eight minutes later. In fact 26,000 million neutrinos pass through each square inch (4000 million per square centimetre) of the Earth, or of our bodies, in every second. An infinitesimal fraction of them react with particles in the atoms they meet.

Astrophysicists have measured the intensity of this flood of neutrinos with special detectors. Paradoxically these 'neutrino telescopes', designed to study the heart of the Sun, are built deep underground. The purpose of this is to screen out other forms of radiation – cosmic rays and background radioactivity. To be sensitive enough to interact with the neutrinos the detectors have to be very large. The world's first solar neutrino detector, as big as a swimming pool, was built at the bottom of a gold mine in South Dakota, USA. The tank was filled with perchloroethylene – dry cleaning fluid. It contained a high proportion of chlorine, with which one of the billions of passing neutrinos would occasionally interact. The interaction would lead to the emission of an electron, which can easily be detected. In the 100,000 gallons (400,000 litres) of the fluid the experimenters calculated that they would catch some 25 neutrinos each month. In fact they observed on average only eight solar neutrinos each month.

The earliest experiments failed to detect *any* neutrinos and some theorists suggested that the Sun might have gone out – the reactions in its centre had ceased but the surface had not yet cooled off.

The solar pinball machine

If this were true, it would take about one million years for the surface to go cold. That is the time it takes electromagnetic energy – light, ultraviolet radiation, and x-rays – to work its way outwards from the centre. The radiation bounces from electron to electron in the densely packed matter at the Sun's core, like a ball bouncing in a pinball machine.

Now that neutrinos have been detected, we know that the Sun has not gone out. But since they are fewer than expected, it may be that the Sun has 'gone off the boil' and cooled off a little at the centre.

If the temperature were 10 per cent lower than the astrophysicists expected the low neutrino intensity would be accounted for. But this temperature is too low to keep up the observed output of heat and light from the surface. It could only be a temporary departure from the Sun's normal long-term state. This raises intriguing possibilities. Has the Sun been off colour for the past few million years? If so, could that possibly tie in with the recent spate of ice ages that has afflicted the Earth during roughly that time?

In the 1930s the physicists had to change their ideas to account for what the astronomers knew of the conditions inside the Sun. The boot may now be on the other foot. The astronomers may have to revise their notions of how stars work to take account of the physicists' knowledge of nuclear reactions. For the standard theories do not admit the possibility of stars varying – temporarily, we hope – in this way.

But should we hope for a return to 'normal'? After all, human beings emerged only during the last million years or so. The conditions on Earth that we regard as normal – ice ages included – may be due to a temporary misbehaviour of the Sun. If so, a return to the Sun's 'normal' state might mean a return to the tropical conditions in which dinosaurs dominated the Earth!

The first solar neutrino detector, at the bottom of a gold mine in South Dakota, USA. Since it has come into use it has registered fewer neutrinos from the depths of the Sun than theorists had expected

Further reading
R.J. Bray and R.E. Loughhead, *Sunspots*, Dover 1979
H.J. Eysenck and D.K.B. Nias, *Astrology: science or superstition?*, Maurice Temple Smith 1982
John Gribbin, *The strangest star*, Fontana 1980
Guy Lyon Playfair and Scott Hill, *The cycles of heaven*, Pan 1979

The pattern of the future

How does one distinguish between prediction and prophecy? Can the concept of free will accommodate predestination? BRIAN INNES takes a look at the principal methods of divination, and begins with the ancient, but still flourishing, art of geomancy

'How now, you secret, black, and midnight hags!' Macbeth and Banquo encounter the Weird Sisters on a heath near Forres. The witches' prophecies were to change Macbeth's life, but they predicted nothing that did not remain in his control

THROUGHOUT THE HISTORY of mankind, those who were concerned about what the future held for them have sought guidance from 'wise' men and women. From the Azande tribesman who offers a chicken to the witch doctor in return for a prognostication of next month's weather, to the investor consulting his astrologer for assistance in forecasting future movements of the stock market, the motives, the means and the advice have always been very similar. But for all those prepared to *prophesy*, few would be prepared to say that they could *predict*.

The dangers inherent in placing too exact an interpretation on prophecy are exemplified very neatly in Shakespeare's *Macbeth*. Macbeth has – as the historian A.L. Rowse very rightly puts it – 'a flawed and ruined nobility – he is the victim of the Weird Sisters' prophecies; or, rather, of the promptings to which their "prophecies" gave confirmation.' In other words, Macbeth is given information that he interprets in one way; but subsequent events show that an entirely different, and equally plausible, interpretation could have been made.

When Macbeth first meets the witches, they hail him as thane of Cawdor, and as 'Macbeth, that shalt be king hereafter'. They also greet Banquo:

First Witch: Lesser than Macbeth, and greater.
Second Witch: Not so happy, yet much happier.
Third Witch: Thou shalt get kings, though thou be none. . . .

Within minutes, Macbeth is named thane of Cawdor, and so, driven by ambition and the conviction that the witches have foretold his future, he murders King Duncan and himself becomes king of Scotland. Then, fearing that the rest of the witches' prophecy will also come true, he engineers the murder of Banquo – but Banquo's son Fleance escapes, and will sire a line of later kings.

But Macbeth must have more:
I will tomorrow,
And betimes I will, to the weird sisters:
More shall they speak; for now I am bent to know,
By the worst means, the worst.

The witches are only too happy to give Macbeth what he asks. They conjure up a succession of apparitions, who advise:

1. Beware Macduff.
2. None of woman born shall harm Macbeth.
3. Macbeth shall never be vanquished until Birnam wood comes to Dunsinane.
4. A line of kings shall follow Banquo's death.

Since he can do nothing about the last

Divination

prophecy, Macbeth determines to deal with the first. Learning that Macduff has already fled to England, he puts Lady Macduff and all her family to the sword. But he is greatly heartened by the other two prophecies, for they seem to imply clearly that no one shall harm him, and that he shall not be vanquished.

In the last scenes of the play, however, he discovers that the witches' words have another meaning. Birnam wood does indeed come to Dunsinane, for Malcolm's army wears its leafy branches as camouflage; and Macduff, who finally kills Macbeth, was not *born* of woman, but 'from his mother's womb untimely ripp'd' – that is, he was born by Caesarean section.

An inescapable fate?

Prophecy is the outcome of divination, and the example of Macbeth, and the advice given him by the witches, should serve to make clear the difference between divination and prediction. What the witches foretold was *not* predetermined: if Malcolm's men had not hidden behind leafy branches from Birnam wood, if Macduff had not returned from England to avenge the murder of his family, then Macbeth might well have lived out his reign and died in his own bed.

Indeed, Macbeth failed principally because of the psychological effect of the prophecies upon his self-confidence. The weird sisters did not make any specific predictions: they made only negative statements: 'None of woman born shall harm Macbeth...' and 'Macbeth shall never vanquished be until...'. They did not say that someone who was not born of woman *would* harm Macbeth; but the effect of their prophecy was that Macbeth's confidence was raised so high that, when he discovered that Macduff was not 'of woman born', he was immediately destroyed by his own guilt and superstitious fear.

If, then, divination is not prediction and is not concerned with predetermined events, what use is it? Why go to a fortune-teller with your problems, if a newspaper 'agony aunt' or even a close friend can provide you with a wealth of good advice? The reason, quite simply, is that the diviner does not make use of information that he or she consciously possesses about the person making the consultation: by the use of some means – whether it is the entrails of a freshly killed animal, arbitrarily chosen objects, a crystal ball, the astrological birth-chart of the subject or certain marks, such as moles, upon his person – the diviner is put in touch with information that is obtainable only by transcendental methods.

To those for whom a belief in the free will of the individual is paramount, the idea of a predetermined future is totally unacceptable. But look at it this way. Someone's birth can be compared to the launching of a space vehicle. At the moment of 'lift-off', all the conditions are known and understood by mission control: the rocket will follow a predetermined trajectory, and at a known time the vehicle will be detached and will follow a predetermined course. The astronaut need do nothing thereafter; he can leave the future manoeuvring of the vehicle to those on Earth. But he is also provided with manual controls that he can use himself; he may become bored and start tinkering with fine adjustments in flight that produce results he did not expect; or, in a fit of rage – or other show of temperament – he may throw himself about the capsule and disturb its equilibrium. Whatever he does, *of his own free will*, will be recorded by mission control; and they can immediately inform him what will be the outcome of his actions, however unplanned.

They can, however, only advise. If he persists in what he is doing he may miss his target and disappear for ever in the depths of space, and nothing that anybody on Earth can do will help him.

This is how divination works. The diviner can give advice on the basis of information that is not available to his subject; he can predict the outcome of a particular course of action and suggest an alternative; but he cannot state that any future event will definitely occur.

All divination, by whatever method, follows the same sequence:

First, a question is formulated. This may range from something very specific – such as 'Will I win today's lottery?' or 'Should I marry this man?' – to general enquiries of the form 'What will my future life be like?' Obviously, the more specific the question, the more specific the answer is likely to be – and, therefore, the more trustworthy it is for the enquirer. Generalised questions usually attract answers that are susceptible of many different interpretations.

Next, some physical means is employed to

Below: a geomancer practises his art. Reading meaning into randomly generated patterns remains popular. In the West, tea leaves are read, in other cultures the throwing of inscribed tablets – similar to the throwing of dice – is a common method of divination (divining tablets from Mashonaland, Zimbabwe, right). The belief persists that a specially gifted person – shaman, witch doctor or fortune teller (a Vietnamese stick thrower, below right) – is needed to practise divination, but it seems that almost anyone can

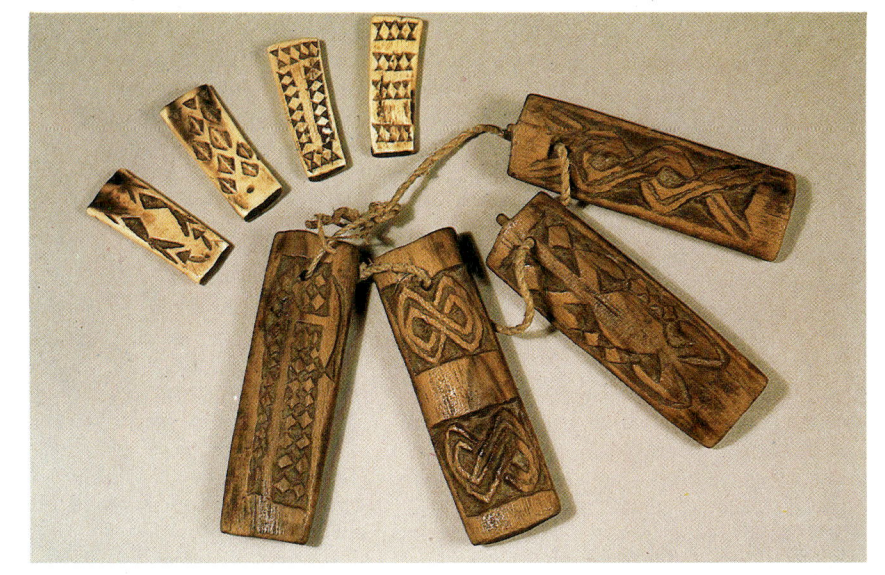

Divination

Left: the life of an individual can be compared to a space mission. Its purpose is known to mission control, who can – and do – manoeuvre the spacecraft from the Earth. Yet the crew could depart from the prearranged programme. Mission control could advise the crew not to, and they could still take no notice. Similarly, *we* have free will; divination can only advise us; it does not actually determine the future of our lives

provide a link between the enquirer and the diviner. The enquirer may be asked to provide an intimate possession, to touch something belonging to the diviner, or to make an arbitrary choice of cards from a pack, objects thrown to the ground, or any random arrangement of things from which he does not make a conscious selection. Or the diviner may employ some device, such as a crystal ball or a pendulum, on which he can concentrate so intensely that consciousness of his surroundings recedes to a point where he is effectively in a trance. Drugs may also be used for this purpose.

Skill – or cunning?

Then, avoiding any temptation to make use of knowledge he may consciously possess about the enquirer, or to reason logically from one premise to another, the diviner *intuitively* produces his 'message'. Depending upon his skill – or cunning – this message may be straightforward advice of a practical nature, or a succession of cryptic statements that only the enquirer can interpret for himself. Frequently, as innumerable tales throughout history have told us, this advice can appear so obscure that the enquirer despairs of it; on occasion, diviners have been killed by their clients in an agony of frustration.

The methods of divination have their own archaic names, from abacomancy – divination from patterns of dust – to zoomancy – the observation of the behaviour of animals. There are, however, five methods of divination that have particularly attracted the attention of practitioners over the centuries, and that have therefore gathered about them a vast amount of literature and working tradition. These are astrology (see page 561), cartomancy, cheiromancy, geomancy, and the Chinese method of divination known as the *I Ching*.

Although astrology has claimed to be the oldest of these, there is little doubt that geomancy is as old – and it is certainly the simplest. In this context, geomancy got its name from the practice of making a pattern of holes in the earth, and should not be confused with the Chinese practice of *feng-shui*, which is concerned with finding propitious places on which to erect tombs, build houses or found cities.

Geomancy, in fact, may be the surviving ancestor of the *I Ching*: the divinatory figures of geomancy are made up of four lines, and those of the *I Ching* of six. Since each line can take one of two forms, the total number of combinations in geomancy is only 16, compared with the 64 of the *I Ching*.

The lines may be marked in the dust or earth – which is how the art of geomancy got its name; or they may be made up of kernels or stones; or they may of course be marked on paper.

The art is said to have originated in Persia, but it is widespread over the whole of the Mediterranean region, the near East and much of Africa, and since its spread over this area followed the spread of Islam it is at least possible that Arab traders had brought it from China. In Malagasy, geomancy is known as *sikidi*; on the west coast of Africa as *djabe* or *fa*. In Europe, the first full description occurs in the second book of the *Occult philosophy* of Cornelius Agrippa (1531).

The right lines

The 'lines' from which the geomantic figure is derived can be obtained in a wide variety of ways. They may be straight horizontal lines traced – randomly and without conscious direction – in the dust, which are distinguished as short or long lines; or they may be either straight or wavy. These two classes of line are then identified as 'odd' or 'even', and are represented conventionally by either one or two stones, palm kernels or dots. Or the lines may be made up of a random succession of dots, the oddness or evenness being determined by the number of dots. In

Divination

fa, a handful of 18 palm kernels is passed from the left to the right hand, and the number of kernels remaining in the left hand is counted as either odd or even.

To make a geomantic figure, four lines are required. If, for instance, the first and third are even, and the second and fourth odd, the resultant figure will be:

Altogether, there are 16 of these figures, each with its own name and significance, as detailed in the accompanying table.

Below: how the geomantic figures are traditionally interpreted in the four main methods – the European, which uses Latin designations; the two West African systems of *fa* and *djabe*; and the *sikidi* of Malagasy

The meaning of the figures

Figure	Latin name	Fa	Djabe	Sikidi
	Puer Yellow; rash, inconsiderate	**Lete** Abscess	**Kaoussadji** Long Life	**Alakarabo** Leads to danger
	Amissio Loss	**Tche** Pearl	**Marili** Sickness	**Adalo** Tears; protection against enemies
	Albus White; wisdom	**Touloukpin** Unripe papaya fruit	**Baiala** Family	**Alohomora** Favourable to thieves
	Populus The crowd	**Yekou** Spirits of the dead	**Djamaha** The crowd	**Asombola** Plenty
	Fortuna major Good luck	**Houolin** Pointed shell	**Adouhi** Victory over an enemy	**Adabaray** Fire
	Conjunctio Joining together	**Holi** Removal of an obstacle	**Dam'hi** Success	**Alatsimay** Protects thieves and enemies
	Puella Girl; pretty face	**Toula** A firing gun	**Nagiha** Soon	**Alikisy** Good fortune in love; riches
	Rubeus Red; passion, vice	**Ka** Canoe	**Oumra** Marriage	**Alabiavo** Riches, jewels
	Aquisitio Success, gains, good fortune	**Fou** Blowing the fire	**Kali** Good fortune on the right; bad on the left	**Alihotsy** Lightness of spirit
	Carcer Prison, delay, confinement	**Di** Resistance	**Sikaf** Law, command	**Akikola** Protects vagabonds
	Tristitia Sorrow, melancholy	**Aklan** Porous stone	**Mankuss** Death	**Betsivongo** Obsession, tears
	Laetitia Joy, health, beauty	**Abla** Connection	**Laila** Riches	**Alahijana** Strength; happy marriage
	Cauda Draconis Exit, lower kingdom	**Gouda** Evil gods	**Sahili or Haridja** Serious intentions	**Karija** Fate
	Caput Draconis Entrance, upper kingdom	**Sa** Between the thighs	**Raia** Health	**Alakaosy** Evil fate, disputes, war
	Fortuna Minor Less good fortune; external aid	**Losso** Riven tree	**Sapari** Journeys	**Soralahy** Pride, domination
	Via The way, journeys	**Gbe** Language	**Dariki** Children	**Taraiky** Loneliness; death

In Africa, these figures are interpreted singly, or in pairs. In the European tradition, the procedure is more complicated. In the first operation 16 lines are produced, and these are used to generate four 'Mother' figures. Suppose for example that the four following Mothers are produced:

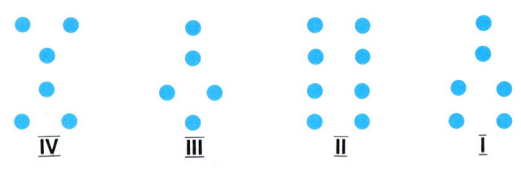

IV   III   II   I

These are respectively: Fortuna Minor, Populus, Puer and Conjunctio.

From these four Mothers four Daughters are produced, by adding the four lines horizontally, from right to left:

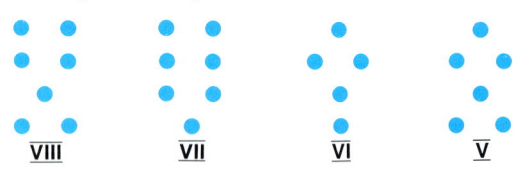

VIII   VII   VI   V

These are, respectively, Amissio, Puella, Tristitia and Albus.

Now four Nephews must be produced. The first Nephew is obtained by adding *together* the first and second Mothers, and marking the sum as before, with one dot for odd and two dots for even. So, from the first two Mothers, we get:

Fortuna minor
IX

And from the second two Mothers:

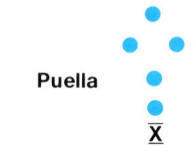

Puella
X

Similarly the third and fourth Nephews are formed by adding together the first and second, and the third and fourth, Daughters:

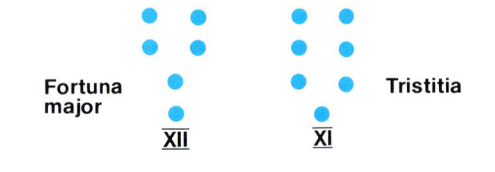

Fortuna major   **Tristitia**
XII   XI

From the Nephews, two Witnesses are obtained by the same process of adding together:

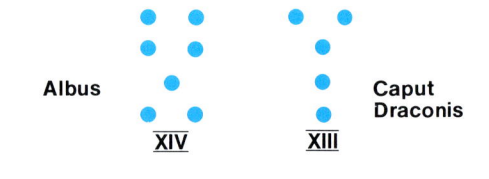

Albus   **Caput Draconis**
XIV   XIII

And finally, a Judge is obtained by adding together the lines of the two Witnesses:

Acquisitio
· ·
 ·
 ·
·
XV

Right: a South African witch doctor casts and reads the 'wise stones'

The final pattern of 15 geomantic figures will provide the answer to one of 16 questions:
1. Will he have a long life?
2. Will he become rich?
3. Should he undertake the project?
4. How will the undertaking end?
5. Is the expected child a boy or a girl?
6. Are the servants honest?
7. Will the patient soon recover?
8. Will the lover be successful?
9. Will the inheritance be obtained?
10. Will the lawsuit be won?
11. Will he obtain employment?
12. How will he die?
13. Will the expected letter arrive?
14. Will the journey be successful?
15. Will good news arrive soon?
16. Will the adversary be overcome?

It can be seen that these questions cover most common preoccupations; with experience, the analysis of the geomantic pattern can be applied to other, rather more specific questions.

How are the figures interpreted, and how is the question answered? Let us suppose that the example above was obtained in answer to the question 'Will the lawsuit be won?'

In this case the Judge is Acquisitio, which signifies success, and the two Witnesses are Caput Draconis and Albus. These are all

Below: on the west coast of Africa, in the geomantic method known as *fa*, palm kernels are passed from hand to hand for a few moments. Those that end up in the left hand are counted and the geomantic figures are then formed from them

fortunate omens, and the implication is that wisdom will prevail and the lawsuit will be won with honour. We can investigate the progress of the lawsuit by considering the pattern of figures from the beginning. The outcome of the suit depends upon others (Fortuna Minor), whom we may suppose are the jury (Populus), likely to behave capriciously (Puer), but finally reaching a common verdict (Conjunctio). Perhaps the possibility of losing the suit (Amissio) is concerned with a girl (Puella), who can be the cause of sorrow (Tristitia) unless wisdom (Albus) prevails. The representative (Fortuna Minor) of the girl (Puella) could be a danger (Tristitia), but good fortune (Fortuna Major) will be the final outcome.

Open to interpretation

Geomancy is the most primitive of all the methods of divination, but this example shows clearly how adaptable it is as a means of interpretation. Because of the sequence of operations by which the Judges and Witnesses are obtained, there are only eight possible Judges – Acquisitio, Amissio, Fortuna Major, Fortuna Minor, Populus, Via, Conjunctio, Carcer – and each of these Judges has a possible eight combinations of Witness, this figure being doubled due to the fact that each Witness may stand on either right or left of the Judge. Altogether, therefore, there are 128 possible configurations of Judge and Witnesses, each of which can be an answer to one of 16 questions.

Methods of divination to be considered in succeeding articles are far more complex. In the *I Ching*, for example, there are 64 basic figures; while in the use of the Tarot cards there are a minimum of 22 cards, which may be disposed in an almost infinite variety of ways.

How effective is the I Ching *as a method of divination today? See page 1926*

Murder by moonlight

Close examination of the Bible yields evidence of an attempt to suppress an ancient tradition of Moon worship. STAN GOOCH argues the remarkable hypothesis that dim but potent echoes of this religion still persist

WHAT WAS THE NATURE of the old religion that was supplanted by Judaism? We have seen that it was probably a fertility religion in which worship of the Moon played an important part (see page 1875). This is strongly implied by certain evidence from the Bible. A new religion generally suppresses those elements of the religion it supplants that it cannot absorb, and the fact that the number 13 appears to have undergone a considerable purging from the Old Testament suggests that 13 may have had some significance in the old religion. Thirteen is the number of houses in the Moon zodiac – it is the number of full or new Moons in the solar year – and is therefore of central importance in Moon worship.

There are passages in the Old Testament that make it clear that a flourishing tradition of Moon worship existed alongside Judaism. In Isaiah 1:13-14, for example, God, speaking through the prophet, says:

> Bring no more vain oblations; incense is an abomination to me; the new moons and sabbaths, the calling of assemblies, I cannot away with; it is iniquity, even the solemn meeting.
> Your new moons and your appointed feasts my soul hateth: they are a trouble unto me; I am weary to bear them.

And in Hosea 2:11, speaking of the iniquitous state of Judaism, he says:

> I will also cause all her mirth to cease, her feast days, her new moons, and her sabbaths, and all her solemn feasts.

Turning to what at first seems to be entirely different evidence, there are some important connections between the numbers 7 – which retains an important place in the Bible – and 13, which has been largely purged. Seven is the midpoint between 1 and 13:

$$1\ 2\ 3\ 4\ 5\ 6\ 7\ 8\ 9\ 10\ 11\ 12\ 13$$

Midpoints are extremely important in all occult thought – midnight, the midwinter solstice, midsummer's day, for instance. The main origins of this general concern about midpoints are probably midwinter (will the slain Sun live again this year?) and midnight (will the hidden Sun come back to us once more?).

The midpoint between one and seven is four, thus:

$$1\ 2\ 3\ 4\ 5\ 6\ 7$$

Multiplying the two mid-numbers and 13 itself together, $7 \times 4 \times 13$, gives 364 – the number of days in a full year – or almost. The number we need is 365 – and this is why, Robert Graves tells us, ancient legends refer not to a year, but to a year and a day $(364 + 1)$. There is more: the number of quarters of the Moon, $4 \times 7 = 28$; and 28, is of course, the average length of the female menstrual cycle.

Ancient Egyptian tombs, dating back to around 3000 BC, contain some very curious magical implements or 'chess boards'. On these boards there is room only for the pieces themselves – none for moving them. There are always either 7 or 13 pieces along each

Holy blood, Holy Grail

side of the board – 49 or 169 pieces altogether – and, more significant, the pieces themselves are always in the shape of half-moons. Osiris, to whose cult these items belong, was one instance of a 'Horned God', and his sister Isis was a 'Horned Goddess' (see page 1875). But Robert Graves tells us that Isis was not originally the sister of Osiris but his mother, and that she ruled before him.

The American researcher James Vogh, aware that there might be a Moon zodiac of greater antiquity than the familiar Sun zodiac, set out to discover the thirteenth sign of the Moon zodiac. He found it to be Arachne, the Cretan spider goddess. One of his major pieces of evidence was a mosaic zodiac from a Jewish gnostic synagogue, Beth Alpha, in the Jezreel Valley in Israel. It is clear that this has been altered from a 13-house to a 12-house zodiac. In the middle sits a spider-like figure, Arachne, with 13 items in her headdress and the crescent Moon on her left shoulder.

Vogh also became fascinated by the many ancient legends in which threads are used to lead people out of labyrinths, and their connections with spiders' webs – and, via them, with the spider goddess Arachne. One of the most important labyrinths of the ancient world was that of Knossos, which flourished with the Minoan civilisation around 2500 BC. At the centre of the labyrinth was said to live the strange creature known as the Minotaur, the offspring of a bull and of the wife of Minos, the king of Crete, herself the daughter of the Moon. Vogh took the name *Minotaur*, split it and reversed the order of the pieces. He now had *taur* and *min* – with the *o*, he conjectured, perhaps representing the Moon. From this and other evidence, advanced in his book *Arachne rising: the thirteenth sign* (1977), he deduces that the sign of Arachne must originally have fallen between the two consecutive signs of Taurus and Gemini.

Many lines of evidence suggest that the spider goddess, the Moon goddess, and the universal earth mother – who seems to have made her appearance somewhat later than these two – are one and the same. But perhaps of more immediate importance is Vogh's suggestion that the many instances of pre-Christian crosses are actually stylised spiders. The variant of the cross we call the swastika is perhaps the most literally suggestive of the spider; and Vogh has many spider amulets from North America with a cross in a circle drawn upon their backs.

Top: a spider's web, symbol of delusion and captivity. Researcher James Vogh believes he has discovered the thirteenth sign of the Moon zodiac – that of the spider goddess Arachne, shown at the centre of a zodiac from the gnostic synagogue at Beth Alpha (above)

Left: the Immaculate Conception, by Murillo (1617–1682). The Virgin Mary is traditionally shown trampling a crescent Moon. Could this be an indication that Christianity superseded a religion of Moon worship?

Baleful Moon dew

As previously mentioned, Moon and menstruation are derived from the same root, and scientific study has shown that the Moon is closely related to the female menstrual cycle. A menstruating woman is a fertile woman, and few things were more important to ancient peoples than a regular supply of new babies to ensure the continued existence of the tribe. Women also apparently dream more at menstruation than at other times, but in any case the connections between menstruation and mysticism are legion. Robert Graves tells us that 'the baleful moon dew of the witches of Thessaly was a girl's first menstrual blood taken during an eclipse of the moon.' The sabbath, both the Christian and the witches' version, was originally the festival of the Moon goddess's menstruation. All early peoples – Europeans, Asians, North

Holy blood, Holy Grail

and South American Indians, Africans and Australian Aborigines – believed that the red soil found throughout the world was the blood of the Moon goddess shed when giving birth to the planet Earth. This red soil is everywhere regarded as a magical substance. Some authors have seen among its various descendants the ash of Ash Wednesday, and the 'red powder' that, in many folk tales from all over Europe, could turn base metals into gold or silver.

It seems much more likely, however, that this belief is a confused memory of the sacrificial blood and the menstrual blood of women, and the goddess who turned the dead land of winter into the gold of summer and autumn. The so-called noble metals of the alchemists, gold and silver, do happen also to be the colours of the Sun and Moon.

In summary, it seems we have evidence of a garbled and distorted memory of a religion of enormous antiquity – a fertility religion in which worship of the Moon played a central part.

Let us now turn our attention to a number of legends and fairy tales.

The story of Sleeping Beauty is as follows. A great king invites 12 good fairies to attend the christening of his daughter. Each bestows a blessing on the child. But a thirteenth, evil, fairy, who has not been invited, now appears and curses the child with death if she should ever prick her finger. Despite all precautions, she does, and falls into a permanent sleep. All around her, the castle and its lands also fall dead. One day, however, a brave knight finds his way to the castle, and at his kiss the princess and her lands come once again to life.

King Arthur of Britain has in his castle a round table at which he sits with his 12 most favoured knights – a total of 13. All the knights are loyal except the rebellious and traitorous Mordred. While Arthur is absent, Mordred usurps the kingdom and marries Guinevere, Arthur's wife. On Arthur's return, he and Mordred fight, and deal each other mortal wounds. Arthur is said not to be dead, however, but only sleeping. One day he will awake and return to lead his people once more.

In Scandinavian mythology, the story of the death of Balder, the most loved of the gods, is as follows. A banquet is held in Valhalla to which 12 of the gods have been invited. While the feast is in progress Loki, the spirit of strife and mischief, who has not been invited, nevertheless turns up as the thirteenth guest. He gives blind Hoder an arrow of mistletoe, and gets him to shoot it. It kills Balder. In the Saxon version of the story, Balder is resurrected, and the golden age of mankind begins.

The story of Christ's crucifixion is this. Christ leads a band of 12 disciples – making a band of 13 altogether. Christ is betrayed by a

Above: a carving of the ancient fertility goddess, known as a Sheila-na-gig, being seduced by the Lord of the Underworld, on the porch of the church of St Mary, Whittlesford, Cambridgeshire. Fertility is immensely important in all primitive societies – the face of this Brazilian girl (left) has been smeared with red ochre to ensure her fertility; it is a symbol of the blood that, her tribe believes, was shed by the Earth mother when she was giving birth to the Earth. In his book The white goddess, Robert Graves (below) argues that the idea of a fertility goddess pre-dates notions of male gods – and the Moon is perhaps the oldest fertility goddess

Holy blood, Holy Grail

Further reading
Michael Baigent, Richard Leigh and Henry Lincoln, *The holy blood and the Holy Grail*, Jonathan Cape 1982
Stan Gooch, *Guardians of the ancient wisdom*, Fontana 1979
James Vogh, *Arachne rising: the thirteenth sign*, Granada 1977

King Arthur and Mordred fight their battle to the death (above left); Loki incites the blind Hoder to kill Balder (above right); the Sleeping Beauty is awakened by a kiss (left); and Christ is betrayed by Judas (below left). In all these stories, the 'best' or most beloved member of a group is killed by the weakest – but comes to life again, heralding a period of joy and well-being. These stories may all mirror the drama of the natural year, in which, in the short or 'weak' lunar month – at the winter solstice – the Sun is 'betrayed' and 'dies', only to come to life again, bringing summer and plenty

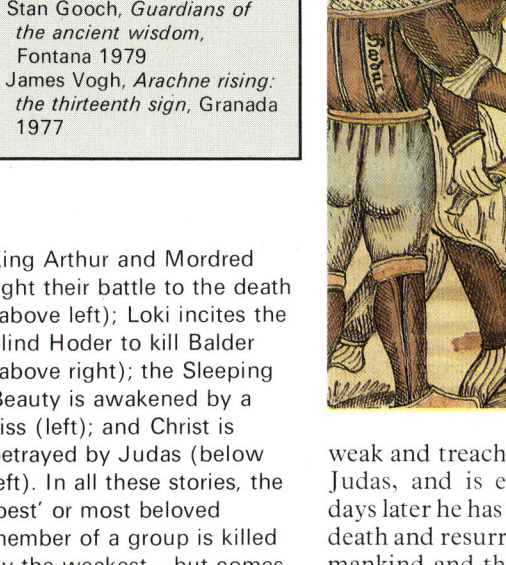

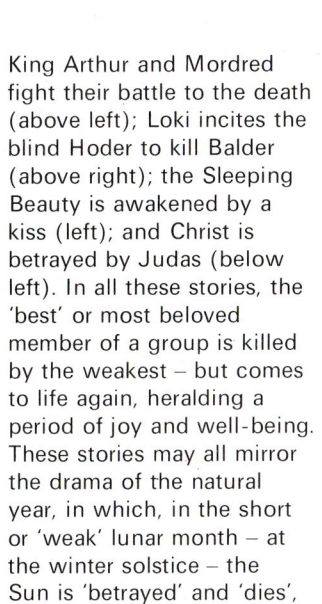

Below: the seal of the English Templars, bearing the device of the crescent Moon – the beginning, and perhaps the end, of the mysteries unravelled in the 1982 bestseller *The holy blood and the Holy Grail*

weak and treacherous member of the group, Judas, and is executed. Nevertheless, two days later he has risen from the dead. Christ's death and resurrection signal redemption for mankind and the promise of eternal life.

The parallels in these stories are obvious. In each of them, the most beloved is killed by the one evil or weak member of a group of 13. The most beloved dies and desolation follows. But the most beloved comes to life again, and all will be well once more.

It seems clear that these stories are all metaphorical representations of the cycle of the year. They are all the story of the Sun who is killed each year by the Moon, but is then immediately resurrected by her to bring another golden summer. The Moon year contains only twelve and a half complete cycles of the Moon. The thirteenth lunar month is therefore short and 'weak'. It is in this 'weak' month that the Sun dies.

Confirmation of this interpretation comes from the Saxon version of the Balder story, where Balder and Hoder die fighting for the hand of the virgin Moon. Moreover, in Scandinavian mythology Balder is the 'god of the summer sunlight', whereas Hoder represents 'darkness and winter'.

The authors of *The holy blood and the Holy Grail* are quite emphatic that Mary Magdalene's role in the Bible story has been heavily censored (see page 1823) – and I entirely agree with them. I go further however: I believe she is the representative of a cult of Moon worship, and that the story of Christ's crucifixion is the story of a ritual killing, a confused relic of a time when sacrifice of the king was believed necessary to ensure the continued fertility of the land and tribe. The Priory of Sion, for whose existence Michael Baigent, Richard Leigh and Henry Lincoln argue so persuasively, is the guardian of this ancient tradition of Moon worship – very old, very powerful and still flourishing to this day right at the centre of Western civilisation.

The British scareship invasion

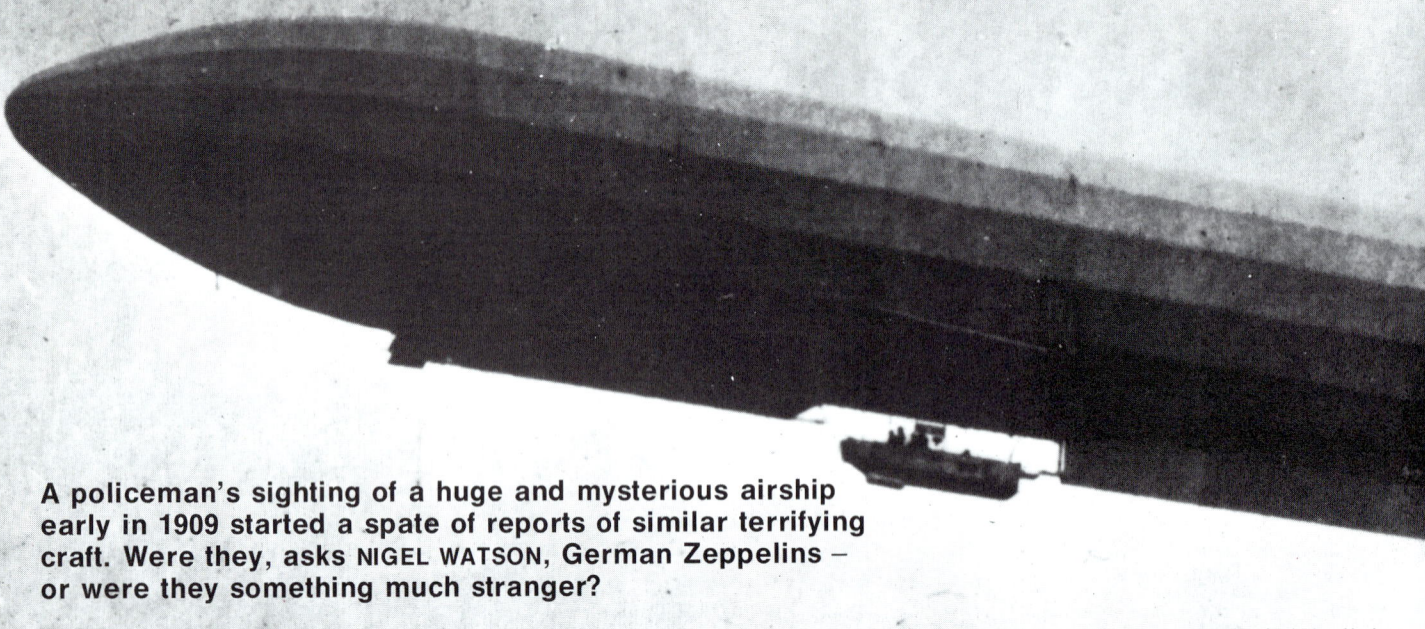

A policeman's sighting of a huge and mysterious airship early in 1909 started a spate of reports of similar terrifying craft. Were they, asks NIGEL WATSON, German Zeppelins – or were they something much stranger?

IN THE EARLY MONTHS of 1909 an aerial horror began to haunt the imaginations of the British people. The first sighting of a phantom airship to have a major impact on the public consciousness was made by a Cambridgeshire policeman, PC Kettle. He was patrolling Cromwell Road in Peterborough on the morning of 23 March when he heard the sound of a distant motor car. As he continued to 'hear the steady buzz of a high power engine' he suddenly realised that the noise was coming from above. On looking up he saw a bright light attached to a long oblong body outlined against the stars. This strange aerial object crossed the sky at a high speed, and was soon lost from sight.

News of this sighting was met with a certain amount of scepticism. Nevertheless, it set the pattern for future 'airship' watchers: reports from people who had seen bright, powerful lamps or searchlights attached to dark bodies making a noisy passage across the night sky soon became numerous. Another common feature of such stories was the happy habit of many self-proclaimed experts of submitting explanations for such marvellous visions. In the case of PC Kettle's sighting, a Peterborough police officer announced to the press that a 'very fine kite flying over the neighbourhood of Cobden

Above: an early dirigible, the Zeppelin Mark 2, in flight over Lake Constance in April 1909. The same year, there was a spate of mystery airship sightings throughout Britain. Many people believed that the aircraft were German Zeppelins making reconnaissance flights in preparation for an invasion of Britain – but German airships were far too unreliable for it to be possible to employ them on such a dangerous mission

Below: Cromwell Road, Peterborough, the site of the first 'scareship' sighting

Street' had been the cause. The bright light was easily explained as a Chinese lantern that had been attached to the kite.

'But how about the matter of the airship going at a tremendous pace?' asked a reporter.

'Oh, that was a little poetic touch on Kettle's part for the benefit of you interviewers. He did not officially report that, and the wind driving the kite would give the impression of movement,' replied the officer.

'But how do you get over the whirring and beating of engines?' asked the still puzzled reporter.

'Oh, that,' responded the officer, as he went to take his leave, 'was the motor which goes all night in the Co-operative Bakery in Cobden Street!'

This bland dismissal of PC Kettle's observation might have carried more weight if it had been released soon after the sighting.

British scareships

Instead, it took the Peterborough police at least six weeks to arrive at this simple answer to the mystery of the airship. It seems they preferred to imply that PC Kettle was a simpleton who could not distinguish between a kite and an airship, rather than to see the Peterborough police force implicated in giving credence to such an unlikely story.

At first PC Kettle's observation seemed an isolated occurrence. But around the beginning of May sightings began to be reported daily throughout south-east England. A typical report was made by a Mr C. W. Allen. As he and some friends were driving through the village of Kelmarsh, Northamptonshire, on 13 May, they heard a loud bang. Then above them they heard the 'tock-tock-tock' sound of a motor engine. Although the sky was dark they were able to see a 100-foot (30-metre) long torpedo-shaped airship that carried lights fore and aft. It was moving swiftly, but this did not prevent the witnesses seeing a platform suspended beneath the craft, which appeared to contain its crew. The airship disappeared in the direction of Peterborough.

There were many more such reports. But what were the aircraft? The fact that the exploits of Count Zeppelin were well-known in Britain (see box), combined with the antagonism between Germany and Britain, soon led people to believe that German airships were making a reconnaissance in preparation for a future invasion.

Right: a clipping from the Cardiff *Evening Express and Evening Mail* of Wednesday, 19 May 1909 describes a sighting of the mystery airship made by Mr C. Lethbridge on 18 May on Caerphilly Mountain. Mr Lethbridge saw a huge 'long, tube-shaped object' lying on the grass at the side of the road. Newspaper cuttings relating to airship sightings and to German military matters were later found scattered over the area

Below: the Wellman airship at the Aero Show of 1909. Prior to the First World War, Britain devoted very little research to airships; government construction was begun in 1907, but at the outbreak of war in 1914 only five British ships had been built

The major flaw in the hypothesis, however, was the sheer number of airship sighting reports, which came from all regions of Britain. At the time, Germany barely had the resources to make even one or two reconnaissance flights over Britain. For this reason, a few newspapers were prepared to discount the entire phenomenon as imaginary, and sent readers who had reported airship sightings to what they picturesquely called 'lunacy experts'. From one expert, they received this diagnosis:

In every thousand men there are always two every night who see strange matters – chromatic rats, luminous owls, moving lights, fiery comets, and things like those. So you can always get plenty of evidence of this sort, particularly when you suggest it to the patient first.

The most puzzling and sensational sighting was made by an elderly Punch and Judy showman, Mr C. Lethbridge. With this report, made on 18 May, the focus for the airship's activities shifted from the east coast to mid Glamorgan, Wales. By now there were well-attested reports of a 'long-shaped

British scareships

A phantom fleet?

Could the mysterious airships seen over Britain during 1909 have been German Zeppelins? It seems unlikely.

The pioneer of German airship research was Count Ferdinand von Zeppelin (right), who launched his first dirigible, the *Luftschiff Zeppelin 1* – or *LZ1* – over Lake Constance in July 1900, shortly before his sixty-second birthday. *LZ1*, simply an enormous bag filled with gas and propelled by an engine, remained in the air for just over 17 minutes – but its short flight was impressive, and the future of airships seemed bright.

Count Zeppelin set in motion an ambitious airship-building programme, but by 1909, owing to a number of crashes and shortage of money, there were only three working Zeppelins in existence – the *LZ3*, rebuilt from an earlier airship that had crashed, the *LZ5* and the *LZ6*. Of these, only two, the *LZ3* and the *LZ5*, were in the hands of the army – and they were very much in their experimental stages, and certainly not capable of long and hazardous journeys, or of carrying out the high-speed manoeuvres reported by the witnesses of the British 'scareships'.

---

object' with red flashing lights seen over Belfast, Ireland, on 17 May, and there seemed to be no area of Britain left unaffected by the scare. A few hours after his sighting – which amounted to a close encounter – Mr Lethbridge told inquisitive reporters:

Yesterday I went to Senghenydd and proceeded to walk home over Caerphilly Mountain. You know that the top of the mountain is a very lonely spot. I reached it about 11 p.m., and when turning the bend at the summit I was surprised to see a long, tube-shaped affair lying on the grass at the roadside, with two men busily engaged with something nearby. They attracted my close attention because of their peculiar get-up; they appeared to have big, heavy fur coats and fur caps fitting tightly over their heads. I was rather frightened, but I continued to go on until I was within twenty yards [18 metres] of them and then my idea as to their clothing was confirmed. The noise of my little spring-cart seemed to attract them and when they saw me they jumped up and jabbered furiously to each other in a strange lingo – Welsh or something else; it was certainly not English. They hurriedly collected something from the ground, and then I was really frightened. The long thing on the ground rose up slowly. I was standing still all the time, quite amazed, and when it was hanging a few feet off the ground the men jumped into

Left: the 'scareship' seen by Mr C. Lethbridge on Caerphilly Mountain on 18 May 1909 'rose in the air in a zig-zag fashion' and sailed away towards Cardiff

Right: Ham Common, on the outskirts of London. Here, on the night of 13 May 1909, a Mr Grahame and a Mr Bond saw a remarkable airship whose pilots, whom they described as a Yankee and a German, apparently steered their craft by pulling beer handles

British scareships

Right: the village of Kelmarsh, Northamptonshire where, on 13 May 1909, a Mr C. W. Allen saw a 100-foot (30-metre) airship moving swiftly north-eastwards

Below: a cartoon published in *Punch* of 26 May 1909. The cartoon shows a sea serpent staring glumly at a headline in the *Daily Scare*: 'Mysterious air-ship seen everywhere by night' – and commenting, 'Well, if this sort of thing keeps on, it'll mean a dull August for me'

a kind of little carriage suspended from it, and gradually the whole affair and the men rose in the air in a zig-zag fashion. When they had cleared the telegraph wires that pass over the mountain, two lights like electric lamps shone out, and the thing went higher into the air and sailed away towards Cardiff.

When Mr Lethbridge, accompanied by reporters, returned to the site where he had his encounter, they found several traces of the airship's presence. The ground where the 45-foot (14-metre) long object had been seen was churned up as though by a plough-share. All over the area they discovered a quantity of newspaper cuttings of accounts of airship sightings and references to the German emperor and army. Along with these items they found a large quantity of papier-mâché packing material, a lid from a tin of metal polish, a few dozen pieces of blue paper bearing strange writing, and a metal pin with a red label attached to it. The label of the pin carried instructions in French and excited attention when some commentators thought that it was part of an explosive device, but further enquiry showed it probably to have been a valve plunger for a motor car tyre.

Several witnesses came forward to support Lethbridge's story. In Salisbury Road, Cathays, Cardiff, residents said that on the same evening, between 10.40 and 10.50 p.m., they saw an airship-like object in the air.

Cigar-shaped 'boat'

Additional testimony came from workers on Cardiff docks who, two hours after Lethbridge's encounter, saw a fast moving 'boat of cigar shape' flying from the direction of Newport, and going eastwards. The airship carried two lights, and its engines made a loud whirring noise. One witness said, 'We could not see those on board. The airship was too high up for that at night, but it was plain that it was a big airship.'

Two gentlemen, a Mr Grahame and a Mr Bond, made some even more extravagant claims, to the effect that they had seen a 200- to 230-foot (60- to 70-metre) long airship 'like a collection of big cigar boxes with the ends out' on Ham Common, London. The occupants of the craft, whom they met on the night of 13 May, they described as a clean-shaven Yankee and a German who smoked a calabash pipe. The German asked for some tobacco, which Mr Grahame supplied out of his own pouch. Although they were blinded by a searchlight that played on their faces, the witnesses were able to see that the 'Yankee' was positioned in a kind of wire cage, and in front of him he had a row of levers similar to draught beer pump handles. In front of the German was positioned a map with pins dotted all over it. The encounter apparently came to an abrupt end when the 'Yankee' pulled one of the levers down, 'and then he switched the light off, and the aeroplane went without either of the men saying good-bye.'

With such a variety of bizarre reports, it is hardly surprising that the mystery of the phantom scareship that plagued Britain in 1909 has proved difficult to solve.

On page 1938: more sightings – and parliamentary questions are asked

A touching story

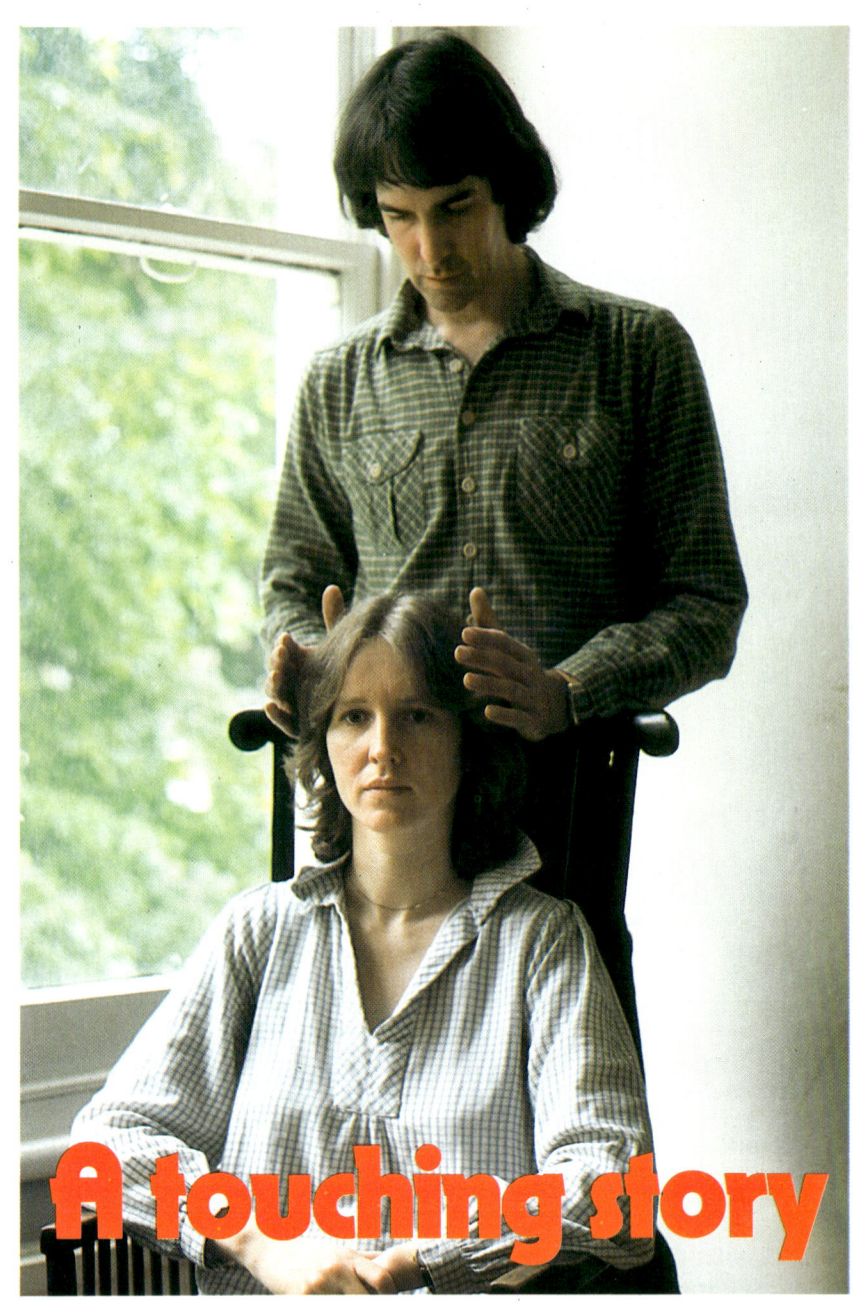

Stroking, pummelling, twisting and massaging – many kinds of touch and manipulation are used in both orthodox and unorthodox therapies. RUTH WEST scrutinises the part that touch plays in healing

A PREMATURE BABY lying in an incubator will put on weight more rapidly if it has a sheepskin, and not an ordinary sheet, to lie on. An asthma sufferer given regular massage ceases to have any serious asthma attacks. An emotionally disturbed teenager cradled by people of his own age and gently rocked in their arms is calmed by this experience of being securely held. What do these three cases have in common? The application of the idea that touch is in itself therapeutic. It may be that underlying some of the alternative therapies are an intuitive use and understanding of the healing value of touch.

Since the 1940s evidence has built up showing that it is of fundamental importance to healthy physical and emotional development to be touched a great deal, especially during the first stages of life. Without adequate tactile stimulation in infancy many physical and behavioural disorders can develop, and such stimulation may in fact be a primary human need.

Classic experiments suggesting that this is so were carried out by Professor Harry Harlow in the 1950s, working with rhesus monkeys. He found that monkeys deprived of contact with a warm, loving mother during their infancy were seriously impaired in their later emotional development.

The anthropologist Ashley Montagu goes one step further back: to the process of birth itself. He suggests that if there is inadequate stimulation of the skin during labour – as in Caesarean or very rapid births – then the infant is inadequately prepared for the period immediately after birth. Respiration, circulation, digestion, elimination and the nervous and endocrine systems are all activated by the prolonged uterine contractions of labour, he believes. He cites studies of Caesarean-born children showing that more disorders and diseases occur among them, and that they have a mortality rate two or three times higher than in ordinary deliveries.

An American behavioural scientist, Dr Donald Barron, studied goat kids delivered by Caesarean section. He found that those that were rubbed dry after birth seemed to be partly compensated for the lack of stimulation during birth. They got up on their legs and prepared to face the world more quickly than those who were not so treated.

Alexander Lowen has attributed schizophrenia to a lack of body contact, leading to failure to establish a sense of personal identity. And there are a number of accounts of breakthroughs being achieved when schizophrenic patients experience warm, human bodily contact. And, of course, there is no

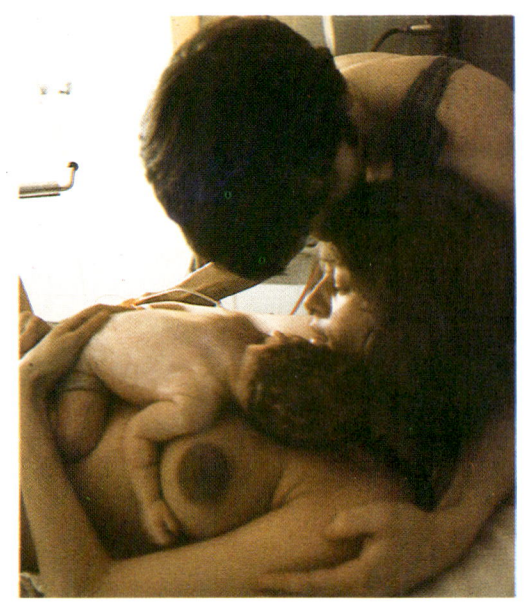

Above: a healer at work with a patient. The rapport between the two is nurtured by gentle touch – a 'laying on of hands' that seems to stimulate the body's own healing powers

Right: parents with their new-born child. Advocates of natural childbirth stress the importance of cuddling and hugging for healthy development

Alternative healing

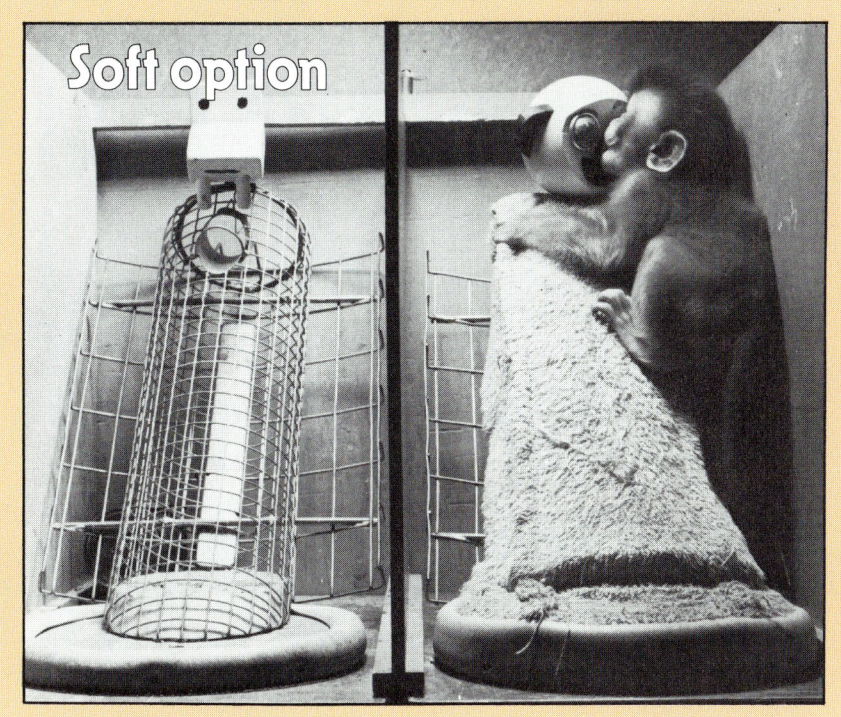

Soft option

The importance to an infant monkey of its mother's touch was studied in the 1950s by an American behavioural scientist, Harry Harlow. In one series of experiments a monkey was brought up in a cubicle with two 'surrogate mothers' (left). One was a cylindrical frame of bare wire, of such a size that the infant could easily cling to it. The other was similar except that it was covered with soft towelling.

In some of the experiments only one 'mother' dispensed milk through a teat; in others both did so. After only a few days of life with these 'mothers', an infant would choose to spend a high proportion of its time climbing over and clinging to the cloth-covered figure while almost ignoring the one made of bare wire. It would do this even when it received all its milk from the bare wire figure alone. Even making the surrogate mother warmer or giving it the ability to rock the infant did not outweigh the importance of its bodily 'feel'.

lack of informal everyday observation to show us that we make use of touch continually to relieve tension. When no one else is available to soothe us, we resort to comforting ourselves by means of touch: tugging ear lobes, telling the rosary, playing with 'worry beads', scratching the chin and so on.

The wisdom of the body

Suppose that sufficient weight of evidence were to accumulate to persuade researchers to take seriously the idea of touch as therapy – how might it be explained? Ainslie Meares, an Australian psychiatrist, explains the therapeutic value of touch through his theory of 'atavistic regression'. There exists, he says, an instinctive level of functioning in human beings, operating through more primitive parts of the brain, a level on which emotional responses occur and thinking is intuitive and non-verbal. Modern Man has forgotten how to listen to this part of the brain: he relies instead on reasoning to cope with the complexities of the 20th century. But he still has occasional access to it, in moments of relaxation or reverie, when he is less alert and his critical faculties are in abeyance. This 'regression' can lead him to a state of mind where he can listen to the 'wisdom of the body' and put in motion his natural healing processes. And touch is one important way of bringing about this regression. Meares has in fact applied 'atavistic communication by touch', as he calls it, in the treatment of cancer patients. He has obtained some impressive results: in some patients the cancer has disappeared, and the lives of other patients have been prolonged.

However, until Meares can test his theory it remains at the level of speculation – with a

It has always been believed that certain privileged individuals could cure the sick by mere touch. It was often the monarch who was thought to have this gift – but sometimes it was a commoner, such as Valentine Greatrakes (below), of County Waterford in Ireland, 'famous for curing several Deseases and distempers by the stroak of his Hand only'

scientific status no different from that of the belief that a witch doctor, or Meares himself, has magic powers that 'make people get better' when touched.

This is not to dismiss Meares's ideas. Others have pointed to the primitive brain as having a wisdom of its own. For example, the French obstetrician Michel Odent, an advocate of 'natural' childbirth, emphasises that

the woman in labour needs first to forget what she has learned, forget what is cultural, to change her conscious level, to become instinctive, and it's easier if she has close contact during the first stage, especially with someone familiar.

But the problem remains of how to put such ideas into a testable form.

An alternative way of explaining the action of touch is to regard it as an example of the placebo effect. This has been defined as

any therapeutic procedure ... which has an effect on a patient, syndrome or disease, but which is objectively without *specific* activity for the symptom being treated.

The placebo effect has generally been associated with tricking a patient into feeling better – for example, by giving him a sugar pill while leading him to believe that it is a carefully chosen, appropriate drug. (*Placebo* is the Latin for 'I will please'.) However, the element of trickery is not an essential part of the idea of a placebo, as the definition above implies.

The effect is firmly established. A placebo is likely to produce a 30 to 40 per cent improvement in symptoms in almost any complaint. When a new drug is tested, its effects must be compared with those of a

Alternative healing

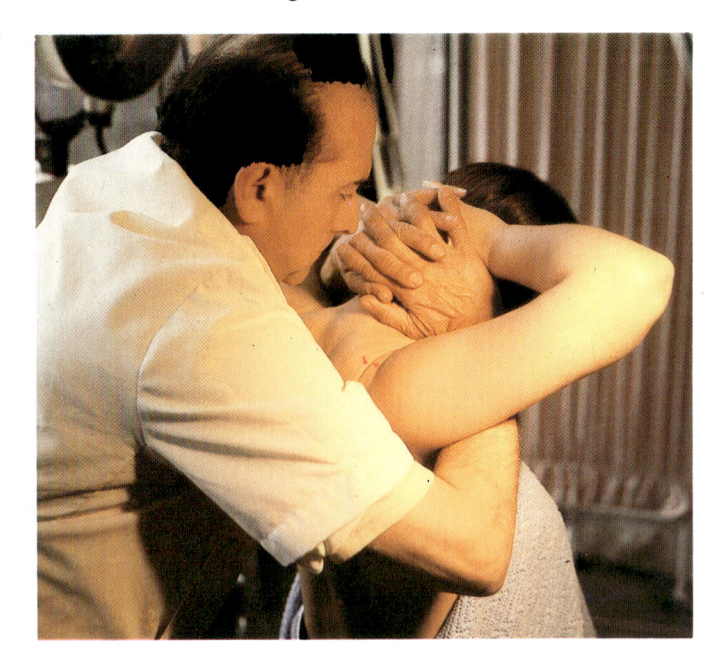

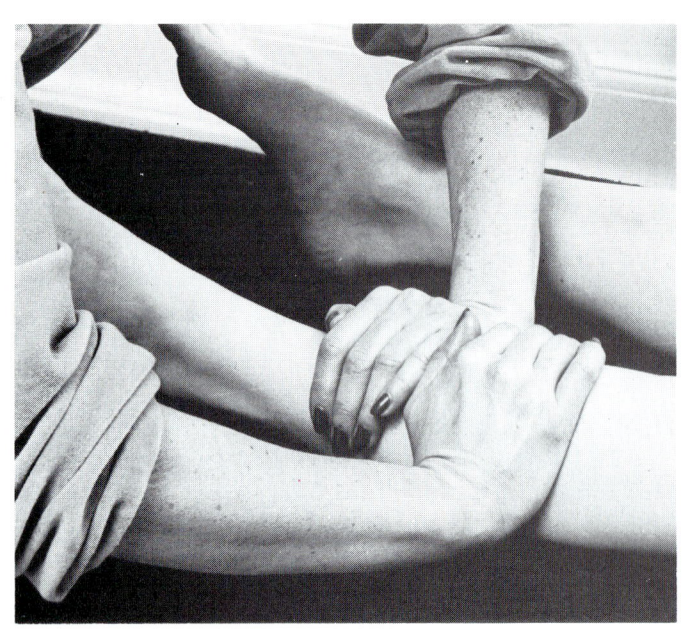

placebo to see whether its benefits are substantially greater than this.

The therapeutic setting has important placebo effects. In one study it was found that patients who talked with a positive, confident anaesthetist before an operation needed only half as much pain-relieving post-operative medication as patients who had not met the anaesthetist.

Herbert Benson, professor of medicine at Harvard Medical School, recommended use of such placebo effects, especially where specific drugs are not clearly indicated for a condition. As he put it: 'Wise physicians recognise that they can often practise an excellent form of medicine by giving a dose of themselves.' He states that this placebo effect is enhanced when the beliefs and expectations of both doctor and patient are positive and when the psychological interaction between doctor and patient is one of firm trust and friendship.

Above left: an osteopath manipulates a patient to relieve tension in the neck. Osteopaths believe that an extraordinarily wide range of disorders can be cured by manipulation

Above right: the value of massage in relaxing muscles is undisputed. But many unorthodox therapists go further and claim that it promotes the flow of beneficial 'vital energies'

Below: shiatsu is a massage technique in which firm pressure is applied to certain areas. In general the same sites are important in acupuncture

These conditions are reminiscent of those that Ainslie Meares stipulates as necessary for effective communication by touch:

First the person touched becomes aware of something of the state of mind of the toucher. For instance, he comes to know if the toucher is anxious or calm . . . understanding or not . . . . Second, the touched one receives a message [that] may be 'I sympathise with you . . . I will stand by you' . . . . Because of the primitive nature of such communication it comes in the form of a vague awareness . . . . The third element . . . is the awakening of primitive psychological processes within the mind of the touched one . . . . In general terms the patient becomes aware that the one touching him is himself profoundly calm and secure. The message that comes is a form of dim awareness that he is being helped. And the reaction evoked in the patient is a regression of psychological and physiological functioning to a simpler level.

Does the technique matter?

Does this mean that when alternative therapies are effective, their success is based upon the placebo effect – initiating and encouraging the operation of the patient's own healing powers with the actual technique of treatment being irrelevant?

There is evidence to indicate that this is not the whole picture. Some has already been discussed in connection with herbal medicine and homoeopathy. To take an example from the range of therapies involving touch, we now discuss the case of chiropractic.

A commission of enquiry appointed by the New Zealand government looked at, among other things, what chiropractors do in the course of treatment. They are normally called upon to deal with localised pain arising

Alternative healing

directly from the malfunctioning of spinal joints. Such pain includes back pain, sciatica, headaches and the like. Chiropractors offer a variety of techniques to correct such musculo-skeletal disorders – from a direct thrust, used to reduce a dislocation, to gentler techniques, involving light or heavy pressure on muscles, ligaments and other soft tissues. Indirect approaches to the correction of disorders are also used, which rely on the belief that 'when the body is held in the correct position long enough, it will do for itself what is best for itself.'

The commission concluded in its final report that:

[although] chiropractors' views on the neurophysiological processes by which [their] results follow often have been scientifically naïve, [it needs] to be understood that the area of spinal mechanics and its implications in neurophysiology has not been explored by orthodox medical science....
Chiropractic today cannot lightly be dismissed.

Clinical evidence, too, demonstrates that manipulation or massage of the spine is of benefit.

Some chiropractors, however, do not stop at saying that they can successfully treat musculo-skeletal disorders (type M disorders, as they term them). They claim that they can be of benefit in a wide range of disorders not normally thought of as being caused by a spinal malfunction: organic, visceral disorders (type O disorders), such as high blood pressure, diabetes and the like. If there were already a spinal problem that a conventional doctor would recognise, the commission could accept that its treatment might have a beneficial effect on the functioning of the rest of the body and so relieve symptoms of a type O disorder. But the commission could not accept the more wide-ranging claim – for that would mean that chiropractic is a complete alternative system of medicine.

According to those advocating the therapeutic use of touch, the chiropractors may be correct in claiming to be able to help all kinds of disorders. Where they are wrong is in saying that spinal adjustments are responsible for successful treatment of type O (organic, visceral) disorders. It is rather the use of touch to enhance a patient's own healing processes that brings the successful results.

Perhaps a combination of these opposed views is correct: what alternative medicine offers to the patient is a combination of genuine skill in its own techniques and use of medicines, together with that something extra – communicated through the normal senses or extra-sensorily – that is required to transform beliefs and hopes into bodily changes. We may be witnessing the rebirth of the Asclepian tradition of healing.

Right: a chiropractor manipulates a patient's upper spine. Chiropractic and osteopathy, originally regarded as quite distinct, have come to resemble each other strongly. There are subtle differences in technique however: roughly speaking, chiropractors are likely to use small, sharp thrusts, whereas osteopaths use slow leverage

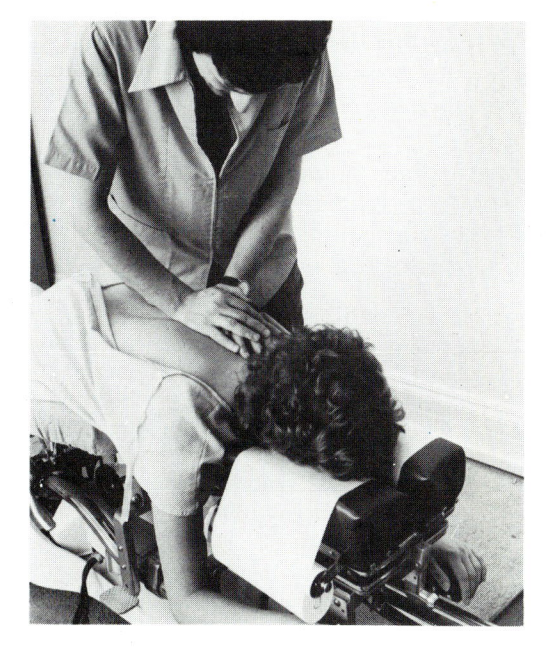

Left: the spine, and the areas on the body that are controlled by nerve connections to the corresponding parts of the spinal cord. Chiropractors and osteopaths regard these connections as of vital importance to their techniques: a disorder in a certain part of the body may need manipulation of the associated part of the spine

cervical vertebrae
- headaches
- insomnia
- migraine
- neuritis
- catarrh
- laryngitis
- tonsillitis

head, eyes, ears, nose, throat, neck

thoracic vertebrae
- asthma
- coughs
- colds
- bronchitis
- influenza
- jaundice
- anaemia
- indigestion
- dyspepsia
- diabetes
- ulcers
- rheumatism
- eczema
- pyelitis
- kidney trouble

shoulders, arms and hands, heart, lungs and chest, liver, stomach, pancreas, spleen, kidneys

lumbar vertebrae
- constipation
- appendicitis
- miscarriages
- impotence
- cramp
- menstrual troubles
- lumbago
- rheumatism

bowels, genital organs, bladder, colon, legs and feet

sacrum
- sacro-iliac conditions
- curvature of the spine

rectum, pelvis

coccyx
- haemorrhoids
- pruritus

Further reading
Norman Cousins, *Anatomy of an illness*, W.W. Norton (New York) 1979
Bernard Dixon, *Beyond the magic bullet*, Allen and Unwin 1978
Brian Inglis, *Natural medicine*, Fontana 1980

Writing on the walls, bells that ring themselves, apparitions and mysterious fires – such were the non-stop paranormal phenomena that occurred after the Foyster family moved into Borley Rectory. Were they real? FRANK SMYTH continues the saga of Borley

IN 1878 A YOUNG WOMAN named Esther Cox became the centre of 'mysterious manifestations' at her sister's home in Amherst, Nova Scotia. Esther saw apparitions visible to no one else. Objects were thrown, furniture was upset, small fires broke out in the house and messages addressed to the girl were found scribbled on the walls. The 'hauntings' became the subject of a book, *The haunted house: a true ghost story . . . the great Amherst mystery* (1879) by Walter Hubbell. The book was a huge success, running through 10 editions and selling over 55,000 copies. But in 1919 the American Society for Psychical Research printed a 'critical study' by Dr Walter F. Prince, suggesting that the Amherst case was not in fact a poltergeist manifestation. Prince said it was all trickery by Esther Cox while in a state of dissociation, or conversion hysteria.

The township of Amherst is about 5 miles (8 kilometres) from the equally small community of Sackville, where another of Esther Cox's married sisters lived and where, 50 years afterwards, the Reverend Lionel Foyster and his wife Marianne lived. The Foysters would have heard of the Amherst case as surely as anyone living in, say, Sudbury today would have heard of the Borley mystery. The fact that Foyster used the pseudonym 'Teed' when writing of the happenings at Borley Rectory during his stay there offers what is tantamount to proof that he not only knew of the Amherst case but was familiar with its details: the unusual name 'Teed' was the married name of Esther Cox's sister. It seems likely, therefore, that his wife also knew of the case, though whether she made deliberate – if unconscious – use of it for her own behaviour is a matter for conjecture. The resemblance between both cases is, in fact, striking; Dingwall, Goldney and Hall in *The haunting of Borley Rectory* offer no less than 19 points of general concurrence, including the ringing of bells, throwing of objects, setting of small fires, and mysterious messages written on walls.

For example, a short time after Marianne Foyster arrived at Borley and took such a dislike to the place, she began to 'see apparitions'. No one else did. Shortly afterwards

Above: Borley Rectory, which seemed to reach the peak of its haunting when Marianne Foyster lived there. It is still an open question as to whether she created the events herself. If so, was it because she suffered from an hysteric disorder she could not control – like Esther Cox in the similar Amherst case? Or did she produce the phenomena through PK?

Below: the cottage that was once part of the Borley Rectory property and in which François D'Arles lived

Borley in ruins?

the manifestations, so similar to the Amherst case, began. Her husband, loyal and devoted, answered villagers who accused her of faking that he could not see the visions because 'he wasn't psychic', but in her 'defence' he began to keep a rough record of events. This was not perhaps as helpful as he hoped it might be because, as he admitted, much of it was written later and many things were confused.

In October 1931, in answer to a plea from the Bull sisters, Harry Price returned to Borley once more. It is interesting to speculate on the motives behind the Bulls' concern: perhaps because they knew the source of the pranks and hoaxes during their own tenancy, they suspected the genuineness of the new 'haunting'. The same could be said of Harry Price, for he returned from his visit convinced that Mrs Foyster was directly responsible for fraud.

In their examination of the alleged phenomena, Dingwall, Goldney and Hall analysed

Below: the ghost hunter Harry Price (left) and Mrs K. M. Goldney of the Society for Psychical Research (right) pose with the Foyster family at Borley Rectory. The Foysters' adopted child Adelaide and an unidentified playmate complete the picture

Bottom: one of several messages that appeared on the walls of the rectory. All of them were scribbled in pencil in a childish hand and were mostly addressed to Marianne Foyster

caught on at least one occasion trying to set fire to bedclothes.

In 1933 when the Foysters went on leave for six months, they left Canon H. Lawton as locum. Nothing untoward happened though the canon, like Major Douglas-Home of the Society for Psychical Research, noted the curious acoustics of the house and surroundings. In any case, by that time Mrs Foyster was spending most of her time in London with Francois D'Arles at their flower shop. An exorcism by a group of Spiritualists the previous year, when Marianne and François first left to open their shop, seemed to have put paid to what the Foysters cosily called 'the goblins'. Or was it that Marianne Foyster was no longer on the premises?

In October 1935 the Foysters left Borley. When the Reverend A.C. Henning was appointed five months later, he chose to live elsewhere, and since his time the rectors of Borley have lived at Liston or Foxearth

the incidents described in Foyster's first record, which he later elaborated upon. Treating the constant bell ringing as a single phenomenon, they isolated 103 different instances. Of these, 99 depended totally on Mrs Foyster's sincerity, three were readily attributable to natural causes, and only one was in any way 'inexplicable'.

Among the most suspicious incidents was the appearance of pencilled writings on the walls. About seven messages appeared during the Foysters' tenancy, most of them addressed to Marianne and appealing for 'light, mass, prayers'. Another, not noted by Price in his Borley books, spelled 'Adelaide', the name of the Foysters' adopted daughter. All the messages were in a childish scribble. Little Adelaide may have been responsible for one or both of the 'mysterious' small fires that broke out in the rectory, for she was

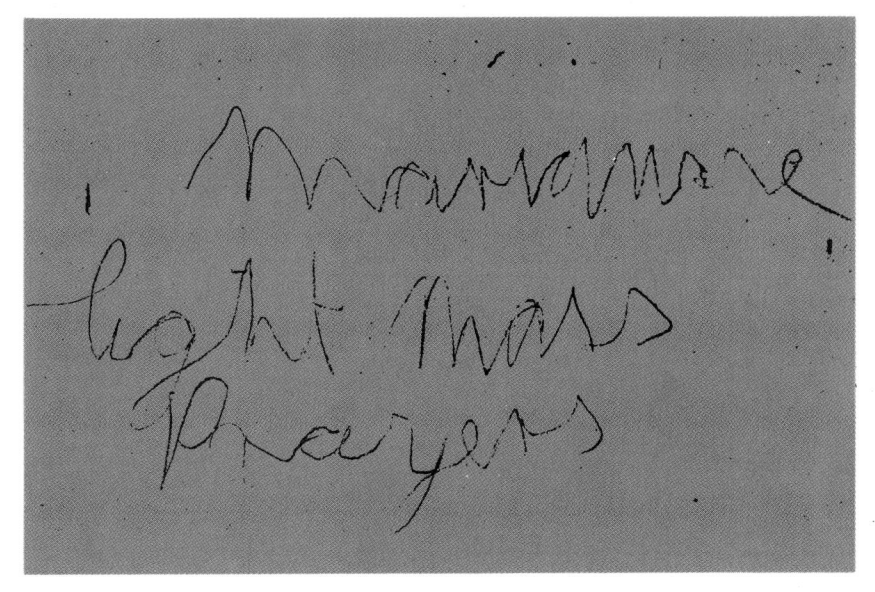

Borley Rectory

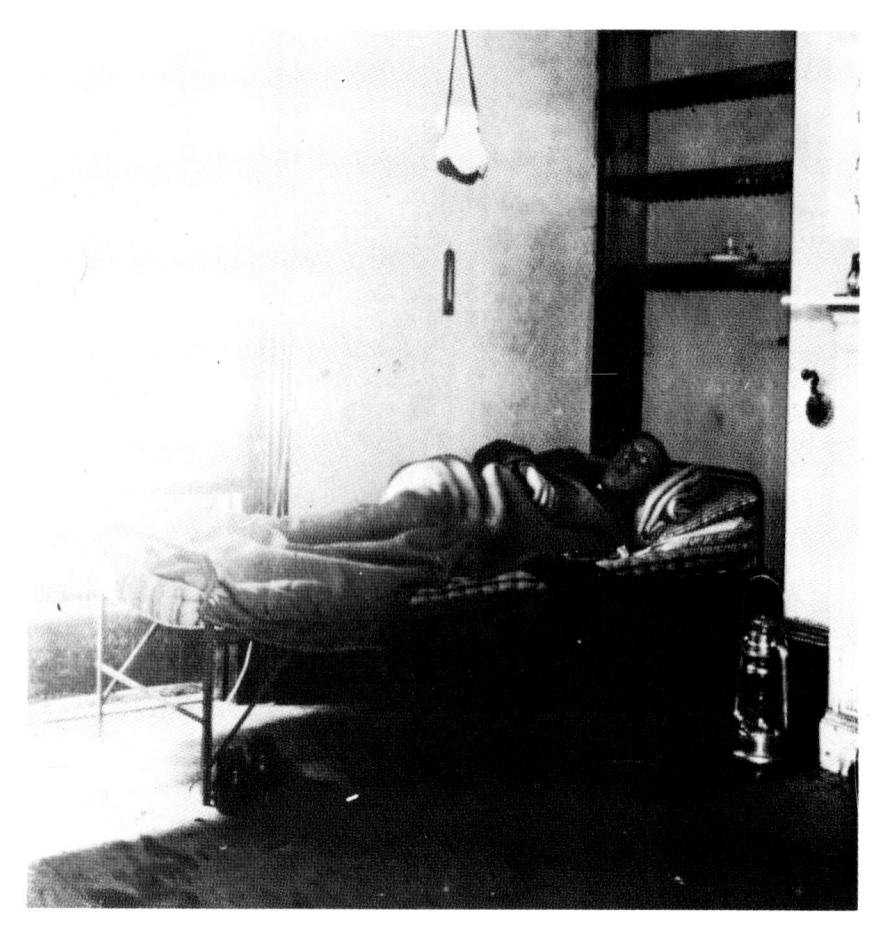

rectories, parishes amalgamated with Borley since the 1930s.

But the battered, drama-ridden old house had still another four years of life to run. On 19 May 1937 Harry Price rented the rectory, and a week later inserted an advertisement in *The Times* asking for 'responsible persons of leisure and intelligence, intrepid, critical and unbiased' to form a rota of observers at the house. If, he later stated, they 'knew nothing about psychical research, so much the better'.

As has been pointed out by Price's critics, ignorance of psychical research is a curious requirement for a team of ghost hunters, but could make it easier to use their 'experiences' to build a good story.

If Harry Price and Marianne Foyster had used fraud for their own personal ends, another trickster who came on the scene in November 1938 was working for purely financial gain. He was Captain William Hart Gregson, who bought Borley Rectory six months after Price's tenancy expired. He immediately asked Price's advice about organising coach trips to see his new property and broadcast on the radio, recounting several minor 'phenomena'. But his coach tour plans were brought to an abrupt end at midnight on 27 February 1939 when fire gutted the building, leaving only a few walls, charred beams, and chimney stacks standing.

Sidney Glanville, one of Price's volunteer researchers of impeccable reputation, said that at a seance at the Glanville home, an entity named 'Sunex Amures' had threatened to burn down Borley Rectory. But the real cause was flatly stated by Sir William Crocker in his autobiography *Far from humdrum: a lawyer's life* (1967). Crocker, a distinguished barrister, and Colonel Cuthbert Buckle, an insurance adjuster, investigated the claim made by Gregson on behalf of the insurers. Crocker states: 'We repudiated his impudent claim for "accidental loss by fire" . . . pleading that he had fired the place himself.'

One of Price's 48 volunteer investigators takes a break from his duties at the rectory. Price rented Borley for a year and gathered a team of 'observers' through an advertisement in The Times to work with him there. He did not ask for experience in psychical research, but required his volunteers to have 'leisure and intelligence' and to be 'critical and unbiased'

'Bare-faced hocus pocus'

The ruins of Borley Rectory were finally demolished in the spring of 1944 and the site levelled. An orchard and three modern bungalows now occupy the spot. During the demolition, Price took a *Life* magazine photographer and researcher Cynthia Ledsham to Borley, and by sheer fluke, the photographer captured on film a brick that was apparently 'levitated' by unseen forces – but was in fact thrown by a worker. *Life* published the photograph over a jokey caption, but Price, in his book *The end of Borley Rectory* (1946), claimed it as a final 'phenomenon'. Cynthia Ledsham was astounded, calling it 'the most bare-faced hocus pocus on the part of . . . Harry Price.'

The truth is that the haunting of Borley Rectory was the most bare-faced hocus pocus from start to finish, with Price feeding his craving for personal publicity from it in the most short sighted way. For, as was shown after his death, his shallow frauds could not hope to withstand investigation.

In a letter to Mr C.G. Glover in 1938, Price wrote: 'As regards your various criticisms, the alleged haunting of the rectory stands or falls not by the reports of our recent observers, but by the extraordinary happenings there of the last 50 years.'

But he wrote to Dr Dingwall in 1946 in reference to the occasion when a glass of water was 'changed' into ink: 'I agree that Mrs Foyster's wine [*sic*] trick was rather crude, but if you cut out the Foysters, the Bulls, the Smiths, etc., something still remains.' It is then logically left that the 'something' is the 'reports of our recent observers'.

As Dingwall, Goldney and Hall said: 'If one wished to dispose of the Borley hauntings on one small piece of paper merely by reference to Price's privately expressed opinions of the evidence', it would be necessary only to quote the two letter extracts in juxtaposition. However, one great irony remains. Despite the demolition of Price's pack of lies, ghost hunters of the 1960s and 1970s doggedly persisted in investigating the area. And they may just have stumbled on something truly paranormal – not at the rectory site, but in Borley church itself.

For the eerie happenings that point to a real haunting at Borley, see page 1954

From a remote hilltop on the Isle of Man there came, in the 1930s, news of an amazing talking animal – a mongoose that was often heard but seldom seen. MELVIN HARRIS **investigates the story of 'Gef' and the family he haunted**

The mongoose that talked

THE AFFAIR of the talking mongoose caused a great deal of excitement in the early 1930s. Initially called the 'talking weasel', this amazing creature lived in a remote place on the Isle of Man and, so the newspaper accounts said, did not just repeat words like a parrot. It used words with an understanding of their meaning. Indeed, according to the family with whom the creature lived, it gave direct answers to questions and made spontaneous comments – some of them quite witty and knowledgeable.

The animal haunted a place called Doarlish Cashen, an isolated farmstead perched over 700 feet (215 metres) up on the west coast of the island. It was a cheerless terrain without trees or shrubs. Even the nearest neighbours were out of view, over a mile (1.6 kilometres) away. Ordinarily there would be little to attract anyone to Doarlish Cashen. But, in September 1931, the rumours of the talking weasel sent the journalists scrambling up the forbidding hill to meet the Irving family who lived at the farm.

A rare picture of Gef, the talking mongoose – centre of a media sensation in the early 1930s. Usually Gef would not show himself even to the family with whom he lived – or whom he haunted – on the Isle of Man. But, so the family said, he allowed this photograph to be taken by Voirrey Irving, the daughter of the house. The wonderful talking animal, often witty and as often insulting, managed to elude all his many investigators

The head of the family was James Irving, a retired commercial traveller approaching 60. An intelligent man with mild, benign features, he was known as an engaging talker and raconteur. He seemed to keep his cheerfulness and good humour despite the fact that his farmstead production had steadily declined, reducing his income to a mere 15 shillings a week.

His wife Margaret was a few years younger than he. She was said to be tallish with a 'dignified bearing, upright and square of carriage'. Her grey hair rose primly above her forehead '. . . to frame her most compelling feature – two magnetic eyes that haunt the visitor with their almost uncanny power'. It was all too easy to draw the conclusion that Margaret Irving was the dominant personality in the household.

The Irvings' daughter Voirrey was 13 but old for her years. She seemed a reserved and undemonstrative child, hardly a scholar but obviously intelligent. And she took an intelligent and eager interest in anything to do with animals, reading any article or book she could get that dealt with them. By contrast, she was also fascinated by mechanical devices such as motor cars, aeroplanes and cameras.

Voirrey's knowledge of animals was not just theoretical but also practical. She was

Talking mongoose

fully experienced in handling sheep and goats. And she had devised a successful way to catch rabbits. She would roam the hills with her sheepdog Mona until a rabbit was sighted. While Mona 'pointed' the prey and put it in a frozen mesmerised state, Voirrey would slowly creep up behind and kill the rabbit with a sharp blow to the head. The significance of her skills in this regard came out later.

Of the many newspaper reporters who met the Irvings, the luckiest came from the Manchester *Daily Dispatch*, for he was the only one to hear the talking weasel. He wrote of his successful mission:

> The mysterious 'man-weasel' . . . has spoken to me today. Investigation of the most remarkable animal story that has ever been given publicity . . . leaves me in a state of considerable perplexity. Had I heard a weasel speak? I do not know, but I do know that I've heard today a voice which I should never have imagined could issue from a human throat.

He left the house puzzled and impressed but fully convinced that the Irvings were honest and responsible – unlikely to be the initiators of an elaborate and sustained practical joke.

His next report, however, was more guarded:

> Does the solution of the mystery of the 'man-weasel' of Doarlish Cashen lie in the dual personality of the 13-year-old girl, Voirrey Irving? That is the question that leaps to my mind after hearing the piercing and uncanny voice attributed to the elusive little yellow beast with a weasel's body. . . . Yesterday I heard several spoken sentences. . . . The conversation was between the 'weasel-voice' and Mrs Irving, who was unseen to me in another room, while the girl sat motionless in a chair at the table. I could see her reflection, although not very clearly, in a mirror on the other side of the room. She had her fingers to her lips. . . . The lips did not move, so far as I could see, but they were partly hidden by her fingers. When I edged my way into the room the voice ceased. The little girl continued to sit motionless, without taking any notice of us. She was sucking a piece of string, I now saw.

Remarkably, none of the eager visitors ever caught sight of the talking animal. They all had to rely on Jim Irving's description to picture it. He judged it to be about the size of 'a three-parts grown rat, without the tail' and thin enough to pass through a 1½-inch (4-centimetre) diameter hole. Its body was yellow like a ferret's, its long bushy tail was tinged with brown, and its face was shaped somewhat like a hedgehog's but with a flattened, pig-like snout. This description was based on the pooled information of the three

Right: the Irving family in their ill-lit home, known as Doarlish Cashen. From the left are Voirrey, her mother Margaret and her father Jim

Below: Voirrey and her dog Mona. Some investigators hinted that Gef might be the creation of this lonely and intelligent girl, but this was not proved conclusively

Talking mongoose

Irvings, for each of them claimed to have seen the animal on separate occasions.

According to Jim Irving, their tiny lodger had first made itself known by barking, growling and spitting – all purely animal sounds. Irving took the sudden notion to try to teach the creature other kinds of noises. So he began to imitate animal and bird sounds and to name each creature as he made its sound. Within days, he claimed, the weasel would repeat the sounds as soon as the relevant animal or bird name was called out. The most astounding part of his experiment soon followed. 'My daughter then tried it with nursery rhymes, and no trouble was experienced in having them repeated.'

From then on there was no stopping the wily weasel. By February 1932 it was freely demonstrating its remarkable cleverness to the Irvings. Jim Irving wrote:

It announces its presence by calling either myself or my wife by our Christian names. . . . It apparently can see in the dark and described the movements of my hand. Its hearing powers are phenomenal. It is no use whispering: it detects the whisper 15 to 20 feet [4.5 to 6 metres] away, tells you that you are whispering, and repeats exactly what one has said.

When the ghost hunter Harry Price learned of the talking weasel, he acted swiftly by asking a colleague to visit the Irvings and file a report. Price called this investigator 'Captain Macdonald' to protect him from any unwanted publicity. Macdonald obliged and turned up at the farmhouse on the evening of 26 February 1932. There he sat around for almost five hours – and heard and saw nothing. But as he left the place, he heard a shrill scream from inside the house – 'Go away. Who is that man?' The words were quite clear at first, then they tailed away into unintelligible squeals. When Macdonald hurried back into the house, the voice ceased. So he arranged to return early the next day.

The next day's vigil started with the Captain being shown some water trickling from a hole in the wall. He was solemnly assured that this was 'the animal performing its natural functions'. The vigil proved more fruitful later. In the evening, Voirrey and her mother went into the bedroom above the living room and within minutes a shrill voice started talking to Margaret Irving. This went on for a quarter of an hour. Then Macdonald appealed to the animal to show itself. 'I believe in you!' he shouted, hoping to charm the evasive weasel. But the squealed reply was final. 'No, I don't mean to stay long as I don't like you!' Macdonald then tried to creep up the stairs but slipped, making a deafening clatter. With that the creature screamed, 'He's coming!' So ended Macdonald's hoped-for ambush.

Ten days later, Charles Northwood –

Doarlish Cashen, high on a cheerless hilltop with the nearest neighbour more than a mile (1.6 kilometres) away. The ramshackle house gave Gef plenty of scope for playing hide and seek

Talking mongoose

again, not his real name – turned up at Doarlish Cashen. An old friend of Jim Irving, he came out of concern for the Irvings, and later he sent a favourable report to Price. By now, the family had christened the talking animal 'Gef' and had discovered that he was an Indian mongoose born in Delhi on 7 June 1852. These details 'came from Gef himself'.

Once Northwood had settled in, Irving called out, 'Come on Gef, Mr Northwood's here. You promised to speak you know!' But not a squeak was heard – until Voirrey went into the kitchen to prepare lunch. Then in a mild voice Gef said, 'Go away Voirrey, go away.' Two minutes later Gef began to speak again. Then, when Irving asked him to bark, he promptly did so. But he refused to sing his favourite song *Carolina moon*, even though the gramophone record was played to inspire him. Later still, Gef shouted, 'Charlie, Charlie, Chuck, Chuck . . . Charlie my old sport! . . . Clear to the Devil if you don't believe!'

Gef's mood changed when he heard that Northwood's son, Arthur, was due to arrive at the Irving farm. He grew threatening. 'Tell Arthur not to come. He doesn't believe. I won't speak if he does come. I'll blow his brains out with a thruppenny cartridge!'

Then he softened a little and returned to domestic small talk. 'Have you ordered the rooster, James, from Simon Hunter? Mind you do so. Have you posted that letter?' But a short while later his vicious side took over again. As Northwood put it:

> . . . from behind the boards in the sitting room, possibly some 25 to 30 feet [8 to 9 metres] away, I heard a very loud voice penetrating, and with some malice in it: 'You don't believe. You are a doubter,' etc. This was very startling, and for the first time put a bit of a shiver through me. Equal to a couple of irascible women's voices put together! I said: 'I do believe.' I had to shout this.

Then came the probing query, 'Charlie. . .is Arthur coming?' followed by a screech and a loud thump.

By this time Northwood had to leave, which meant the end of the encounter. But on his way down the hill he heard some screeches behind him and each of these was identified by Irving as having been made by Gef.

Northwood made a second visit a few days afterwards, bringing his sister-in-law and niece. This time, he claimed, his sister-in-law and her little girl heard the talking mongoose as well. 'Gef said the name of my sister-in-law's child and said that she had a powder puff in her bag.' He conceded that this was not very telling because both these facts were well-known to Voirrey. Despite that, he remained convinced that Gef was not Voirrey, but 'some extraordinary animal which has developed the power of speech by

Right: Jim Irving points to Gef's fingers appearing through the slats on the bedroom wall. All the pictures of the talking mongoose were uniformly poor and indistinct, leaving as much to the imagination as to the eye

Below: the wooden box-like structure known as 'Gef's Sanctum', located in Voirrey's room. On top is a chair that, according to the Irvings, the mongoose pushed around for exercise

Talking mongoose

some extraordinary process.'

The Northwood visits were the last productive ones for the next three years. But that long timegap did not mean that Gef had gone to earth. On the contrary, the Irvings stated that he became more entertaining and more adventurous during those years. And Jim Irving was able to produce a diary that recorded many of the mongoose's new sayings and antics.

From this account we learn that Gef began killing rabbits to help the family budget. After killing them he would leave them near the house and report the exact position to the family. Then he started bringing home other useful things: a paintbrush one day, then a pair of pincers, then a pair of gloves.

In the house itself, he grew increasingly playful. He would bounce a rubber ball up and down in time with gramophone records and push a lightweight chair around to get exercise. According to the diary, all these events were staged on top of a wooden boxlike structure in Voirrey's room, known as 'Gef's Sanctum'.

As a return for his services and entertainment he expected, in fact demanded, choice titbits. For him the orthodox mongoose diet was out. Gef insisted on offerings of lean bacon, sausages, bananas, biscuits, sweets and chocolates. These were carefully placed on one of the crossbeams of the roof so that he could sneak up and grab them when he chose. For Gef continued to be abnormally shy and hated being watched. The family had only brief glimpses of him on rare occasions.

During this period, Gef demonstrated both that he could speak in other languages, even if he used only the odd word and short phrase, and that he could perform some elementary arithmetic. He showed that he could read by yelling out some of the items printed in the newspapers left around the house. He also increased his repertoire of songs and delighted the family with his renderings of *Home on the range*, *The Isle of Capri* and the Manx national anthem, as well as some Spanish and Welsh ditties.

More surprisingly, Gef allowed himself to be handled – though he still refused to show himself in full. Margaret Irving was permitted to place her finger in his mouth and feel his teeth. She was also graciously allowed to shake one of Gef's paws – which, she said, had 'three long fingers and a thumb'. These paws were obviously extremely versatile, since Irving claimed that Gef had opened drawers with them, struck matches and operated an electric torch.

The irascible Gef grew very free with his insults. When Irving was slow at opening his mail, Gef shouted, 'Read it out you fatheaded gnome!' When a visitor said she was returning to South Africa, he screamed, 'Tell her I hope the propeller drops off!'

A fascinating mystery

The formerly shy and retiring talking mongoose finally even agreed to pose for some photographs taken by Voirrey. But these were of poor quality and revealed almost no details. Then boldness prompted Gef to leave samples of his fur for examination. These samples were forwarded to Captain Macdonald who passed them on to Harry Price. In turn, Price sent them for examination to F. Martin Duncan, an authority on fur and hair at the Zoological Society of London.

While Price waited for the expert's opinion, Captain Macdonald visited Doarlish Cashen once more. Yet again, he heard Gef's voice but saw nothing of the elusive creature. This helped Price to decide to make an inspection of the house himself.

What sealed Price's decision to visit Doarlish Cashen was a revealing report from Duncan on the alleged mongoose hairs. Duncan's letter of 23 April 1935 read:

I have carefully examined them microscopically and compared them with hairs of known origin in my collection. As a result I can definitely state that the specimen hairs never grew upon a mongoose, nor are they those of a rat, rabbit, hare, squirrel or other rodent, or from a sheep, goat or cow. . . . I am inclined to think that these hairs have probably been taken from a longish-haired dog or dogs. . . . When you visit the farm keep a look-out for any dog . . . with a slight curly hair and a fawn and dark colour.

On 30 July 1935 Harry Price trudged up the hill to the Irving home on the trail of the talking mongoose. With him went R.S. Lambert, editor of the *Listener*. The two hoped to solve a fascinating mystery. And they bore Duncan's final words well in mind.

For the bemusing aftermath of the talking mongoose sensation, see page 1946

Top: a drawing of Gef from Harry Price's book on the talking mongoose affair. Irving said that he had got the description he gave to the artist from Gef himself, since the mongoose so shyly stayed out of sight

Above: two mongooses in their natural habitat. The Indian species, of which Gef claimed to be one, is famous for its snake-killing skill. But the mongoose is a predator of small mammals as well, and Gef concentrated on killing rabbits

I Ching: enquire within

One of the oldest and most flexible of divinatory methods is also the most fascinating. BRIAN INNES **continues his discussion of divination with a brief look at the Chinese Book of Change**

CONFUCIUS SAID: 'If some years were added to my life, I would give 50 to the study of the *I Ching*, and might then escape falling into great error.' That was in 481 BC, when he was already nearly 70 years old, and had written a series of commentaries on the text of the book the Chinese call *I Ching*, which means 'the Book of Change'.

The *I Ching* is one of the oldest and most respected oracle books in the world. In its present form it can be traced back at least 3000 years – and even at that time it was already considered venerable, being based upon more primitive forms of oracle.

The Book of Change draws its basic philosophy from the ancient Chinese faith known as Tao. The word 'tao' is most usefully translated as 'way' – as in the Christian expression 'I am the Way, the Truth, the Life' – but no English word provides a really satisfactory equivalent, and even in Chinese it is susceptible of a variety of meanings. Indeed, as one Chinese inscription puts it: 'the Tao that can be put into words is not Everlasting Tao.'

Taoist writings are full, in fact, of negative definitions: 'power and learning is adding more and more to oneself, Tao is subtracting day by day; rigour is death, yielding is life; as laws increase, crimes increase.'

To the Taoist sage the world is not made up of discrete particles of time and space: everything is part of everything else, and reality consists of ceaseless change. The river that one paddled in yesterday is not the river one swims in today; and so the Universe is seen as a moving pattern in which nothing is permanent. So the *I Ching* is different from other oracle books: it does not regard the past, the present and the future as fixed; instead, it treats time and fate as dynamic and flowing, never the same from one moment to the next. The advice that one obtains by consulting the *I Ching*, therefore, is of possibilities: if you act in a particular way it is likely to result in such-and-such an outcome.

As a tool of divination, the *I Ching* is very similar to geomancy in principle (see page 1901); but the divinatory figures that are generated are composed of six lines instead of four, and therefore there are a possible 64, rather than 16, figures. Moreover, where the

Far right: K'ung Fu-tzu, the great Chinese philosopher known to us as Confucius

Below: a romanticised Western view of the ceremony involved in consulting the *I Ching*: the sticks are being passed through the smoke from an incense burner, while the enquirer makes his kowtows before them

Below: the philosophy of Tao contains a strong sexual element, and intercourse is regarded as the interchange of yin and yang between the two partners. The cup represents Autumn Days, the last of the Thirty Heaven and Earth postures: 'The lord Yang lies on his back, his hand at the back of his head, and lady Yin sits on his stomach, but turning her face to his feet'

Witness-Judge procedure of geomancy results in only 128 different interpretations, each of the *I Ching* figures contains within itself 64 possible variations, and can generate at least one further figure: the total number of interpretations, therefore, is:

$$64 \times 64 + 64 = 4160.$$

Taoist philosophy classifies all the energies of the Universe under two headings, yin and yang. Yin is passive, watery, pertaining to the Moon, essentially female; yang is active, fiery, pertaining to the Sun, essentially male. The lines that make up the divinatory figures are described as either yin or yang lines; a broken line represents yin, a continuous line yang.

The six-line figures are known as hexagrams. Each can be regarded as made up of two three-line figures called trigrams. Since each line of each trigram can be either continuous or broken, the number of trigrams is $2 \times 2 \times 2 = 8$. And since each hexagram is made up of two trigrams, the number of hexagrams is $8 \times 8 = 64$.

The traditional way in which these figures are generated is long and complicated. A bundle of 50 dried yarrow stalks is required; yarrow was used because it had a certain holy significance to the Chinese. One of the stalks is set aside, and is not used in obtaining the hexagram; there is some dispute among Western writers as to whether the fiftieth stalk plays any part in the tradition of the *I Ching* or not.

The remaining 49 stalks are then separated into two piles. After this, the procedure is as follows:

1. One stalk from the right-hand pile is placed between the little finger and ring finger of the left hand.
2. Stalks are removed four at a time from the left-hand pile until four or less are left. These stalks are placed between the ring finger and the middle finger of the left hand.
3. Stalks are removed four at a time from the right-hand pile until four or less are left. These stalks are placed between the middle finger and the index finger of the left hand.

The stalks held between the fingers of the left hand will now total either 5 or 9:

$$1 + 1 + 3 = 5$$
$$\text{or } 1 + 3 + 1 = 5$$
$$\text{or } 1 + 2 + 2 = 5$$
$$\text{or } 1 + 4 + 4 = 9$$

These stalks are then put aside, and the process is repeated with the remaining 40 or 44 stalks. At the end, the stalks held between the fingers will total either 4 or 8:

$$1 + 1 + 2 = 4$$
$$\text{or } 1 + 2 + 1 = 4$$
$$\text{or } 1 + 4 + 3 = 8$$
$$\text{or } 1 + 3 + 4 = 8$$

This pile is also set aside, and the process repeated with the remaining stalks. Once more, the stalks held in the left hand will total either 4 or 8.

There are now three little piles: the first contains 5 or 9 stalks, the second and third each contain 4 or 8. There are therefore eight possible combinations of these three quantities. These provide a yin or yang line:

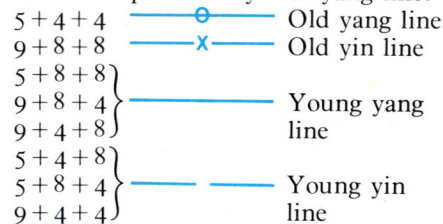

5 + 4 + 4 ——○—— Old yang line
9 + 8 + 8 ——×—— Old yin line
5 + 8 + 8
9 + 8 + 4 } ———— Young yang line
9 + 4 + 8
5 + 4 + 8
5 + 8 + 4 } ———— Young yin line
9 + 4 + 4

The 'old' lines are also known as 'moving' lines: an Old yang line is seen to be changing into a Young yin line, and an Old yin line into a Young yang line. Each of the four types of line is also given a 'ritual number':

Old yin line   6
Young yang line   7
Young yin line   8
Old yang line   9

So far, only a single line has been generated. This is drawn as the bottom line of the hexagram, and then the procedure must be repeated five times more, the lines being drawn in ascending order.

Producing a single hexagram, therefore, can take five minutes or more. Those who let the *I Ching* govern their lives have developed a simpler and quicker method that requires only three coins. Chinese coins traditionally had an inscribed face and a blank or 'reverse' face – the side of a modern coin that gives the value is considered the inscribed side: if the blank face is given the value 3, and the inscribed face the value 2, tossing the three coins will provide a total of 6, 7, 8 or 9 – and so, taking this as the ritual number, the first line is obtained. It is possible, in this way, to obtain the hexagram in less than a minute.

What follows the obtaining of the hexagram? The texts of the *I Ching* are of several different periods and different kinds. First comes a description of the hexagram itself, in terms of the two trigrams of which it is composed; then comes the Judgement, which is said to have been composed by King Wen, the founder of the Chou dynasty (*c.*1100 BC). This is a rather brief analysis of the hexagram as a whole.

'The superior man'

The next text, the Commentary, is traditionally attributed to Confucius, although it is improbable that he himself wrote it. This is generally longer than the Judgement, and takes note of the significance of the individual lines making up the whole hexagram. The third text, the Image, is succinct; it describes the kind of action that the sensible person – referred to usually as 'the superior man' – should take. This text has also been attributed to Confucius.

The final group of texts were composed by King Wen's son, the Duke of Chou, who destroyed the Shang dynasty in 1027 BC. These were written about 40 years after Wen's text: they are brief and rather cryptic, and they deal with the occurrence of Old

Divination

yang and yin lines within the hexagram.

One or two specific examples will illustrate the nature of these different texts, and the way in which they are interpreted.

In hexagram 63, Chi Chi – Climax and After – the upper trigram is K'an, which symbolises dangerous deep water, the Moon, the winter season, the north, the middle son, an ear, the 'element' wood and the colour red; the lower trigram is Li, representing fire, the Sun, summer, the south, the middle daughter, the eye, and the colour yellow.

The text of *I Ching* describes Chi Chi as being an evolutionary phase of hexagram 11, T'ai, which means Peace. Hexagrams are read from the bottom, and the 'strong' positions are considered to be lines 1, 3 and 5. In T'ai, lines 1, 2 and 3 are occupied by yang lines, while lines 4, 5 and 6 are yin; in Chi Chi, the yang lines have migrated upward to their appropriate positions, displacing the yin lines to position 2, 4 and 6. Thus, says the text, everything is in its proper place. But although this is a very favourable hexagram, it still gives grounds for caution: for it is when equilibrium has been reached that any sudden displacement may cause order to revert to disorder.

The Judgement on Chi Chi reads: 'After the climax there is success in small matters. Righteous persistence brings its reward. Good fortune in the beginning, but disorder in the end.'

Now comes the Commentary. 'Chi Chi indicates progress in small matters. The proper position of the yang and yin lines shows that righteous persistence will be rewarded; the weak line at the centre of the lower trigram indicates good fortune in the beginning, but the way peters out, efforts come to an end, and disorder returns.' This is one of a number of cases in which the Commentary seems to add very little to the Judgement, but in other cases it can be of considerable value in elucidating the often obscure phrases of the Judgement.

The verses of the Duke of Chou refer to the occurrence of 'moving' lines, the Old yang and Old yin lines. The bottom line of Chi Chi is a yang line: if it is an Old yang line, with a ritual number 9, then the verse for that line should also be read.

These Old lines are also moving into Young lines. Suppose, for instance, that the hexagram Chi Chi was obtained as follows:

When the old lines have changed into their opposites, the hexagram will be:

This is a very different hexagram. It is 62,

Above right: how the sticks are held between the fingers of the left hand

Above far right: in this porcelain dish the shepherdess, a yin symbol, is surrounded by two male and one female sheep: these sheep represent the trigram Tui, or Joy

Right: an example of an English translation of the text of the I Ching, giving the Judgement, the Commentary and the typically cryptic verses written on the individual lines

63 Chi Chi Climax and After

The trigrams:
above: K'an dangerous deep water
below: Li fire, brightness

This hexagram represents an evolutionary phase of hexagram 11, T'ai, Peace. The strong yang lines have moved upward into their appropriately strong positions, displacing the yin lines into their proper weak positions. Everything is in its proper place. But although this is a very favourable hexagram, it still gives grounds for caution: for it is when equilibrium has been reached that any sudden movement may cause order to revert to disorder.

The Judgement
After the climax there is a success in small matters. Righteous persistence brings its reward. Good fortune in the beginning, but disorder in the end.

Commentary
Chi Chi indicates progress in small matters. The proper position of the yang and yin lines shows that righteous persistence will be rewarded; the weak line at the centre of the lower trigram indicates good fortune in the beginning, but the way peters out, efforts come to an end, and disorder returns.

The Image
Water over the fire, the image of Chi Chi. The superior man, accordingly, gives due thought to the misfortunes to come, and takes precautions in advance.

The Lines
In the bottom line, NINE signifies:
Like a driver who brakes his chariot,
Or a fox with a wet tail.
No blame.

In the second line, SIX signifies:
She loses her carriage curtain.
Do not run after it.
For in seven days it will be recovered.

In the third line, NINE signifies:
The Illustrious Ancestor
The emperor Wu Ting
Attacked the country of devils.
Three years he took in subduing it.
Small men are not fit for such enterprises.

In the fourth line, SIX signifies:
The finest clothes turn to rags.
Be careful all day long.

In the fifth line, NINE signifies:
The neighbour in the east sacrifices an ox
But it is the neighbour in the west,
With his small spring sacrifice,
Who is blessed for his sincerity.

In the sixth line, SIX signifies:
His head is in the water.
Misfortune.

1928

Divination

Hsiao Kuo. The Judgement, Commentary and Image for this second figure should also be read for interpretation, but since the lines have now moved the verses of the Duke of Chou are not significant.

One can go further: if the lines are moving independently of one another, there are two possible intermediate hexagrams between Chi Chi and Hsiao Kuo. These are:

The first is 49, Ko; the second is 39, Cheng. Reading the texts for these two hexagrams, but remembering that only one can be the true intermediate, may help in the interpretation.

One has to be very careful in trying to present an imaginary worked example of the use of the *I Ching*: too often, indeed, one finds that the hexagram obtained is Meng:

> I do not seek out the inexperienced; he comes to find me. When he first asks my advice, I instruct him. But if he comes a second or a third time, that is troublesome, and I do not advise the troublesome. . . .

As an experiment, I asked the *I Ching* 'whether it would be wise for me to finish this article tonight'. The hexagram I obtained was 20, Kuan:

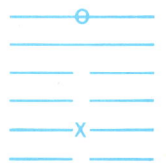

Kuan signifies contemplation: 'the worshipper who has washed his hands, but not yet made the offering'. The upper trigram of Kuan is Sun, representing wind and gentleness; the lower trigram is K'un, the Earth, the passive. The Image of Kuan is the wind moving over the Earth. 'So did the kings of old visit all parts of their kingdom, to see their people and give them instruction.

There is an Old yin line in the second line, which signifies:

> Contemplation through the crack of the door
> Is sufficient only for a housewife

and the Old yang line in the sixth line signifies:

> Contemplating himself
> The superior man is without reproach.

It seems that *I Ching* is advising me not to continue with the article until I have had time to think about it some more; it also suggests that my time would be better occupied in assertaining whether the editorial staff have any problems.

Now the moving lines must be allowed to develop, and the resultant hexagram is 29, K'an:

This is one of only eight hexagrams in which the trigram is doubled. In each trigram a strong yang line has plunged into the deep between two yin lines, as water lies in a deep ravine. The Judgement reads: 'Abyss upon abyss, danger piled on danger. But if you are sincere there is success locked up within.' The Commentary continues the theme, and the Image of K'an is: 'The water flows on and on to its destination; the image of the abyss upon the abyss. So the superior man walks in eternal virtue, instructing others in the conduct of their affairs.'

The last part of this text clearly relates to the advice given above – although the warnings of danger seem unnecessarily strong in such a minor matter. Can the intermediate hexagrams throw any light on the matter?

The two possible intermediates are:

These are, respectively, 59, Huan, and 8, Pi.

Huan signifies dispersal, and the advantageousness of travel. In the sixth line, the Old yang line signifies:

> He disperses bloodiness
> Keeping evil at a distance
> Departing without blame.

Pi, on the other hand, is the image of holding together; it signifies those who follow the lead of the superior man.

It was only a light-hearted question, and it deserves a light-hearted answer. The *I Ching* has told me that it is time for me, and my staff, to stop work and go home!

Understanding the Tarot cards – and how they understand us. See page 1966

Ghostly 'extras', spirit messages and materialisations of people and objects – these were the hallmarks of the professional psychic photographer. Were the spirit manifestations they produced genuine? FREDERICK GOODMAN weighs the evidence

BY ITS VERY NATURE, psychic photography has from its beginnings been open both to the accusation of fraud and to fraud itself. Not a single established spirit photographer was free of taint – all, at one time or another, were the object of bitter intrigue, legal action or both. Yet many had genuine psychic abilities.

The Bostonian William Mumler was almost certainly the first person in the United States to earn a living as a professional spirit photographer. He became very well-known, and it is clear from surviving pictures that his mediumistic abilities were quite remarkable. Several investigations failed to unearth any fraud on his part. Nonetheless, Mumler fell foul of the law in 1869 – but it was as a result of a journalistic campaign whose aim was to create scandal. The spirit photographer was eventually charged as a swindler, but the evidence brought to the court was so overwhelmingly in his favour that the case was dismissed.

Mumler's most famous spirit picture is one taken towards the end of 1865, about four years before his trial. The sitter, who visited Mumler incognito, was no less a person than Mary Todd Lincoln, then recently widowed by the assassination of President

An enterprising spirit

Abraham Lincoln. In the print is a recognisable image of Lincoln, standing behind her and laying his hands upon her shoulders.

After Mumler's death in 1884, another spirit photographer came to notice on the west coast of the United States. This was the Californian Edward Wyllie. Dr H.A. Reid, who was a specialist in the history of 19th-century psychic photography, said of him:

> As to the work of Edward Wyllie, the medium photographer, the proofs and testimonies that the phenomena were genuine and not trickery, were all so open, untrammelled, fair and conclusive that to reject them is to reject the validity of all human testimony.

Wyllie led an adventurous life of travel in India and New Zealand before settling in Pasadena, California, in 1886 as a photographer. He had been psychic since childhood and his psychic leanings came to the fore rapidly with the appearance of unwanted 'extras' on his photographs. These spirit forms at first threatened to interfere with his business, but when he realised that the extras were often recognisable to his sitters, he changed his line of business accordingly. Wyllie was able to photograph spirit forms 60 per cent of the time. The number of 'recognitions' among these was substantial. His highly distinctive style is characterised by several extras upon a single plate. For example, a portrait of J.R. Mercer contains the spirit forms of his mother and his wife, a bunch of flowers and a spirit message signed 'Elisabeth B. Mercer'.

In the decades in which Wyllie was the foremost of spirit photographers in the United States, the most famous and versatile of English mediums was William Eglinton. Though Eglinton was from time to time unmasked as a fraud (see page 1847), he had undoubted psychic powers. Unlike the majority of Spiritualists of his day, he was able at times to work in daylight. He would often permit photographs to be made and one

Spirit photography

Left: the widowed Mary Todd Lincoln with the spirit of President Abraham Lincoln. The picture was taken in Boston, Massachusetts, USA, by William Mumler, the first professional spirit photographer, the year that Lincoln was assassinated

Below: the English medium William Eglinton (right) seen with the remarkable materialisation he produced in full view of witnesses and a photographer

Below right: the sitter's mother and wife, a spirit message and some flowers are the kind of 'extra' that typify Edward Wyllie's distinctive style of psychic photography

remarkable picture shows a complete materialisation. This was witnessed and described by Eglinton's biographer, John S. Farmer:

> At this time his breathing became increasingly laboured and deep. Then, standing in full view, by a quick movement of his fingers, he gently drew forth, apparently from under his morning coat, a dingy white-looking substance. He drew it from him at right angles and allowed it to fall down his left side. As it reached the ground it increased in volume and covered his left leg from the knee downwards. The mass of white material on the ground increased in bulk and commenced to pulsate, move up and down and sway from side to side. Its height increased and shortly afterwards it quickly grew into a form of full stature, completely enveloped in the white material. The upper part of the medium then drew back and displayed the bearded face of a full-length materialised spirit, considerably taller than himself....

The only method of making photographs of materialised figures in the seance room was by means of the magnesium light, which was said to have a deleterious effect on the medium as well as on the spirit. Even so, some of the most impressive of 19th-century spirit photographs were made by means of the magnesium flare. Among these pictures is a series made during the seances of the Spiritualist Madame d'Esperance, who left fascinating memoirs of her dealings with leading Victorian mediums, investigators and spirit photographers. In her archives there is a picture taken in March 1890 of the fully materialised form of a beautiful 15-year-old Arab girl called Yolande, who would materialise frequently (see page 1846). Indeed she became the medium's most constant spirit companion. Yolande would take approximately 15 minutes to materialise into human form. A description of the process has been left by one of the members of the d'Esperance circle:

> First a flimsy, cloudy, patch of something white is observed on the floor, in front of the cabinet. It then gradually expands, visibly extending itself as if it were an animated patch of muslin,

Spirit photography

Left: a spirit, perhaps of a Spanish girl called 'Ninia', taken during one of the many successful photographic seances conducted by Madame d'Esperance in the 1890s

Right: a spirit portrait of the American poet Walt Whitman (right) compared with his living likeness. It was taken by the English medium William Hope

Below: this ghostly nun is a partial materialisation photographed in 1918 by the medium Castelwitch

lying fold upon fold, on the floor, until extending about 2½ by 3 feet [75 by 90 centimetres] and having a depth of a few inches. . . . Presently it begins to rise slowly in or near the centre, as if a human head were underneath it, while the cloudy film on the floor begins to look more like muslin falling into folds about the portion so mysteriously rising. By the time it has attained two or more feet [60 centimetres], it looks as if a child were under it and moving its arms about in all directions. . . . Presently the arms rise considerably above the head and open outwards through a mass of cloud-like spirit drapery, and Yolande stands before us unveiled, graceful and beautiful, nearly 5 feet [1.5 metres] in height, having a turban-like headdress, from beneath which her long black hair hangs over her shoulders and down her back.

The dematerialisation was no less dramatic, though it took only between two and five minutes. The form suddenly fell 'into a heaped patch of drapery'. The drapery – Yolande's clothes – 'slowly but visibly melt into nothingness', said the witness.

The picture of Yolande is pleasant to the eye, but not all materialisations are quite so lovely to behold. They can be repulsive, both in the process of formation by the medium and in their final form.

The material by which spirits are given visible form is the mysterious substance called ectoplasm. It is exuded from the medium's body, most usually from one of the orifices, and the extrusions from the mouth of the medium – or, in one case, from the nipples – are often repellent. Even when a materialised form has the power to walk in the manner of a living being, it may be only partially formed. One example of an unpleasant partial manifestation was photographed by the medium Castelwitch during seances in Lisbon in 1918. The spirit form was that of a nun, and it was so ghastly in appearance that one of those taking part in the seance actually broke down, begging the spirit not to come closer. A description by one witness to these seances and the nun's several materialisations captures something of the atmosphere:

> We saw at first a kind of vapour, through which it was possible to distinguish the picture on the wall. This vapour grew a little longer, became thicker, and took the form of a spirit which gave us the impression of being a monk [sic] dressed in white. It advanced and drew back three times towards the red light, on its way it knocked on the table. Three times it disappeared and then reappeared, making the same movement.

Even the clinical description of this spirit nun by the psychologist and psychical researcher Baron von Schrenck-Nötzing carries a sense of the macabre into the textbooks:

> The phantom is flat, in spite of the very vivid facial expression. The face of the nun is veiled, and the upper body draped in a white fabric. It is remarkable in the fact that in this figure the whole right side (including the right ear, shoulder and arm) is entirely

Spirit photography

missing, as if this part had, from top to bottom, been ripped off a life-sized portrait.

The hallmark of the professional spirit photographer is the ability to capture images of the dead that are recognisable to living relatives or friends. The professional with the highest record of such recognitions was the Frenchman Jean Buguet. While Mumler could claim 15 recognitions, and the Englishman Frederick Hudson 26, Buguet could claim 40 recognitions in his spirit photographs. Even had Buguet miraculously discovered a new way of making double exposures that would fool the photographic experts of his day, fraud on that scale would have been almost impossible. For many of the Buguet spirit forms were of people who had died before the invention of photography, so there were no originals to use for double exposures.

Buguet was, like Mumler, brought to trial. And as in Mumler's case, hundreds of favourable testimonials poured into the court. The trial was almost certainly rigged. Buguet was found guilty but, as one writer later commented, this 'did not and could not efface the facts of genuine psychic photography'. No more did it efface the fact of Buguet's ability as a spirit photographer.

Some of the stories attached to recognition photographs are extraordinary. A particularly interesting one concerns the production of a picture of a Chinese man and his son, made by Wyllie for one of the psychical research societies on the west coast of America. The society had expressed a hope that Wyllie might be able to obtain a spirit form on a photograph of someone who was wholly ignorant of Spiritualism. Accordingly, when Charlie, a Chinese laundryman, came in on his usual round, Wyllie asked him if he would like to sit for his portrait.

He was very much scared. I made his mind easy and asked him to come in a few days, and I would give him the picture. When I developed the negative, there were two extras on it – a Chinese boy and some Chinese writing. When Charlie came round I showed him the print, and he said, 'That my boy; where you catchee him?' I asked him where his boy was, and he said, 'That my boy. He's in China. Not seen him for three years.' Charlie did not know that his son was dead.

Such pictures and such stories point strongly to the genuineness of spirit photography, whether by amateurs or professionals and in spite of the fact that the mysterious extras have never been fully explained. And the phenomenon is not limited to human spirit forms, for animal extras appear regularly - if less frequently – in psychic photography.

Are all the animal extras in spirit photography family pets? See page 1958

Above right: Charlie and the 'extra' of his son, taken by Edward Wyllie as a test for psychical researchers. They wondered if a spirit would appear when the sitter was completely ignorant of Spiritualism – and Charlie, who was Chinese, filled the bill

Left: a typical early photograph by the Frenchman Jean Buguet, who produced a high percentage of 'extras' that were recognised by the living as being of the dead. Buguet was brought to trial and convicted of fraud, but still has many defenders of his abilities as a true psychic photographer

The gospel truth?

'The third day he rose again from the dead': thus the Christian creed asserts the miracle of Christ's bodily resurrection. But is this a religious myth – or a literal truth? DAVID CHRISTIE-MURRAY reviews the evidence

THE GREATEST MIRACLE – or the greatest illusion in history? Under which heading comes the resurrection from the dead of Jesus, called the Christ? The story is contained in all four gospels, and a reference to it in 1 Corinthians 15:3-7 probably embodies a creed dating from a period soon after Jesus's death. Here follows a summary of each account so they can be compared and contrasted.

Mark relates that Jesus was scourged and brutally treated by Roman soldiers, who buffeted him, crowned him with thorns and crucified him. He died at the ninth hour (3 p.m.) and had to be buried before the Sabbath began at 6 p.m., so that his corpse should not profane it. Joseph of Arimathea, a secret disciple of Jesus, boldly asked Pilate, the Roman governor, leave to bury the body. Pilate, surprised that Jesus was already dead, checked with the centurion in charge before granting Joseph's request.

Joseph wrapped the body in 'fine linen' (was this the Turin shroud? see page 287) and hurriedly laid it in a sepulchre hewn out of a rock, the entrance of which was blocked by a great stone. Mary Magdalene and Mary, mother of Jesus, noted where Jesus's body was laid.

Part of Friday, all of Saturday (the Sabbath) and part of Sunday, totalling about 36 hours, comprised three days according to Jewish reckoning. Very early on Sunday, Mary Magdalene, Mary the mother of James, and Salome went to the sepulchre to anoint the body properly with spices. They wondered who should roll away the stone from the tomb for them, and on their arrival were surprised to see a young man sitting there, clad in white. He said,

> Be not affrighted: Ye seek Jesus of Nazareth, which was crucified: he is risen he is not here: behold the place where they laid him.
>
> But go your way, tell his disciples and Peter that he goeth before you into Galilee: there shall ye see him, as he said unto you.

Terrified and bewildered, the women fled and told no one.

The risen Christ, Mark continues, appeared first to Mary Magdalene, who told the disciples and was not believed. Then he appeared 'in another form' to two disciples walking into the country, and finally to the 11 Apostles as they ate, reproaching them for their unbelief and exhorting them to preach

Below: the crucified Christ is lifted from the cross. The gospels tell of his suffering: he had been brutally scourged, crowned with thorns, nailed in hands and feet (above right) and pierced in his side – too much, surely, to survive by any normal means, especially in an age when medical care was primitive at best

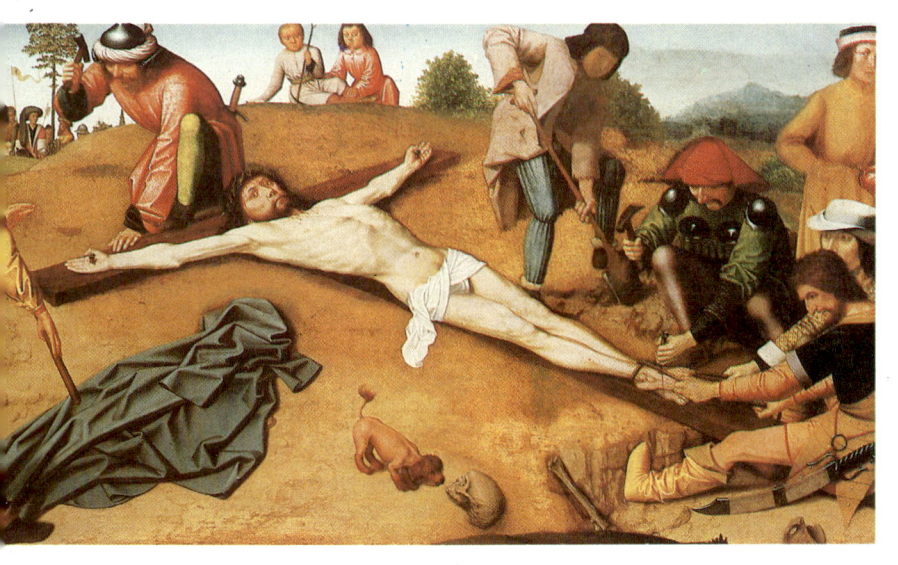

Bible mysteries

the gospel throughout the world. Afterwards he 'was received up into heaven'.

Matthew adds a buffeting from the Sanhedrin (the Jewish council) to Jesus's other physical hurts. He also relates how the Jewish authorities, recalling Christ's claim that he would rise again after three days, asked Pilate to guard the body to prevent the disciples stealing it by night and claiming a miraculous resurrection. Pilate told them to use their own men, probably Jews from the Temple police, who kept order inside the Temple precincts where no gentiles were allowed.

Matthew omits Salome, mentioning only two women visiting the tomb at first light on Sunday. A great earthquake marks the descent from heaven of an angel with a face 'bright as lightning' and 'snow-white raiment', who rolls back the stone and sits upon it, terrifying the guards into stupefaction. He addresses the women in the same words as Mark's 'young man'. Filled with awe and great joy, they run to tell the disciples. On the way there they are greeted by Jesus himself. He repeats the message that the disciples should go to Galilee where he and they will meet. Meanwhile the guards report what has happened to the chief priests, who bribe them to say that while they slept, the body was stolen by the disciples.

The disciples then meet Jesus as arranged on a mountain in Galilee, worshipping him – 'but some doubted' – and receive instructions to evangelise the world.

Luke asserts that the women (unnamed) not only beheld the sepulchre when Jesus was buried but 'how his body was laid'. On Sunday Mary Magdalene, Joanna, Mary the mother of James, and other women found the stone rolled away and were perplexed by the absence of the body. Suddenly, 'two men stood by them in shining garments' who gave them approximately the same message as reported by Mark and Matthew, adding a reminder that Jesus had prophesied his death and resurrection. The women told the disciples and were disbelieved, but Peter ran to the sepulchre, saw the discarded graveclothes, and departed, puzzled.

Luke then describes the two disciples' walk to Emmaus, $7\frac{1}{2}$ miles (12 kilometres) outside Jerusalem. Jesus joined them but 'their eyes were holden that they should not know him'. They told him of the crucifixion and that certain women had found the tomb empty and had seen a vision of angels who affirmed that Jesus was alive. Other disciples visited the sepulchre and verified that the body was no longer there. Jesus expounded to them the scriptures 'concerning himself', was invited to share their evening meal and was recognised by them when, probably using characteristic gestures, he blessed and broke bread. Then he vanished from their sight. They returned post-haste to Jerusalem

Right: a florid 19th-century depiction of Christ rising from his tomb, triumphing over death and corruption. On Pilate's orders a large boulder had been placed across the mouth of the tomb to ensure that the body could not be stolen, and its disappearance taken by Christians as evidence of the promised resurrection. But when some female disciples went to the tomb to anoint Jesus's body in the Jewish tradition, they found the boulder had unaccountably been rolled away, and a 'young man' was sitting there (below left). The gospels vary on this point: there are 'two young men', 'two angels', 'a young man' and 'an angel'. Whoever was sitting there was unknown to the women. According to Luke, the 'two men...in shining garments' said to the women: 'Why seek ye the living among the dead? He is not here, but is risen'

1935

Bible mysteries

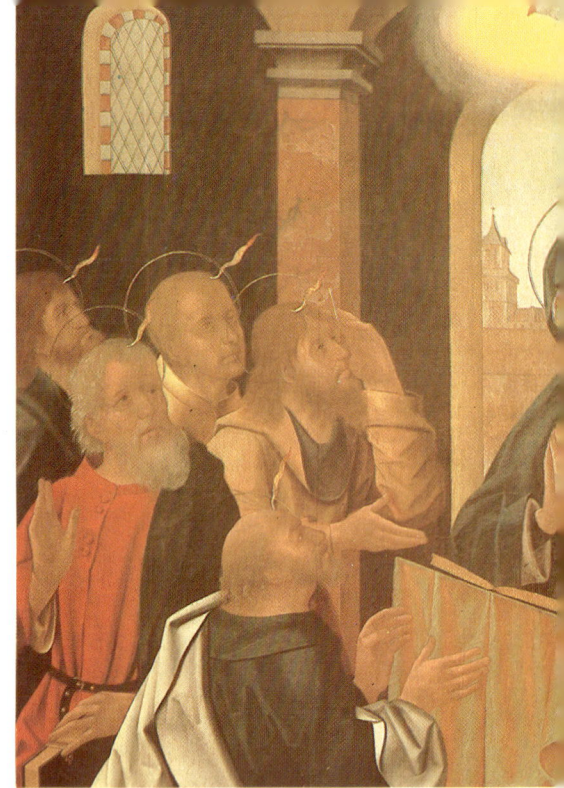

and told the 11 Apostles, who reported in their turn that the Lord had appeared to Peter. While they were talking, Jesus appeared suddenly in their midst. Thinking they were seeing a ghost, they were terrified; but he invited them to touch him, showing them his wounded hands and feet and proving his material nature by eating before them. He told them to 'tarry in Jerusalem until power came upon them' – there is no mention of meeting in Galilee – and, leading them out of the city to Bethany, ascended from their sight 'into heaven'. The disciples remained joyfully in Jerusalem, worshipping daily in the Temple.

John adds that a soldier pierced Jesus's side with a spear while he was on the cross and that there came out 'blood and water', a medically accurate description of the piercing of the pericardium – a fatal wound if Jesus had not already died. John mentions a visit on Sunday morning 'while it was yet dark' of Mary Magdalene only. Seeing the stone rolled away, she ran to tell Peter and John that Jesus's body had been removed and 'we' (clearly indicating the presence of others with her) 'know not where they have laid him.' The two ran off together. John, outstripping Peter, looked into the sepulchre and saw the linen clothes lying there but remained outside. Peter pushed past him, John followed and, noting that the headcloth was lying apart from the grave-clothes, they left, 'wondering'.

Mary Magdalene, returning to the tomb, stood outside it weeping and, stooping down,

Top: the resurrected Christ meets two disciples on the road to Emmaus, 'But their eyes were holden that they should not know him.' Seeing the risen Jesus as a stranger, the disciples told him enthusiastically of the resurrection. Later, when sharing an evening meal at Emmaus, the 'stranger' suddenly revealed himself as the risen Jesus (above). The real mystery is why no one recognised him

saw two 'angels' – whom she seems, nevertheless, to have accepted as normal human beings at the time, for when they asked her why she was weeping, she replied, 'Because they have taken away my Lord and I know not where they have laid him.' Turning, she saw Jesus but (perhaps because her eyes were dimmed with tears) did not recognise him. Mistaking him for a gardener, she asked him where he had put Jesus's body. He replied, 'Mary' – in such a way that she instantly recognised him. He told her not to touch him, but to tell the disciples that he was alive.

The same evening Jesus appeared among the disciples. Thomas, who was absent at the time, later refused to believe that Christ had been resurrected unless he could touch Christ's wounds. Eight days later Jesus appeared again, and Thomas was convinced.

Besides its innate improbability, the

Bible mysteries

Left: the 'Holy Ghost' (or Holy Spirit) descends upon the Apostles at Pentecost, in the form of tongues of fire. The writers of the scriptures could well have been writing symbolically, but there is no reason why real tongues of fire should not have been the 'outward and visible sign of an inward and spiritual grace'

Right: not unnaturally, one of Jesus's disciples, Thomas, doubts that the abused and tortured Jesus could possibly have been resurrected. Understanding Thomas's scepticism, the risen Jesus prompts Thomas to feel the reality of the resurrected body, by probing the wound made by the centurion's spear

resurrection story can be attacked in several ways. First, perhaps the women watching the burial mistook the tomb. However, such an error would almost immediately have been discovered and rectified.

Or perhaps Jesus did not die on the cross, but only swooned, recovered in the tomb, escaped from it and was seen afterwards by one or two followers. A Roman scourging was so terrible that many victims died under it; even a short crucifixion could be fatal; the spear thrust in itself would have been lethal; the centurion – presumably experienced in such matters – confirmed Jesus's death. And how could Jesus have possibly escaped from the tomb after such ill-treatment?

Another explanation is that the body was stolen by some of the disciples who deceived the others into thinking Christ had risen. But it is highly unlikely that a religion that spread throughout the Roman Empire so rapidly, against intense persecution, could have been founded on a deception, especially as the leaders who presumably engineered the conspiracy themselves went heroically to martyrdom without one of them revealing the plot.

Or was the body removed by the Romans or the Jews, to nip Christianity in the bud? But in that case, why was it not produced the moment Christ's resurrection was begun to be preached? Or, if the body had been hidden in the wrong grave just a few minutes' walk outside Jerusalem, why was it never revealed? Peter's first preaching of the resurrection resulted in 3000 conversions – an unlikely outcome for a sermon based on a lie that could have been so easily exposed.

Critics point out that the gospel stories are full of discrepancies. However, this can be seen as a strength, as it shows there was no collusion among the writers. They also show their confidence in their case by admitting, unnecessarily, details that weaken it, such as the temporary non-recognition of Jesus and their doubts. Moreover, the stories can be substantially reconciled, as a renowned scholar, N.P. Williams, has shown in his *The first Easter morning*. However, the events recorded in the New Testament may have been telescoped by writers whose conventions did not include rigorous adherence to chronology.

Of the nature of Christ's resurrection body, which could apparently materialise or dematerialise at will, psychical research perhaps has something to say. Matter through matter – the teleportation of objects and even people – is a well-attested phenomenon, common in reports of poltergeist cases and said to occur frequently at seances. And bilocation – the appearance of a live human being in two places simultaneously – has been reported in the lives of Sister Mary of Agreda (see page 281) and more recently, Padre Pio who died in 1968.

Believers may also find supporting evidence of the resurrection in the Turin shroud, while sceptics still maintain that some unknown, but rational, factor convinced the first disciples of something that simply never happened.

Yet the annals of psychical research and the archives of collectors of anomalous phenomena point to the reality of 'miracles' – so perhaps there is no reason to doubt that the miracles of the New Testament did happen exactly as recorded.

Further reading
F. Duncan M. Derrett, *The Anastasis: the resurrection of Jesus as an historical event*, P. Drinkwater 1982
Charles Gore (ed.), *A new commentary on Holy Scripture*, SPCK 1937
Frank Morison, *Who moved the stone?*, Faber & Faber 1930
Michael C. Perry, *The Easter enigma*, Faber & Faber 1959
N.P. Williams, *The first Easter morning*, SPCK 1920

Who sent the scareships?

When the 1909 epidemic of 'scareship' sightings died down, it seemed to be the end of the story – until, in 1912, new and more mysterious sightings began to be reported. NIGEL WATSON continues his investigation

RUMOURS OF A FLIGHT by a Zeppelin airship over Sheerness, Kent, on the evening of 14 October 1912 caused questions to be asked in the House of Commons. On 27 November 1912, opposition MP Mr William Joynson-Hicks asked the First Lord of the Admiralty, Mr Winston Churchill, if he knew anything about this matter. Mr Churchill affirmed that an unidentified aircraft had been reported on that date. It was heard flying over the district at 7 p.m., and caused flares to be lit at nearby Eastchurch in anticipation of a landing by the craft. However, nothing descended from the night sky, and the nationality and origin of the craft, Mr Churchill had to admit, remained a mystery.

Enquiries by the press in Eastchurch revealed that the townspeople had heard a buzzing noise between 6.30 and 7 p.m. on 14 October. But at the time it was assumed to be the sound of an airship or aeroplane making its way to the naval aviation school at Eastchurch. This was not the case, however, for no aircraft made any night flight on the date in question, from or to that base.

The public discussion that followed in the wake of the exchange between Mr Joynson-Hicks and Mr Churchill had many unforeseen consequences.

Almost immediately the German *L1* Zeppelin, which had started a 30-hour proving flight on 13 October, was blamed as the cause of the Sheerness incident. Whether or not the *L1*, or any other of Germany's airships, visited Sheerness in 1912 is still a matter for debate. Whatever the reason for the incident, the British government decided to strengthen the Aerial Navigation Act of 1911, in order to pacify public and official disquiet. The bill was quickly passed through parliamentary channels and was given the royal assent on 14 February 1913. It gave the Home Secretary the power to prohibit aerial traffic over areas of the United Kingdom and its territorial waters. It also meant that if an aerial vehicle failed to respond to ground signals, or violated the prohibited areas, it was liable to be fired at.

Not everybody was pleased with the amended act. Feverish efforts were made to construct an efficient sky gun – but while the project remained in its experimental stages,

British scareships

The state of the art

The government of the day claimed it knew nothing of the 'scareships' of 1913. Could this really have been the case? The first two army airships, the *Nulli Secundus* I and II, had been dismantled by 1909; the first of the smaller airships that followed them, the *Beta*, made its maiden flight in 1910. Clearly whatever caused the 1909 sightings could not have been an army machine. The same applies to the 1913 sightings. The successors of the *Beta* – the *Gamma* and *Delta* – were too small to be mistaken for 'scareships', and two airships ordered from France, and one made in Britain by Vickers, had met with disaster.

There remains the possibility that some of the Welsh sightings may be explained as misidentifications of airships built by the only private manufacturer of note, E.T. Willows of Cardiff. But these ships were familiar to local people; Captain Lindsay, for example, actually compared the 'scareship' he saw over Cardiff on 17 January 1913 with the Willows airship. The mystery remains.

Left: the Krupp 6.5-centimetre gun, designed in Germany in 1909 for shooting down airships, shown with an artist's impression of a Zeppelin. Sightings of an unidentified airship over Kent in October 1912 led opposition MP Mr William Joynson-Hicks (inset) to ask questions in the House of Commons; and in 1913 parliament passed a bill that meant that any unauthorised foreign aircraft found in Britain's airspace was liable to be fired at. Unlike Germany, however, Britain lacked an effective long-range anti-airship gun

Below: Clyne Woods, Swansea, scene of an impressive scareship sighting in January 1913

many argued that the act was like a dog with a loud bark, but with no teeth to bite with. It was against this background of events that a new wave of phantom airship sightings began in January 1913.

Early in the morning of 4 January three witnesses, including a police constable, saw and heard an airship flying over Dover. It came from the direction of the sea and disappeared from sight to the north east. Despite a strong westerly wind, the craft, which displayed a light and made a distinct droning sound, flew at a great speed. In this case it was alleged that a French airship from a base at Verdun, 120 miles (200 kilometres) away, had been the culprit, though it is hard to imagine why the craft would have made such a perilous journey at such an early hour in poor weather conditions.

Another significant sighting was made by Captain Lionel Lindsay, Chief Constable of Glamorganshire, on 17 January. At 4.45 p.m. he saw an airship pass over Cardiff. He said:

> It was much bigger and moved faster than the Willows airship and left in its trail a dense volume of smoke. I called the attention of a bystander to the object, and he agreed with me that it was some large aircraft. It disappeared quickly so giving evidence of speedy movement.

Steven Morgan, of Merthyr, saw a similar object from his bedroom window, half an hour after Captain Lindsay. He was also impressed by the trail of smoke the airship left behind it. Before he could obtain the use of a powerful telescope the craft went out of view over the Aberdare Valley.

These sightings encouraged more witnesses to come forward. One such observer was a postman from Sketty, Swansea, who saw what looked like a very bright light hovering over Clyne Woods on 21 January at 7 p.m. Four days later, a mysterious aircraft going at a speed of 25 miles per hour (40 km/h) was seen by several people in Liverpool. Although members of a local flying club had been in the air earlier in the day, they said that at the time of the sighting it had been too windy for an extended flight. On several nights at the end of January many witnesses reported seeing a bright light moving over Manchester, which puzzled them.

Epidemic 'airshipitis'

The sightings of the airship, or airships, spread throughout the land to such an extent that a newspaper nicknamed the epidemic of reports 'airshipitis'.

When MP Mr Joynson-Hicks was asked about Captain Lindsay's sighting, he replied:

> I don't doubt the report at all, for though our own aircraft can only do thirty or forty miles [50 or 65 kilometres], the Zeppelin vessels can cross the Channel. I believe, in fact, that foreign dirigibles are crossing the English Channel at will. It is a very serious matter.

Yorkshire became a new focal point for the sightings in February. Two young people in Scarborough were the first to see anything unusual in the night sky. At some time early in the month, Mr Taylor and Miss Hollings saw a light hovering over Scarborough racecourse. They were attracted by the sound of

British scareships

machinery, which they attributed to the light. After a few minutes a conical beam of white light descended from the craft and was played upon the racecourse for six or seven minutes. The beam of light vanished and then reappeared briefly before the thing flew away towards Selby.

Another Yorkshire sighting occurred on 21 February, between 9 and 9.30 p.m., when two men on the sand barge *Star* were dredging the river Ouse at Beningborough, and saw a light in the sky. One of the witnesses, Mr Riply, said: 'It went round and round and then stopped. It stood stationary for a short time, and then went over Billington Locks. It stood there again for some time, and then went round and round as if surveying the country.' It repeated this activity several times before finally disappearing.

At the same time in Selby, a solicitor named Mr March saw from his home a bright star over Hambleton. The star moved up and down, and backwards and forwards, as if surveying the area, or looking for something. After 45 minutes it rapidly sailed towards Leeds.

It seems that 21 February must have been a busy night for the crew of the airship – if there was, indeed, only one – for not only did many people throughout Yorkshire report seeing its lights and hearing its motors, but it was also seen over Exhall, Warwickshire and Hunstanton, Norfolk.

It was at this stage in the proceedings that the War Office began to take an interest in the sighting reports, and efforts were made to discover the identity of the mystery airship; the results of their investigations were, however, never disclosed.

Hundreds of sightings were made at the end of February by people throughout the United Kingdom. Many of these observations were, however, explained as visions of Venus, or balloons sent up by jokers. This was, indeed, true in many instances.

An impressive sighting that was not so easily explained was made by Captain Lundie and his crew aboard the *City of Leeds* steamer on 22 February at 9.15 p.m. As they were leaving the mouth of the Humber they saw high over the Yorkshire coast something that 'resembled a shark in appearance', said the captain. 'It had wings on either side, and we saw the tail of the machine. No lights were visible, but owing to the rays of the moon these were not necessary. . . . We had it under observation for about five minutes. It maintained a high altitude all the time, and finally disappeared over Grimsby.'

Mystery biplane

An intriguing sighting, possibly connected with the 'scareship' incidents, was made by a Mr Collins on board his yacht in Killary Harbour, Ireland. In late February he heard a droning sound above the bay, and saw an aeroplane coming from the direction of the sea. Suddenly it descended and landed inland. Mr Collins said:

> I ran to shore thinking they might want help or information, as it might be a breakdown. I saw it was of the bi-plane type. The occupants were three in number, and one apparently a mechanic whom I could not see, tinkering at the engines. the other two were foreigners pretty stout, with florid complexions, and very intelligent foreheads, apparently Germans.

When he asked them, in German, if he could help them, one of the men answered him in French saying he did not understand, and then brusquely told him to go away as they had everything under control. Mr Collins did not see the aircraft take off again, but he did see a steamer on the horizon, which appeared to be waiting for the return of the aircraft and its impolite aeronauts.

The sheer number of sightings made in the beginning of 1913 makes this wave difficult to research and analyse, especially since there are nearly as many explanations put forward by the pundits of the period. However, mystery still shrouds many of these sightings, though UFO researchers have made a determined effort to come to terms with this material. The result of these researches should have interesting implications for modern-day UFO studies, when the data is finally collated.

A spectacular airship was seen by two men who were dredging the river Ouse at Beningborough, Yorkshire, between 9.00 and 9.30 p.m. on 21 February 1913. The men saw the same airship again close by at 4 a.m. the next day, and kept it under observation for around an hour and a half

Further reading
Christopher Chant, *Aviation: an illustrated history*, Orbis 1978
Edward Horton, *The age of the airship*, Sidgwick & Jackson 1973